"Well, Any, Child, How Can I Help You"

# FIVE LITTLE PEPPERS GROWN UP

# FIVE LITTLE PEPPERS GROWN UP

A SEQUEL TO

FIVE LITTLE PEPPERS MIDWAY.

BY

MARGARET SIDNEY

AUTHOR OF

"An Adirondack Cabin," "The Golden West," " What the Seven Did," " Rob ; A Story for Boys," and others.

ISBN: 978-93-5128-960-9(PB)

First Published in 1893
Indian Reprint in 2017

*Published by*

Kalpaz Publications
C-30, Satyawati Nagar,
Delhi – 110052
E-mail: kalpaz@hotmail.com
Website: kalpazpublications.com
Ph.: +91-9212142040

# CONTENTS

# CHAPTER I

# POLLY GIVES MUSIC LESSONS

"Miss Pepper—Miss Pepper!"

Polly turned quickly, it was such an anxious little cry.

"What? Oh, Amy Loughead."

Amy threw herself up against Polly's gown.

"Oh, if I may," she began, flushing painfully.

"You see my brother is coming to-morrow—I've a letter—so if you will let me."

"Let you what?" cried Polly, with a little laugh; "go on, Amy, don't be afraid."

"You see it is just this way," Amy twisted her fingers together, drew her breath hard, and rushed on nervously; "Jack—he's my brother, you know—promised me—I never told you—if I would only learn to play on the piano, he'd take me to Europe with him next time, and now he's coming to-morrow, and—and, oh! what shall I do?"

Amy was far gone now, and she ended with a little howl of distress, that brought two or three of the "Salisbury girls" flying in with astonishment.

"Go back," said Polly to them all, and they ran off as suddenly as they had popped in, to leave Amy and the music teacher alone.

"Now, Amy," said Polly kindly, getting down on her knees beside the girl where she had thrown herself on the broad lounge, "you must just understand, dear, that I cannot help you unless you will have self-control and be a little woman yourself."

"You told me I would be sorry if I didn't practice," mourned Amy, dragging her wet little handkerchief between her fingers, "but I didn't suppose Jack was coming for six months, and I'd have time to catch up, and now—oh dear me!" and she burrowed deeper into Miss Salisbury's big sofa-pillow.

"Take care!" warned Polly, with a ready hand to rescue the elaborate combination of silk and floss, "it would be a very dreadful thing if this should get spoiled."

Amy Loughead brought her wet cheek off suddenly. "There isn't a single tear on it, Miss Pepper," she gasped.

"That's very fortunate," said Polly, with a relieved breath. "Well, Amy child, how can I help you?" She sat down now, and drew the girl's hot little hand within her own.

"I can almost play that horrible 'Chopin,'" said Amy irrelevantly; "that is, I could, if—oh Miss Pepper," she broke off suddenly and brought her flushed face very near to the one above her, "could you help me play it—just hear me, you know, and tell me things you did, over again, about it, if I practice all the afternoon? Could you?"

"This evening, do you mean?" asked Polly, a trifle sharply.

"Yes," said Amy faintly, and twisting her handkerchief. "Oh dear me, I know you're so tired. What shall I do?"

"But you don't understand," cried Polly, vexed with herself that she couldn't help her annoyance from being seen. "I shall put some one else out if I give up my evening. I have an engagement, Amy. No, I don't see how I can do it, child; I'm sorry." And then before she knew how, she put both arms around the little figure. "Don't cry, dear, I suppose I must. I'll get out of the other thing. Yes, fly at Chopin, and keep your courage up, and I'll be over at seven. Then to-morrow Brother Jack will say 'How fine!' and off you'll go over the seas!"

Outside, Polly, after enlisting Miss Salisbury's favor for the evening's plan, was hurrying along the pavement, calling herself an hundred foolish names for helping an idle girl out of a scrape. "And to think of losing the only chance to hear D'Albert," she mourned. "Well, it's done now, and can't be helped. Even Jasper when he hears of it, will think me a silly, I suppose. Now to make my peace with Pickering."

She turned down the avenue running out from the street that had the honor to contain "Miss Salisbury's Boarding and Day School for Young Ladies," and met face to face, suddenly, a young man, about whose joy at meeting her, there could be no doubt.

"Oh, Polly!" he cried, "here, let me take that detestable thing!" trying to get the music-roll out of her hand.

"Take care how you talk against this," cried Polly, hugging it closer. "Indeed you shall not touch it, till you are glad that I am a music teacher. Oh, I must tell you—I was on my way to your house because I was afraid you wouldn't understand a note. I can't go to-night."

"Can't go to-night?" repeated Pickering, in his astonishment forgetting all his manners.

"Why, Polly Pepper, what do you mean?"

***" Why, Polly Peppeb, What Do Mane ?"***

"Why, I must give it up," cried Polly nervously; "don't ask me—or perhaps I ought to tell you, Pickering, then you'll see I can't help myself." And Polly rapidly unfolded her plan for the evening, omitting all details as to Amy's careless waste of her lessons despite all efforts to make her practice. At the end of the recital, Pickering Dodge came to a full pause on the sidewalk, regardless of all passers-by, and turned a glowering face on Polly, who was forced to stand still also, and look at him.

"What idiocy!" he exclaimed, "to give up D'Albert for that ignoramus! Polly, are you losing your senses?"

"I don't know," said poor Polly, who had lost the first flush of enthusiasm over her plan, and to whom nothing now seemed so delightful as the sight and sound of D'Albert and his wonderful melody. "Well, it's done, so don't tempt me to feel badly, Pickering."

"Indeed, and it's not done," said Pickering angrily; "you made the engagement, Polly.

I never knew you to break one before," he added stingingly.

The tears flew into Polly's brown eyes, and every bit of color deserted her round cheek. "Don't call it that, Pickering," she implored, putting out her hand.

"I shall call it just what it is," declared Pickering, in his stiffest fashion. "It's a broken engagement, Polly Pepper, nothing more nor less."

"Then," said Polly, all her tears dried, "I must go with you, if you hold me to it." She raised her head, and looked him full in the eyes.

"I will be ready," and she moved off with her most superb air, without deigning a good-by.

"Oh, Polly," cried Pickering, starting forward to overtake her, "see here, if you very much wish it, why, of course, Polly—Polly, do look around!"

"What do you wish to say?" asked Polly, not looking around as he gained her side.

"Why, of course," cried Pickering, his words stumbling over each other, "if you can't go, I'll—I'll give it up, and stay at home."

"And why should you stay at home?" cried Polly, suddenly giving him a glimpse of her face; "you've lovely seats; do ask Alexia."

"Alexia!" exclaimed Pickering angrily. "Indeed I will not. I don't want any one if I can't have you, Polly." He was really miserable now, and needed comfort, so she turned around and administered it as only Polly could.

By the time the talk was over, she hurried off with a radiant face, and Pickering with an expression only one remove from that of absolute gloom, retraced his steps to lay one of "the lovely seats" for the D'Albert concert, before Miss Rhys, for her acceptance.

Phronsie came slowly down the hall to meet Polly as usual; this day with one of her company white gowns on. Polly always knew when these were donned that something unusual was to be expected from the daily routine of the household.

"Are you really and truly home, Polly?" asked Phronsie, taking the music-roll to tuck it under her own arm.

"Yes, Pet;" Polly set a kiss on the red lips. "And I am as hungry as a beaver, Phronsie."

"So you must be," said Phronsie, with a little sigh, "for you were so long in coming home. Well, do hurry now, Polly." This last as Polly was skipping over the stairs to her own room to freshen up a bit. Then Phronsie turned into the dining-room to be quite sure that the butler had made the belated luncheon as fine as Polly could desire it.

"She didn't ask why I had on this gown," mused Phronsie, softly disposing again the flowers at Polly's plate, "and it's funny, I think, for Polly always sees everything;" and she began to look troubled at once.

***Phronsie Came Slowly Down The Hall,,***

"This is just as splendid as it can be," cried Polly, coming in, and picking up one of the roses at her plate. "Phronsie, you are just a dear to have everything so nice," and she fastened it at her belt. "Why, dear me! You've a fine gown on! What is going to happen?"

"And you didn't see it," said Phronsie, a bit reproachfully, as she gently smoothed the front breadth of mull.

"Forgive me, dear," begged Polly. "Well, what is it, Pet? Do tell me; for I'm dying of curiosity, as the Salisbury girls say."

Phronsie stood up on tiptoe, and achieved Polly's ear.

"Who do you think is coming to-night?" she whispered impressively.

"To-night? Oh, dear me! I can't possibly guess," said Polly, beginning to think that this one evening of all the year held supreme moments for her. "Who is it, Phronsie? do tell me quickly."

"Well," said Phronsie, drawing off to see the surprised delight sure to come on Polly's face, "it's Jasper himself."

"Not Jasper?" exclaimed Polly, quite gone with joy. "Oh, Phronsie Pepper, you can't mean that?"

"But I do," said Phronsie, forgetting her age, to hop up and down on the rug, "we've a letter while you were at the school, and I wasn't to tell you suddenly, so I put on one of my nice gowns, so you would know."

"But how could I possibly suppose that Jasper would come now," cried Polly, seizing Phronsie's hands to execute one of the old-time dances. "Now I almost know he is going to stay over Christmas."

"He is—he is!" cried Phronsie in a little scream; "you've guessed it, Polly. And Mamsie said—she's gone down town with Grandpapa; he's going to get tickets for the concert to-night, so that you can all go together, even if you can't sit together, and she said that"—

"Oh, Phronsie!" exclaimed Polly in dismay and she stood quite still.

"Aren't you glad?" asked Phronsie, her joy suddenly hushed.

"And I've done it myself—spoiled all this loveliness," cried Polly passionately, little white lines coming around her mouth, "and Jasper here!"

"Oh, Polly, Polly!" Phronsie clasped her gown imploringly,"don't, Polly."

"I just won't go to the school," declared Polly at white heat; "I don't care for the concert, but I'll send a note over to say that I am detained at home."

"What is it, Polly?" begged Phronsie, all sorts of dreadful surmises seizing her, "do tell me, Polly, won't you?"

"It's—nothing; you wouldn't understand, child," said Polly quickly. "There, don't ask."

Phronsie crept away in a grieved fashion, to be presently folded into Polly's warm arms. "I'm bad to-day, Phronsie dear. There, Pet, now you are all right, aren't you?" as she hugged her close.

"I am, if you are, Polly," said Phronsie doubtfully.

"Well, I'm all right now," said Polly, her brow clearing; "the bad has gone at last, I hope, to stay away, Phronsie. Now I must hurry and eat this nice luncheon you've fixed for me;" and she sprang toward the table.

"Don't you want to write a note first?" asked Phronsie, wondering at Polly's strange mood, and following her to the table-edge, "you said so."

"No; I've given it up," said Polly, sitting down and beginning on her chop and toast. "Bless you, dear, you've given me an orchid," glancing down between her mouthfuls to the bouquet at her plate; "you should have saved them all for Jasper."

"Turner said I might have it," said Phronsie triumphantly, "and I knew you'd give it to Jasper, so it's all right."

"It surely shall do double duty," said Polly merrily, with a tender glance for the orchid. "Well, how's Baby?"

"He is very nice," said Phronsie, with a grown-up air, "and didn't cry a bit for Mamsie. And now if you are really all right, Polly, I'll go up to the nursery and look at him."

"So I would," said Polly approvingly. "Yes, I'm all right; see, I'm on my chop No. 2."

Phronsie smiled with great satisfaction at this, and went off. At a quarter of seven, Polly, in a storm of remonstrance from all but one, hurried off to help poor Amy Loughead through her Slough of Despond.

Jasper alone, just arrived for dinner, was the only one who remained silent when the storm of disapproval broke forth over Polly and her doings. After the first astonished exclamation, he had absolutely refused to say anything save "Polly knows best."

"I don't know how to thank you," said Polly out in the wide hall, where he hurried to meet her, as she ran downstairs with her plainest walking things on, "for I don't believe they would have let me go. I never saw Mamsie feel so, Jasper." And now Polly could not keep the tears back.

"She'll see it all right to-morrow," said Jasper soothingly.

He put his hand out and grasped hers, as in the old days in the little brown house, and Polly answered through her tears, "I know, Jasper."

And then the maid appearing, who was to accompany her to Miss Salisbury's, Polly came out from her tears, and said, "I'm ready, Barbara."

"You are not needed, Barbara," said Jasper, reaching up for his top-coat from the oaken rack.

"What are you going to do?" gasped Polly, her hand on the door-knob, and glancing back.

"Walk over with you to that center of culture and wisdom," said Jasper coolly, close beside her now, his hat in his hand.

"O, Jasper!" exclaimed Polly in dismay, her face growing quite pale, "don't; you'll be late for the concert. Barbara, Barbara!" Polly looked past him to summon the departing maid.

"Barbara is a good girl, and understands the duty of obedience," said Jasper laughingly. "There's no help for it, Polly; you must accept my escort," and he opened the door.

"But Grandpapa! he will be terribly disappointed not to have you go to the concert with him," cried Polly, getting down the steps with a dreadful weight at her heart.

"I made it all right with father," said Jasper, "as soon as I heard of your plan; and Mr. Alstyne is on his way over to take my place; at least he ought to be in response to my note. Don't worry, Polly; come."

"Oh! what perfectly elegant seats," exclaimed Alexia Rhys, waving her big ostrich fan contentedly, and sweeping the audience with a long gaze. "Everybody is here to-night, Pickering."

"That's not so," said Pickering savagely, and bestowing a thump on his unoffending opera hat, already reduced to the smallest possible bulk.

"Don't spoil it," advised Alexia coolly, with a sidelong gaze at his face. "Well, of course I mean everybody except Polly; and I'm sure, Pickering, it isn't my fault that she didn't come; Polly always was queer about some things."

Pickering did not answer, but bestowed his glance on the programme in his hand.

"And now she is queerer than ever," said Alexia, glad to think that the dainty blue affair on her head, she called a bonnet, was already doing its work, as she heard a lady in the seat back of them, question if it were not one of the newest of Madame Marchaud's creations. So she sat more erect, and played nonchalantly with her fan. "Yes, and it's all because of those dreadfully horrid music lessons."

Pickering coughed, and rattled his programme ominously, which Alexia pretended not to hear.

"Why Mr. King lets her do it, I can't see," she went on.

"Do stop," said Pickering shortly, and casting a nervous glance back of her shoulder.

"Never mind if they do hear," said Alexia sweetly, "all the better; then they'll know we don't approve of her doing so, at any rate."

"I do approve," said Pickering, his face flaming, "if she wants to; and we've got to, any way, because we can't help ourselves. I do wish, Alexia, you wouldn't discuss our friends in this public way."

"And I don't think it is a very sweet thing to invite a girl to a concert, and then get up a fight," said Alexia, back at him.

"Goodness—who's fighting?" exclaimed Pickering under his breath.

"You are—I wish you could see your face; it's as black as a thunder cloud," said Alexia, with the consciousness that her own was as calm as a June morning. "And I'm sure if you don't want to attract people to our conversation, you might at least look a little pleasanter."

Pickering threw two or three nervous glances on either side, to prove her words, and was by no means reassured to see the countenance of Billy Harlow, one of his young business friends, across the aisle, suffused with an attempt to appear as if he hadn't been a witness to the little by-play.

"Well, I'm morally certain I won't trouble you with another invitation to a concert," he said, too furious to quite know his own words.

"You needn't," said Alexia, swinging her fan with an even hand, and still smiling sweetly, this time including in it Billy, who had no girl with him. "I really could endure life at home better than this bliss." And then D'Albert came on the stage, and it was the proper thing to keep quiet, so the hostilities died down.

Going out of the Opera House, Billy Harlow ran up to the two. "Lovely time you've had," he said on Alexia's side, and with a little grimace.

"Haven't I?" said Alexia back again, with the air of a martyr. Pickering stalking along by her side, had the air of a man who didn't care what was being said about him.

"Just look at him now," said Alexia softly, "isn't he sweet? And fancy my bearing it for two hours. I don't think any other girl in our set, could."

"Why didn't Miss Pepper come this evening?" asked Mr. Harlow curiously; "Pickering said he'd asked her."

"Oh! she gave it up to help some girl," said Alexia carelessly. "She's the music teacher at Miss Salisbury's school, you know."

"Oh! is she?" asked Mr. Harlow innocently, forgetting to mention the daily interviews he sustained with his sisters Kitty and Grace who were "Salisbury girls," on Miss Pepper's movements.

"And at the last minute he asked me to take her place," said Alexia with perfect frankness, "and I was goose enough to do it."

"Isn't Miss Pepper going to give a Recital pretty soon?" asked Mr. Harlow, incidentally, as they worked their way along to the entrance.

"Yes, she is," said Alexia sharply, "at the Exeter—we can't stop her; she says she's proud to do it, and it shows the girls' wonderful ability; and all that sort of thing—and—and—oh dear me! after she's once done that, she'll always be 'Miss Pepper the music teacher.' Isn't it horrid!"

"I believe that is our carriage," said Pickering stiffly, and without so much as a half-glance at Billy. "Come, Alexia."

# CHAPTER II

# GETTING READY FOR CHRISTMAS

"Baby ought to have a Christmas Tree," said Phronsie slowly.

"Ah—King-Fisher, how is that? Do you want a Christmas Tree?" Jasper dropped to all-fours by the side of the white bundle in the center of the library rug, as he propounded the momentous question.

The Baby plunged forward and buried both fat hands in the crop of brown hair so suddenly brought to his notice.

"Is that the way to show your acknowledgment, sir?" cried Jasper, springing to his feet, Baby and all. "Well, there you go—there, and there, and there!" tossing the white bundle high in the air.

"Goodness! what a breeze you two contrive to raise," exclaimed Joel; "Mamsie," as Mother Fisher put her head in the doorway, "the little chap is getting the worst of it, I tell you."

"Joel's jealous," said Jasper, with a laugh. "Take care, King-Fisher, that really is my hair, sir."

Mrs. Fisher nodded and chuckled to the baby, and hurried off.

"He didn't really mean to pull your hair, Jasper," said Phronsie in a worried way; and getting up from the floor where she had been deserted by the baby, she hurried over to the two flying around in the center of the room.

"But he does pull dreadfully, though," said Polly, laughing, "don't you, you little King!" pinching Baby's toes as Jasper spun him past her.

"My goodness!" exclaimed Mr. King, coming in the opposite doorway, "I should think it was a menagerie here! What's the matter, Phronsie?"

"Baby is pulling Jasper's hair," said Phronsie slowly, and revolving around the two dancers, "but he really doesn't mean to, Grandpapa."

"Oh! I hope he does," said old Mr. King cheerfully, coming in and sitting down in his favorite chair. "I'm sure it speaks well for the young man's powers of self-defense, if he gives Jasper a good tweak."

"Father!" cried Jasper in pretended astonishment. "Well, King-Fisher, as popular opinion is against me, I'll set you down again, and nurse my poor scalp," and down went the white bundle again to the floor, Phronsie going back to her post as nurse.

"There's been a terrible scheme worked up since you were out, sir," announced Joel to the old gentleman.

"Hey—what's that?" demanded Mr. King, staring at Polly.

"Oh! it isn't Polly this time," said Joel with a laugh. "Generally it is Polly that sets all dreadful things going; but this time, it is some other ringleader."

"Then I am sure I sha'n't approve if Polly isn't in it," declared the old gentleman flatly.

"But I am in it, Grandpapa," Polly made haste to say. "I think it is very, very nice."

"That alters the case," said Mr. King. "So what is it, Joe? Out with it."

"It's nothing more nor less than to upset this house from top to bottom," said Joel, "and get up a dreadful howling, tearing Christmas Tree."

***"Baby Ought To Have A Christmas Tree, " Said Phronsie Slowly.***

"Oh, Joe Pepper!" ejaculated Polly reproachfully, "and you've always had such fun over our Christmas Trees. How can you!"

"It's for Baby," cried Phronsie, with a pink flush on her cheek. "He's never seen one, you know, Grandpapa."

"No, I should think not," said the old gentleman, looking down at the white bundle. "Well, and so you want a Christmas Tree for him, Phronsie child?"

"I think we ought to have one," said Phronsie, "because you know, he's never, never seen one. And we all have had so many beautiful Trees, Grandpapa."

"To be sure, to be sure," said Mr. King. "Well now, Phronsie child, come here and tell me all about it," and he held out his hand.

Phronsie cast an anxious glance at the bundle. "Can I leave him, Grandpapa?" she asked.

"Leave him? Mercy, yes; it does babies good to be left alone. He'll suck his thumbs or his toes."

"I'll stay with him," said Polly, running out of her corner to get on her knees before the baby. "There now, sir, do you know what a blessed old care you are?" smothering him with kisses.

"Yes, I really think we ought to have a Christmas Tree," Phronsie was saying, "Grandpapa dear," huddling up against his waistcoat as usual.

"Then we surely will have one," declared old Mr. King, "so that is settled. Do you hear, young people," raising his voice, "or does that little scamp of a baby take all your ears?"

"We hear, Grandpapa," said Polly from the floor, "and I'm very glad. It will be good fun to get up a Christmas Tree."

"Seeing you never have had that pleasing employment," said Jasper *sotto voce*, on the rug before the fire.

"Never mind; it'll be just as good fun again," said Polly.

"And not a bit of work—oh, no!"

"Don't throw cold water on it," begged Polly under her breath, while the baby scrambled all over her, "don't, Jasper; Phronsie has set her heart on it."

"All right; but I thought you wanted every bit of time to get ready for your Recital, and the other things; and then, besides, there's Phronsie's performance down at Dunraven."

"Well, so I did," confessed Polly, with a sigh, "but I can get the time some way."

"Out of 'the other things,'" said Jasper grimly. "Polly, you'll have no fun from the holidays. It isn't too late to stop this now." He darted over toward his father.

"Jasper!" cried Polly imploringly.

"What is it, my boy?" asked Mr. King, quite deep in the plans for the Tree, Joel having added himself to their company.

"Oh, nothing; Polly wants it, and we must make it a good one," said Jasper, rather incoherently, and beginning to retreat.

"Of course it will be a good one," said his father, a trifle testily, "if we have it at all. When did we ever get up a poor Tree, pray tell?"

Polly drew a relieved breath, and gathering the baby up in her arms, she hurried over to the old gentleman's chair with a "Now when do you want to have the Tree, Phronsie?"

"Must we have it Christmas Day?" asked Phronsie, looking at her anxiously.

"Christmas Day? Dear me, no! Why, what would the Dunraven children do, Phronsie, if you took that day away from them?" cried old Mr. King in astonishment.

Phronsie turned slowly back to him. "I thought perhaps we ought to let Baby have the Tree Christmas Day," she said.

"No, indeed," again said Mr. King. "Come here, you little scamp," catching the baby out of Polly's hand, to set him on his other knee; "there now, speak up like a man, and tell your sister that you are not particular about the time you have your Tree."

"Ar—goo!" said the Fisher baby.

"That's it," said the old gentleman with approval, while the others shouted. "So now, as long as your brother says so, Phronsie, why, I should have your Tree the day before Christmas."

"Oh, Polly wants to go"—began Jasper.

"Ugh!" cried Polly warningly to him. "Yes, Phronsie; you much better have it the day before, as Grandpapa says."

"And you don't suppose Baby will feel badly afterwards when he gets bigger, and cry because we didn't give him Christmas Day," said Phronsie, "do you, Grandpapa?"

"Indeed, I don't," declared the old gentleman, pinching the set of pink toes nearest to his hand; "if he does, why, we'll all let him know what we think of such conduct."

"Then," said Phronsie, clasping her hands, "I should very much rather not take Christmas Day from the Dunraven children, because you know, Grandpapa, they expect it."

"Of course they do," said old Mr. King. "Bless me! why, we shouldn't know it was Christmas at all, if we didn't go down to Bedford and carry it; and as for those children"—

The picture that this brought up, of Dunraven without a Christmas, threw such a shadow over Phronsie's face, that Polly hastened to say reassuringly:

"Oh, Grandpapa! we wouldn't ever think of not carrying a Christmas to Dunraven, would we, Pet?" and she threw her arms around Phronsie.

"Of course not," chimed in Jasper and Joel, in a way to bring back the smiles to the little downcast face.

And the baby crowed, and seized Phronsie's floating yellow hair with both hands, and they all got in one another's way to rescue it; and Mrs. Pepper hurried in again, this time for Baby; and he was kissed all around, Phronsie giving him two for fear he might think she was hurt; and one of the maids popped in with "There is a gentleman in the reception room to see Miss Mary."

Jasper turned off with an impatient gesture.

"I do suppose it is Mr. Loughead," said Polly, "for he wanted to come some time and talk about Amy. O, dear! I hope I shall say the right thing."

"Doesn't the fellow know better than to come when we are home for the Christmas holidays?" grumbled Joel. Jasper looked as if he could say as much, but instead, walked to the window, and looked out silently.

"He's very anxious about Amy," said Polly, running off to the door, where she paused and looked back for sympathy toward her little protege.

"I should think he would be," grunted Joel; "she's a goose, and beside that, she doesn't know anything."

"O, Joe! she hasn't any father nor mother," cried Polly in distress.

Joel gave an inaudible reply, and Polly ran off, carrying a face on which the sunshine struggled to get back to its accustomed place.

"Beg pardon for troubling you," said a tall young man, getting off from the divan to meet her, as she hurried into the reception room, "but you were good enough to say that I might talk with you about my sister, and really I am very much at sea to know what to do with her, Miss Pepper."

It was a long speech, and at the end of it, Polly and the caller were seated, she in a big chair, and he back on the divan opposite to her.

"I am glad to see you, Mr. Loughead," said Polly brightly, "and I hope I can help you, for I am very fond of Amy."

"It's good of you to say so," said Jack Loughead, "for she's a trying little minx enough, I suspect; and Miss Salisbury tells me you've had no end of trouble with her."

"Miss Salisbury shouldn't say that," cried Polly involuntarily. Then she stopped with a blush. "I mean, I don't think she quite understands it. Amy does really try hard to study."

"Oh!" said Jack Loughead. Then he tapped his boot with his walking-stick.

"So you really think my sister will amount to something, Miss Pepper?" He looked at her keenly.

Polly started. "Oh, yes, indeed! Why, she must, Mr. Loughead."

He laughed, and bit his moustache.

"And really, I don't think that Amy is quite understood," said Polly warmly, and forgetting herself; "if people believe in her, it makes her want to do things to please them."

"She says herself she has bothered you dreadfully," said Jack, with a vicious thrust of the walking-stick at his boot.

"She has a little," confessed Polly, "but not dreadfully. And I do think, Mr. Loughead, now that you have come, and that she sees how much you want her to study and practice, she will really do better. I do, indeed," said Polly earnestly.

Outside she could hear the "two boys," as she still called them, and Grandpapa's voice in animated consultation over the ways and means, she knew as well as if she were there, of spending the holidays, and it seemed as if she could never sit in the reception room another moment longer, but that she must fly out to them.

***" Oh !" Said Jack Loughead. Then He Tapped His Boot With His Walking Stick.***

"Amy has no mother," said Jack Loughead after a moment, and he turned away his head, and pretended to look out of the window.

"I know it." Polly's heart leaped guiltily. Oh! how could she think of holidays and good times, while this poor little girl, but fifteen, had only a dreary sense of boarding-school life to mean home to her. "And oh! I do think," Polly hastened to say, and she clasped her hands as Phronsie would have done, "it has made all the difference in the world to her. And she does just lovely—so much better, I mean, than other girls would in her place. I do really, Mr. Loughead," repeated Polly.

"And no sister," added Jack, as if to himself. "How is a fellow like me—why, I am twenty-five, Miss Pepper, and I've been knocking about the world ever since I was her age; my uncle took me then to Australia, into his business—how am I ever to 'understand,' as you call it, that girl?"

It was impossible not to see his distress, and Polly, with a deaf ear to the chatter out in the library, now bent all her energies to helping him.

"Mr. Loughead," she said, and the color deserted her round cheek, and she leaned forward from the depths of the big chair, "I am afraid you won't like what I am going to say."

"Go on, please," said Jack, his eyes on her face.

"I think if you want to understand Amy," said Polly, holding her hands very tightly together, to keep her courage up, "you must love her first."

"Hey? I don't understand," said Jack, quite bewildered.

"You must love her, and believe she's going to do nice things, and be proud of her," went on Polly steadily.

"How can I? She's such a little beggar," exclaimed Jack, "won't study, and all that."

"And you must make her the very best friend you have in all this world, and let her see that you are glad that she is your sister, and tell her things, and never, never scold." Then Polly stopped, and the color flew up to the waves of brown hair on her brow.

"I wish you'd go on," said Jack Loughead, as she paused.

"Oh! I've said enough," said Polly, with a gasp, and beginning to wish she could be anywhere out of the range of those great black eyes. "Do forgive me," she begged; "I didn't mean to say anything to hurt you."

Jack Loughead got up and straightened himself. "I'm much obliged to you, Miss Pepper," he said. "I think I'm more to blame than Amy, poor child."

"No, no," cried Polly, getting out of her chair, "I didn't mean so, indeed I didn't, Mr. Loughead. Oh! what have I said? I think you have done beautifully. How could you help things when you were not here? Oh! Mr. Loughead, I do hope you will forgive me. I have only made matters worse, I'm afraid," and poor Polly's face drooped.

Jack Loughead turned with a sudden gesture. "Perhaps you'll believe me when I say I've never had anything do me so much good in all my life, as what you said."

"What are those two talking about all this unconscionable time," Joel was now exclaiming in the library, as he glanced up at the clock. "I could finish that Amy Loughead in the sixteenth of a minute."

Old Mr. King turned uneasily in his chair. "Who is this young Loughead?" he asked of Jasper.

Jasper, seeing that an answer was expected of him, drew himself up, and said quickly, "Oh! he's the brother of that girl at the Salisbury School, father. You know Polly goes over there to help her practice."

"Ah!" said his father, "well, what is he doing here this morning, pray tell?"

"That's what I should like to know," chimed in Joel.

"Well, last evening," said Jasper, with an effort to make things right for Polly, "he was there when they were playing, and he seemed quite put out at his sister."

"Don't wonder," said Joel; "everybody says she's a silly."

"And Polly tried to help Amy, and make the best of her. And the brother asked if he might have a talk some time about his sister. Polly couldn't help telling him 'yes,'" said Jasper, but with a pang at the handsome stranger's delight as she said it.

"A bad business," said the old gentleman irritably. "We do not want your Lougheads coming here and taking up our time."

"Of course not," declared Joel.

"And I suppose he is an idle creature. Polly said something about his traveling a good deal. It's a very bad business," repeated Mr. King.

"Oh! he's all right in a business way," said Jasper, feeling angry enough at himself that he was sorry at Jack Loughead's success. "He has to travel; he's a member of the Bradbury and Graeme Company."

"The Sydney, Australia, house?" asked Mr. King in a surprised tone. "So you've looked him up, have you, Jasper?"

"Oh! I happened to run across Hibbard Crane yesterday," said Jasper carelessly, "and he gave me a few facts. That's about all I know, father."

And in came Polly, looking like a rose; and following her a tall young man, with large, black eyes, whom she immediately led up to Mr. King's chair. "Grandpapa," she said, "this is Mr. Loughead, Amy's brother, you know"—

And Jasper went forward and put out his hand, as an old acquaintance of the evening before, and Joel was introduced, and mumbled something about "Glad to know you," immediately retreating into the corner, and then there was a pause, which Polly broke by crying: "O, Grandpapa! I am going to ask Amy to play at Dunraven for Phronsie's poor children. Why, where is Phronsie?" looking around the room.

"Oh! she went out a little while after Baby's exit," said Jasper, trying to speak lightly.

"Mr. Loughead thinks she'd do it, if I asked her," Polly went on in her brightest way. "Now, that will be lovely, and the children will enjoy it so much."

"Isn't there anything I could do?" asked Jack Loughead, after the Dunraven entertainment had been a bit discussed.

Mr. King bowed his courtly old head. "I don't believe there is anything. You are very kind, I'm sure."

"Don't speak of kindness, sir," he said. "My time hangs heavy on my hands just now."

"He would like to be with his sister," said Jasper, after a glance at Polly's face, and guilty of an aside to his father.

"Oh!—yes," said Mr. King, "to be sure. Well, Mr. Loughead, and what would you like to do for these poor children of Phronsie's Christmas Day? We shall be very glad of your assistance."

"I could bring out a stereopticon," said Jack; "no very new idea, but I've a few pictures of places I've seen, and maybe the children would like it for a half-hour or so."

"Capital, capital," pronounced the old gentleman quite as if he had proposed it. And before any one knew how it had come about, there was Jack Loughead talking over the run down to Bedford with them all on Christmas morning, as a matter of course, and as if it had been the annual affair to him, that it was to all the others.

"Quite a fine young man," said Mr. King, when Jack had at last run off with a bright smile and word for all, "and Phronsie will be so pleased to think of his doing all this for her poor children. Bless her! Well, David, my man, are you back so soon?"

"So soon, Grandpapa?" cried David, hurrying in from a morning down town with another "Harvard Fresh," also home for the holidays. "Why, it is luncheon time."

"Impossible!" exclaimed old Mr. King, pulling out his watch. "Er—bless me! the boy is right. Now, Polly, my child, you and I must put off our engagement till afternoon. Then we'll have our Christmasing!"

# CHAPTER III

# CHRISTMAS AT DUNRAVEN

"Grandpapa," cried Phronsie, flying down the platform, "the box of dolls isn't here!"

"Goodness me!" exclaimed old Mr. King, whirling around, "'tisn't possible, child, that we've come off without that. It must be with the other luggage."

"O, no, Grandpapa dear!" declared Phronsie in great distress, and clasping her hands to keep the tears back, "it really, surely hasn't come; Polly says so."

"Well, then, if Polly says so, it must have been left at home," said the old gentleman, "and there's no use in my going to look over the luggage," he groaned.

"What's the matter?" cried Joel, rushing up, his jolly face aglow.

"The worst thing that could possibly happen," said Mr. King irritably; "Phronsie's box of dolls is left behind." Then he began to fume up and down the platform, wholly lost to everything but his indignation.

"Whew!" ejaculated Joel, "that is a miss!" and he looked down at Phronsie, but her broad hat had drooped, the brown eyes seeking the platform floor. "See here, Phronsie."

Phronsie didn't speak for a breathing-space. "What is it, Joey?" then she said, not looking up.

"I'll go back after it; don't you worry, child."

"Oh, but you can't," cried Phronsie, throwing her head back quickly, "the train will come, and then you won't be here."

"I'll take the next train; of course I can't get back for this," said Joel, swallowing hard. "I'll bring the box all right," and he dashed off.

"Joel—oh, Joel!" cried Phronsie, running after him, "don't go!" she implored.

"Here! here! what's the matter?" cried old Mr. King, forgetting his indignation to hurry after her. "Phronsie, wait; what is it, dear?"

"Joel's gone," panted Phronsie, flying back, her broad hat falling off to her shoulders, "oh, do stop him, Grandpapa dear! I'd rather not take the dolls than to have Joel left."

"Stop him? I can't. Bless me, here—somebody!" turning off to the little knots of his party scattered over the platform, "where are you all?"

Polly came running up at this, with a pale face. "Oh, Grandpapa!" she began at sight of him.

"Joel's gone home," announced Phronsie, clasping her hands in distress, "after the box of dolls, and"—

"Joel's gone home!" echoed Polly, standing quite still.

"Yes," said Phronsie, "oh, Polly, do stop him and bring him back."

"She can't," cried the old gentleman; "that boy's legs have carried him half over the town by this time. Nobody could stop him, child."

And then, most of the little knots heard the commotion, and came hurrying up with "What is it?" and "Oh dear, what's the matter?" in time to hear Polly groan, "And Joe thought so much of going down to Dunraven with us!"

*"Joel's Gone," Panted Phronsie, Flying Back.*

"Well, where is he?" cried Jasper, whirling around to look in all directions; while Ben took a few long strides to peer around the station, and David and the other "Harvard Fresh." who had been invited to keep him company, ran, one up, and the other down, the long platform.

"See here now," shouted old Mr. King so sharply that all the flying feet were arrested at once, "every one of you come back! Goodness me, the idea of the Bedford party being scattered to the four winds in this fashion!"

"I'd help if I could," said Mr. Hamilton Dyce, "but I really don't know what it's all about yet."

"Oh dear—dear!" Polly was yet wailing. Then she remembered, and threw her arms around Phronsie who was standing quite still by her side. "Phronsie, precious pet," and she picked up her pretty stuff gown to kneel on the platform-floor to look into the little face, "don't feel badly, dear. Joel will come on the next train."

"But he won't be with us," said Phronsie slowly, and turning her brown eyes piteously to Polly.

"I know it," Polly smothered a sigh, "but we can't help it now. Grandpapa is feeling dreadfully; oh, Phronsie, you wouldn't make him sick, dear, for all the world!"

Phronsie unclasped her hands, and went unsteadily over to the old gentleman. "Joel will come on the next train, Grandpapa," she said.

"Bless me, yes, of course," said Mr. King, seizing her hand; "I don't see what we are making such a fuss for. He'll come on the next train."

"What's the riot?" asked Livingston Bayley, sauntering up, and whirling his walking-stick, "eh?"

"Joel's absconded," said Mr. Dyce briefly.

"Eh?"

"Gone back after Phronsie's box of dolls," explained somebody else.

"Oh dear me," cried Alexia Rhys, trying to get near Polly, "just like that boy." She still called him that, in spite of his being a Harvard man, "He's always making some sort of a fuss."

"Perhaps the train will be late," suggested Mrs. Dyce, who, as Mary Taylor, never could bear to see Phronsie unhappy. "Hamilton, if you don't do something to help that child, I shall be sorry I married you," she whispered in her husband's ear.

"Late? it's late already," said Ben, pulling out his watch, "it's five minutes past time."

"Well, it may be our luck to have it late enough," said Jasper, with a glance at Polly, "as it's Christmas day and a big train; so he may possibly get here—he'll find a cabby that can make good time," he added, with a forlorn attempt at comfort.

Jack Loughead sauntered up and down, on the edge of the group, longing to be of service, but feeling himself too new a friend to offer his sympathy.

"Who the Dickens is that cad?" asked Mr. Bayley in smothered wrath, to Mrs. Dyce.

"Why, don't you know? He's another friend of Polly's," said Mary Taylor Dyce, smiling up sweetly into his face, "and he's going down to help entertain Phronsie's poor children. Isn't he nice?"

"Nice?" repeated Livingston Bayley with a black look at the tall figure stalking on. "How do I know? Who is the fellow, any way?"

But there was no time to reply.

"Here comes the train!" cried Alexia. The warning bell struck, and the rush of travelers from the waiting-room, began. "Oh dear me!" Then she forgot all about her late unpleasantness with Pickering Dodge, and running up to him, she seized his arm, "Oh, Pickering, do make the conductor wait for that horrid boy."

"I can't," said Pickering, "the train's late, any way. There, get on, Alexia," putting out his hand to help her up the steps.

"Oh, I forgot," she cried, drawing back, "that we'd had a fight. Tisn't proper for you to help me, Pickering, and you oughtn't to ask it, till you've begged my pardon."

"Then it will be a long day before you receive my assistance," said Pickering, lifting his cap, and turning on his heel at the same time.

Jasper tried to get up to Polly's side, as she was hurrying Phronsie to the car, old Mr. King holding fast to Phronsie's other hand, but Livingston Bayley got there first.

"Allow me, Miss Phronsie," he was saying, with extended hand. "'Pon me word, it's a beastly crowd going to-day, sir."

"She will do very well with my assistance," said the old gentleman, still holding Phronsie's little glove. "And I suppose Christmas Day belongs to everybody, eh, Bayley?" hurrying in.

Polly, her foot on the lower step, turned and sent a despairing glance down the platform, and Jasper who saw it through the crowd, fell back a little to give a last look for Joel.

"All aboard!" sang out the conductor, waving his hand.

"Come—oh, come!" called Polly with a frantic gesture, from the doorway of the car, as the train moved off. "Oh, Jasper!" as he swung himself up beside her.

"The next train runs down in an hour; don't feel badly, Polly," Jasper had time to beg before they were drawn into the confusion of the car.

But no one could pretend, with any sort of success, that Joel wasn't missed;

and Polly had all that she could do to chase away the sorrowful expression of Phronsie's little face. And everybody tried his and her best to make it as festive a time as possible; and the other passengers nudged one another, and sent many an envious glance at the merry party.

"It's Mr. King's family going down to Bedford," said the conductor to one inquiring mind. "I take 'em every year," proudly. "He's powerful rich; but this ain't his affair. It all b'longs to that little girl with the big hat." Then he dashed off, and called a station; and after the stopping and moving of the train again, he came back and sat on the arm of the seat to finish his account.

"You see, there was an old lady, a cousin of the old gentleman's, and she made a will in favor of this child with the big hat." The conductor pointed his thumb at Phronsie, leaning over Mr. King's shoulder, the better to hear a wonderful story he was concocting for her benefit. "Why, she's got some two or three millions."

*Joel Swinging A Big Box Rushed Into Dunraven Hall.*

"What—that child?" cried the listeners, in amaze.

"Yes—the old lady was tough, but"—he dashed off again, called a station, slammed the door, and was back in position in less time than it takes to tell it—"she was took sudden, while Mr. King's folks was in Europe, and now that child has turned a handsome old place down yonder"—he pointed with his thumb in the direction of Bedford— "Dunraven Lodge, the old lady always called it, into a sort of a Home, and she's chucked it full of children, mostly those whose fathers and mothers are dead; and every Christmas Day Mr. King takes down a big crowd, and"—

Here somebody called him off, not to be seen again till he put his head in the doorway, and shouted "Bedford!"

Joel, swinging a big box as only Joel could, rushed into the spacious hall at Dunraven Lodge. "How are you all!"

Phronsie disentangled herself from a group around the big fire-place where the long hickory logs snapped and blazed.

"Oh, Josey!" she cried, precipitating herself into his long arms.

"Here is the toggery," cried Joel, setting down the doll-box, while he gathered Phronsie up in his arms.

"And you, Josey," cried Phronsie, with a happy little hum, "you are all here yourself," as the group left the fire, and surrounded them.

"Well—well—well!" cried old Mr. King, lifting his head in its velvet lounging cap from the sofa where he had been napping. "Are you really here, Joe!"

"Just like you," greeted Alexia, running down the broad oaken stairs. "Here, he's come!" to Polly, appearing at the head. "We were finishing the tree, and we heard the noise. Dear me, Joe, I should think it was a cyclone," as she joined the group, Polly close behind.

Joel tossed her a saucy answer, while Polly got on her tiptoes and caught his crop of short black hair in her two hands. "Oh, Joe," she said, dropping a kiss on it, "it was lovely in you to go back."

Joel felt well repaid for losing the jolly run down, and the grand *entree* into Dunraven, his soul loved, but he covered up what he thought, by pulling Phronsie into the middle of the hall. "Come on, Phron," he said, "for a spin like old times."

"See here," cried Alexia, "we ought to get back to that Tree, Polly Pepper, or it won't be ready. Dear me, I dropped a box of frost all over the stairs; Joel made such a noise."

At the mere mention of such a possibility as the Tree not being ready, everybody started; the last one in the procession, picking up the doll-box, their movements somewhat quickened, as loud calls were now set up above stairs, for "Polly—Polly!"

"Come on," sang out Joel, who had paid his respects in a flying fashion to Grandpapa's sofa, and leaping the stairs. "Goodness me, Alexia, I should think you did spill this frost. Why didn't you go over more ground?"

"I don't believe we can save one bit," mourned Alexia, peering up the stair-length, each step sparkling with myriad little frosty gems, as if Jack Frost himself had sprinkled it with a Christmas hand. "Oh, dear, why did you come in with such a noise, Joe Pepper?"

"Just like a girl," said Joel; "jumps at everything and drops whatever she has in her hand. You all go up the other stairs; I'll sweep this in a minute, and save what I can."

"Oh, Joe, don't stop; we want you for the Tree," begged Polly. "Phronsie has been waiting downstairs all this time for you to come. Let one of the maids do it;" Joe already had his head in a closet he knew of old, opening into the big hall.

"Give me the broom," said a voice close beside him.

"Eh—what?" cried Joel, pulling out what he wanted—a soft floor brush. "Oh, is that you, Loughead?" turning around.

"I believe so," said Jack, laughing. "Here, give me the broom. I'm no help about a Tree; I'll have the stuff up there soon," and before Joel knew it, he was racing over the back stairs, wondering how it was he had let that disagreeable Jack Loughead get hold of that broom.

"It makes me think of our first Tree, in some way," said Polly softly, with glistening eyes, looking up at the beautiful branching spruce, its countless arms shaking out brilliant pendants, and gay with streamers and candles, wherever a decoration could be placed, the whole tipped with a shining star. "Oh, Bensie, can you ever forget that?"

Ben looked down from the top of the step-ladder where he was adjusting some last bit of ornament.

"Never, Polly," he said, his eyes meeting hers.

"That was so beautiful," cried Polly. "And we had it in our 'Provision Room,' and Mrs. Henderson brought my bird over, and the other things the last minute, and"—

"I had to," broke in Mrs. Henderson with a laugh, and shaking the snips of green from her white apron, "for you and Ben would have discovered the whole surprise. You were dreadful that day."

"I'm glad somebody else was dreadful in those times, besides me," observed Joel from among the branches, where he was tying on the several presents Alexia handed to him.

"Well, you see," said Polly, with rosy cheeks, "it was our first Tree, and we were so afraid the children would find it out, and spoil all the surprise."

"And did we?" cried Phronsie, in intense excitement, emerging from the depths of the Tree, the better to look at Polly, "did we, Polly, and spoil it all?"

"No, Pet," cried Polly, "you were just as good as could be."

"I remember," said Joel, "you told us stories, Polly, in the kitchen, and"—

"We tooted on our tin horns," finished David; "oh, Joe, do you remember those horns?"

"And that molasses candy," said Joel, smacking his lips, "I remember I ate mine up before breakfast."

"And did I have any?" asked Phronsie, turning from one to the other.

"Yes, indeed, you did," answered Joel.

"Why, did you think we'd forget you, Phronsie?" asked Polly, a bit reproachfully.

"And don't you remember it?" said David.

"No," said Phronsie. "I don't; but I remember Seraphina's bonnet."

"It was trimmed with some of Grandma Bascom's chicken's feathers," said Joel.

"And Mamsie made it out of an old bonnet string," said Polly. "Oh dear, if only Mamsie were here to-day!" And a cloud came over her face.

"But we've Baby Fisher now," said Ben cheerfully, looking down at her. "He's worth staying at home for, Polly."

*"And did we," cried Phronsie "find it out, Polly, and spoil it all?"*

"Of course he is," said Polly, her gayety returning. "And dear Papa Fisher was master of ceremonies then; but he wouldn't enjoy it to-day without Mamsie. So we oughtn't to wish him here."

"I wish you wouldn't begin about that Little Brown House, and what elegant times you had in it," exclaimed Alexia, twitching at a present Joel had just tied on, to be sure it was secure; "I shall think this Tree is perfectly horrid, if you do, Polly Pepper."

"Go on—do go on," begged several voices. Meanwhile, Jack Loughead had come silently up into the long hall, and deposited a neat boxful of the gleaming frost on the table, without any comments.

"Dear me, there is so much to tell," cried Polly, with a little laugh, "if we begin about Jappy's Tree."

"Who's Tree?" cried Livingston Bayley, who had been wrinkling his brows in great perplexity all through the recital.

"Why, Jasper's," said Polly and Ben together; Joel and David coming in as echoes.

"You see," said Phronsie distinctly, "that Jasper and dear Grandpapa sent the beautiful things to us."

"Mrs. Pepper and Polly and Ben had gotten the Tree ready before," said Jasper hastily. "Oh! didn't I want to be there!" he added.

"Yes; Polly almost cried because you couldn't be," said Joel in among the branches.

"But she couldn't quite cry," said Davie, "because you see we children would have found it out. Polly always sang in those days."

"Do you remember how we used to run behind the wood-pile when we wanted to plan the Tree, Polly," asked Ben, "to get away from Joel and Dave?"

"You spent most all your time in the Little Brown House in sneaking off from us," said Joel vindictively.

"Well, we had to, if we ever did anything," said Ben coolly.

"I should think so," remarked Livingston Bayley, delighted to give a thrust at somebody.

"And weren't the gilt balls pretty?" cried Polly, quite gone now in the reminiscences, though her fingers kept on at their task; "you did cover those nuts beautifully, Bensie. I don't see how you could, with such snips of paper."

"How did he make the balls?" asked Alexia, forgetting herself in her interest, and coming up to Polly.

"Why, we had some bits of bright paper, little bits, you know, and Ben covered hickory nuts with them, and pasted them all as smoothly; you can't think!"

"Oh, my!" exclaimed Alexia.

"And Polly strung all the pop-corn, and fixed the candle-ends somebody gave Mamsie, and"—

"Candle-ends? Why didn't you have whole ones?" cried Alexia.

"Why, we couldn't," said Polly, "and we were glad enough to get these. Oh! the Tree looked just beautifully with them, I tell you."

"You see," said Phronsie, drawing near to look into Alexia's face, "we were very, very poor, Alexia. So Polly and Bensie made the Tree. Don't you understand?"

"It was really Bensie's Tree," said Polly honestly, "for I didn't believe at first we could do it."

"Oh, yes, you did, Polly," corrected Ben hastily; "at any rate, you saw it in a minute."

"And it's the first time you didn't believe a thing could be done, I imagine," declared Jasper, with a bright nod at Polly.

"Well, Bensie thought of this Tree, and made me see that we could do it," persisted Polly, giving a little quirk to a rebellious pendant.

Mrs. Henderson put the corner of her white apron to her eyes. "I always have to," she said to Mrs. Dyce, "when the Little Brown House days bring those blessed children back to me."

Jack Loughead drew nearer yet; so near that he lost never a word.

"You ought to have seen what a Santa Claus Ben made!" Polly was saying.

"I cut your performance yesterday at Baby's Tree, all out, old fellow," declared Ben, descending from the step-ladder and bestowing an affectionate clap on Jasper's shoulder.

"I don't doubt it," Jasper gave back.

"We made the wig out of Mamsie's cushion hair," laughed Polly. "And we had such a piece of work putting it all back the next morning."

"And Polly shook flour all over me, for the snow," said Ben, laughing.

"Come back, Alexia, and hand me some more gimcracks, do," cried Joel, poking his head out of the branches to look at his late assistant.

"Well, do go on about your Tree in the Brown House," begged Alexia, tearing herself away to answer Joel's demands, "seeing you have begun. What did you do next, Polly?"

"Well, we all marched into the 'Provision Room,'" went on Polly, her cheeks aglow, "expecting to see our Tree just as we had left it; all but Ben, he was going to jump into the window at the right time, when the first thing"—

"Polly sat right down on the floor, saying, 'Oh!'" cried Joel, taking the words out of her mouth.

"I couldn't help it, I was so surprised," said Polly, with shining eyes. "There was a most beautiful Tree, full of just everything; and there was Mamsie, almost crying, she was so happy; and there was Cherry singing away in his cage, and the corner of the room was all a-bloom with flowers, and"—

"And Grandma Bascom was there—wasn't she funny? She used to give us hard old raisins sometimes," said Joel, afraid to show what he was feeling.

"And Phronsie screamed right out," went on Polly, "and Davie said it was Fairyland."

By this time, Alexia had dropped the present she was holding, and had run back to Polly's side again, and somehow most of the other workers followed her example, the circle of listeners closing around the little bunch of Peppers. "And Jasper sent a Christmas greeting, beside the Tree," Polly ended, "and it was perfectly lovely."

"And Santa Claus and Polly took hold of hands and danced around the Tree," said Joel; "I'll never forget that."

"Well, you would better take hold of hands and dance down to the recitation room," said Parson Henderson's deep voice, as he suddenly appeared in their midst, "the children are all ready to give their carols. Come."

# CHAPTER IV

# THE FESTIVITIES

Phronsie looked down into the sea of eager faces "Oh, Grandpapa," she exclaimed softly, and plucking his sleeve, "don't you think we might hurry and begin?"

"Dear me, Phronsie," cried the old gentleman, whirling around in his big chair to look at her, "why, they aren't all in, child," glancing down the aisle where Jasper as chief usher with Ben and the others were busily settling the children. "Bless me, what is Joel doing?"

Phronsie looked too, to see Joel hurrying up to the platform with a little colored child perched on his shoulder. She was crying all over his new coat, and at every step uttered a sharp scream.

"Toss the little beggar out," advised Livingston Bayley, as Joel shot by with his burden.

"Here, Joe, I'll give her a seat" cried David from a little knot of children, all turning excitedly around at the commotion, "there's just one here."

"Much obliged," said Joel, stalking on, "but she says she wants to see Phronsie about something."

Polly, who caught the last words, looked down reproachfully at him from the platform where Phronsie always insisted that she should sit close to her. "Can't help it," Joel telegraphed back, "I can't stop her crying."

Phronsie heard now, and getting out of her chair, she stepped to the platform edge. "Let me take her," she begged.

"Phronsie, you can't have her up here!" Polly exclaimed, while old Mr. King put forth an uneasy hand to stop all such proceedings, and two or three of the others hurried up to remonstrate with Joel.

"She wants to see me," said Phronsie, putting her cool cheek against the dark little one; "it's the new child that came yesterday," and she took her off from Joel's shoulder, and staggered back to her seat by Polly's side.

"Phronsie, do put her down," whispered Polly, "it's almost time to begin," glancing off at the clock under its wealth of evergreen at the farther end of the hall. "Here, do let me take her."

But Phronsie was whispering so fast that she didn't hear.

"What is it? Please tell me quickly, for it is almost time to have the Tree."

At mention of the Tree, the little creature sat straight in Phronsie's white lap. "May I have some of it, if I am black?" she begged, her beady eyes running with tears.

"Yes," said Phronsie, "I've tied a big doll on it for you my very own self." Then she put her lips on the dark little cheek. "Now you must get down, for I have to talk to the children, and tell them all about things, and why they have a Christmas."

But the little thing huddled up against Phronsie's waist-ribbons. "I'm the only one that's black," she said. "I want to stay here."

"Now you see, Joel," began old Mr. King harshly. Phronsie laid a soft hand on his arm. "Please, Grandpapa dear, may she have a little cricket up here? She feels lonely down with the other children, for she's only just come."

"Oh, dear—dear!" groaned Polly, looking down at the little black object in Phronsie's lap."Now what shall we do?" This last to Jasper as he hurried up.

"I suppose we shall have to let her stay," he began.

"When Phronsie looks like that, she won't ever let her go," declared Ben, with a wise nod over at the two.

"She's just as determined as she was that day when she would send Mr. King her gingerbread boy," cried Polly, clasping her hands.

Jasper gave her a bright smile. "I wouldn't worry, Polly," he said. "See, Joel has just put a cricket—it's all right," looking into Polly's troubled eyes.

Phronsie, having seated her burden on the cricket at her feet, got out of her own chair, and took one step toward the platform edge, beginning, "Dear children." But the small creature left behind clutched the floating hem of the white gown, and screamed harder than ever.

"Bless me!" ejaculated Mr. King in great distress. "Here, will somebody take this child down where she belongs?" While Polly with flushed cheeks, leaned over, and tried to unclasp the little black fingers.

"Go up there, Joe, and stop the row," said Livingston Bayley from the visitor's seat at the end of the hall; "you started it."

Jack Loughead took a step or two in the direction of the platform, then thought better of it, and got back into his place again, hoping no one had noticed him in the confusion.

Phronsie leaned over as well as she could for the little hands pulling her back. "Jasper," she begged, "do move the cricket so that she may sit by me."

And before anybody quite knew how it was done, there was the new child sitting on her cricket, and huddled up against the soft folds of Phronsie's white gown, while Phronsie, standing close to the platform edge, began again, "Dear children, you know this is Christmas Day—your very own Christmas Day. And every Christmas Day since you came to the Home, I have told you the story of the dear beautiful Lady; and every single Christmas I am going to tell it to you again, so that you will never, never forget her."

Here Phronsie turned, and pointed up to a large, full-length portrait of Mrs. Chatterton hanging on the wall over the platform. It was painted in her youth by a celebrated French artist, and represented a beautiful young woman in a yellow satin gown, whose rich folds of lace fell away from perfectly molded neck and arms.

All the children stared at the portrait as usual in this stage of the proceedings. "Now you must say after me, 'I thank my beautiful Lady for this Home,'" said Phronsie slowly.

"I thank my beautiful Lady for this Home," said every child distinctly.

"Because without her I could not have had it," said Phronsie. "You must always remember that, children. Now say it." She stood very patiently, her hands folded together, and waited to hear them repeat it.

"Because without her I could not have had it," said the children, one or two coming in shrilly as a belated echo.

***"Will you?" asked Phronsie, looking down into their faces.]***

"And I thank her for the beautiful Tree," said Phronsie. "Now say it, please."

"I thank her for the beautiful Tree," shouted the children, craning their necks away from the portrait to get a glimpse of the curtain-veiled Tree in the other room. "Please can't we have it now?" begged several voices.

"No; not until you all hear the story. Well, now, God took the beautiful Lady away to Heaven; but she is always going to be here too," again Phronsie pointed to the portrait, "just as long as there is any Home. And she is going to smile at you, because you are all going to be good children and try to study and learn all that dear Mr. Henderson teaches you; and you are going to obey every single thing that dear Mrs. Henderson tells you, just as soon as she speaks," said Phronsie slowly, and turning her head to look at the different rows.

"I hope we'll be forgiven for sitting here and listening to old lady Chatterton's praises," whispered Mrs. Hamilton Dyce to her husband. "It makes me feel dreadfully wicked to swallow it all without a protest."

"Oh, we've swallowed that annually for three years now," said Mr. Dyce with a little laugh, "and grown callous. Your face is just as bad as it was the first time Phronsie eulogized her."

"I can't help it," declared his wife, "when I think of that dreadful old"—

"Oh, come," remonstrated her husband, "let's bury the past; Phronsie has."

"Phronsie!" ejaculated Mrs. Dyce. "Oh, that blessed child! Just hear her now."

"So on this Christmas Day," Phronsie was saying in clear tones, "you are to remember that you wouldn't have had this Tree but for the beautiful Lady; and on every single other day, you must remember that you wouldn't ever have had this Home; not a bit of any of it"—here she turned and looked around the picture-hung walls, and out of the long windows to the dark pines and firs of the broad lawn, tossing their snow-laden branches, "but for the beautiful lady. And you must every one of you help to make this Home just the very best Home that ever was. Will you?" And then she smiled down into their faces while she waited for her answer.

"Oh, yes, yes," screamed the children, every one. The little black creature got off from her cricket at Phronsie's feet to look into her face. "And I will too," she cried.

"And now you all want to thank Miss Phronsie for her kind words, we know," Jasper cried at this point, hurrying into the middle of the aisle, "and so, children, you may all stand up and say 'Thank you,' and wave your handkerchiefs."

Up flew all the rows of children to their feet, and a cloud of tiny white squares of cambric fluttered in the air, and the children kept piping out, "Thank you—Thank you." And old Mr. King began a cheer for Phronsie, and another for the children; and then somebody down at the end of the long hall set up another for Mr. King, and somebody else started one for Mr. Henderson, and another for Mrs. Henderson, and there was plenty of noise, and high above it all rang the peals of happy, childish laughter. And when it was all done, everybody pausing to take breath, then Amy Loughead sent out the finest march ever heard, from the grand piano, and Polly and Jasper and all the rest marshaled the children into a procession, and Phronsie clinging to old Mr. King's hand on the one side, and holding fast to the small black palm on the other, away they all went, the visitors falling into line, around and around the big hall, till at last—oh! at last, they turned into the Enchanted Land that held the wonderful Christmas Tree. And when they were all before it, and Phronsie in the center, she lifted her hand, and the room became so still one could hear a pin drop. And then the little children who had sung the carols in the morning stepped forward and began, "It came upon the midnight clear, that glorious song of old"—

And Phronsie drew a long breath, and folded her hands, not stirring till the very last word died on the air.

And then Jasper and the others slowly drew aside the white curtain; and oh! the dazzling, beautiful apparition that greeted every one's eyes! No one could stop the children's noisy delight, and the best of it was, that no one wanted to. So for the next few moments it was exactly like the merry time over the Tree in the "Provision Room" of the Little Brown House years ago, just as Polly had said; only there was ever so much more of it, because there were ever so many more children to make it!

And Polly and Ben were like children again themselves; and David and Joel were everywhere helping on the fun; in which excitement the other Harvard man and even Livingston Bayley were not ashamed to take a most active part, as Jasper, who had borrowed Santa Claus' attire for this occasion, now made his appearance with a most astonishing bow. And then the presents began to fly from the Tree, and Jack Loughead seemed to be all arms, for he was so tall he could reach down the hanging gifts from the higher branches, so that he was in great demand; and Pickering Dodge, one eye on all of Polly's movements, worked furiously, and Alexia Rhys and Cathie Harrison didn't give themselves hardly time to breathe; and there was quite enough for Mr. Alstyne and the Cabots and Hamilton Dyce to do, and everybody else, for that matter, to pass around the presents. And in the midst of it all, a big doll, resplendent in a red satin gown, and an astonishing hat, was untied from the tree.

"O, I want to give it to her myself!" cried Phronsie.

"So you shall," declared Jasper, handing it to her.

"Susan, this is your very own child," said Phronsie, turning to the little colored girl at her side. "Now you won't feel lonely ever, will you?" and she laid the doll carefully into the outstretched arms.

And at last the green branches had shaken off their wealth of gifts, and the shining candles began to go out, one by one.

"Grandpapa," cried Polly, coming up to old Mr. King and Phronsie, with a basket of mottoes and bonbons enough to satisfy the demands of the most exacting Children's Home, "we ought to get our paper caps on."

"Bless me!" ejaculated old Mr. King, pulling out his watch, "it can't be time to march. Ah, it's a quarter of four this minute. Here, child," to Phronsie, "pick out your bonbon so that I can snap it with you."

Phronsie gravely regarded the pretty bonbons in Polly's basket. "I must pick out yours first, Grandpapa," she said slowly, lifting a silver paper-and-lace arrangement with a bunch of forget-me-nots in the center. "I think this is pretty."

"So it is; most beautiful, dear," said the old gentleman, in great satisfaction. "Now we must crack it, I suppose." So he took hold of one end, and Phronsie held fast to the other of the bonbon, and a sharp little report gave the signal for all the bonbons to be opened. Thereupon, everybody, old and young, hurried to secure one, and great was the snapping and cracking that now followed.

"Oh, Grandpapa, isn't your cap pretty?" exclaimed Phronsie in pleased surprise, drawing forth a pink and yellow crinkled tissue bit. "See," smoothing it out with a gentle hand, "it's a crown, Grandpapa!"

"Now that's perfectly lovely!" cried Polly, setting down her basket. "Here, let me help you, child—there, that's straight. Now, Grandpapa, please bend over so that Phronsie can put it on."

Instead, the old gentleman dropped to one knee. "Now, dear," he said gallantly. So Phronsie set the pink and yellow crown on his white hair, stepping back gravely to view the effect.

"It is so very nice, dear Grandpapa," she said, coming back to his side. So old Mr. King stood up, with quite a regal air, and Phronsie had a little blue and white paper bonnet tied under her chin by Grandpapa's own hand. And caps were flying on to all the heads, and each right hand held a tinkling little bell that had swung right merrily on a green branch-tip. And away to Amy Loughead's second march—on and on, jangling their bells, the procession went, through the long hall, till old Mr. King and Phronsie who led, turned down the broad staircase, and into the dining-room; and here the guests stood on either side of the doorway while the little Home children passed up through their midst.

And there were two long tables, one for the Home children, with a place for Phronsie at its head, and another for old Mr. King at the foot. And the other table was for the older people; both gay with Christmas holly, and sweet with flowers. And when all were seated, and a hush fell upon the big room, Phronsie lifted her hand.

*We Thank Thee, oh Lord,*
*For this Christmas Day,*
*And may we love Thee*
*And serve Thee alway.*
*For Jesus Christ*
*The Holy Child's sake.*
*Amen.*

It rang out clear and sweet in childish treble, floating off into the halls and big rooms.

"Now, Candace," Phronsie lifted a plate of biscuits, and a comfortable figure of a colored woman, resplendent in the gayest of turbans and a smart stuff gown, made its appearance by Phronsie's chair.

"I'm here, honey," and Candace's broad palm received the first plate to be passed, which opened the ceremony of the Christmas feast.

Oh, this Christmas feast at Dunraven! It surpassed all the other Dunraven Christmases on record; everybody said so. And at last, when no one could possibly eat more, all the merry roomful, young and old, must have a holly sprig fastened to the coat, or gown, or apron, and the procession was formed to march back to the hall; and Mr. Jack Loughead's stereopticon flashed out the most beautiful pictures, that his bright descriptions explained to the delighted children; and then games and romps, and more bonbons, and favors and flowers; and at last the sleighs and barges for Mr. King's party were drawn up in the moonlight, at the door of Dunraven, and the Christmas at the Home was only a beautiful memory.

"Miss Mary"—Mr. Livingston Bayley put out his brown driving glove—"this way," trying to lead her off from the gay group on the snow-covered veranda.

"Why, I don't understand," began Polly, in the midst of trying to make Phronsie see that it was not necessary to go back and comfort Susan with another good-by, and turning a bewildered face up at him.

"Why, I certainly supposed you accepted my offer to drive you to the station," said Mr. Bayley hurriedly, and still extending his hand. "Come, Miss Pepper."

"Come, Polly, I've a seat for you," cried Alexia, just flying into the biggest barge. "Do hurry, Polly."

"Polly," called Jasper. She could see that he stood by one of the sleighs, beckoning to her.

Meantime, Phronsie had been borne off by old Mr. King, and Polly could hear her say, "Somebody get Polly a seat, please."

"I considered it a promise," Livingston Bayley was saying under cover of the gay confusion. "And accordingly I prepared myself. But of course if you do not wish to fulfill it, Miss Pepper, why, I"—

"Oh, no, no," cried Polly hastily, "if you really thought I promised you, Mr. Bayley, I will go, thank you," and without a backward glance at the others, she moved off to the gay little cutter where the horse stood shaking his bells impatiently.

"Where's Polly?" somebody called out. And somebody else peered down the row of vehicles, and answered, "Mr. Bayley's driving her."

And they were all off.

Polly kept saying to herself, "Oh, dear, dear, what could I have said to make him think I would go with him?" And Livingston Bayley smiled happily to himself under the collar of his driving coat; and the sparkling snow cut into little crystals by the horse's flying feet, dashed into their faces, and the scraps of laughter and merry nonsense from the other sleighs, made Polly want nothing so much as to cower down into the corner of the big fur robes, for a good cry.

And before she knew it, Mr. Bayley had turned off, leaving the gay procession on the main road.

"Oh!" cried Polly then, and starting forward, "Mr. Bayley, why, we're off the road!"

"I know a short cut to the depot," he answered hastily, "it's a better way."

"But we may miss the train—oh, do turn back, and overtake them," begged Polly, in a tremor.

"This is a vastly better road," said Mr. Bayley, and instead of turning back, he flicked the horse lightly with his whip. "You'll say, Miss Mary, that it's much better this way." He tried to laugh. "Isn't the sleighing superb?"

"Oh, yes—oh dear me!" cried poor Polly, straining her eyes to catch a sight of the last vehicle with its merry load. "Indeed, Mr. Bayley, I'm afraid we sha'n't get to the depot in time. There may be drifts on this road, or something to delay us."

"Oh, no, indeed!" cried Livingston Bayley confidently, now smiling again at his forethought in driving over this very identical piece of roadway, when the preparations for the Christmas festivity were keeping all the other people busy at Dunraven, and leaving him free to provide himself with sleighing facilities for the evening. "Don't be troubled, I know all about it; I assure you, Miss Mary, we shall reach the depot as soon as the rest of the party do, for it's really a shorter cut."

Polly beat her foot impatiently on the warm foot-muff he had wrung with difficulty from the livery keeper, and counted the moments, unable to say a word.

"Miss Mary"—suddenly Mr. Livingston Bayley turned—"everything is forgiven under such circumstances, I believe," and he laughed.

Polly didn't speak, only half hearing the words, her heart on the rest of the party, every instant being carried further from her.

"And you must have seen—'pon me word it is impossible that you didn't see that—that"—

"Oh, dear," burst out Polly suddenly, and peering anxiously down the white winding highway. "If there should be a drift on the road!"

Livingston Bayley bit his lip angrily. "'Pon me word, Miss Mary," he began, "you are the first girl I ever cared to speak to, and now you can't think of anything but the roads."

Still Polly peered into the unbroken whiteness of the thoroughfare, lined by the snow-laden pines and spruces, all inextricably mixed as the sleigh spun by. It was too late to turn back now, she knew; the best that could be done, was to hurry on—and she began to count the hoof-beats and to speculate how long it would be before they would see the lights of the little station, and find the lost party again.

"I might have spoken to a great many other girls," Livingston Bayley was saying, "and I really don't know why I didn't choose one of them. Another man in my place would, and you must do me the justice to acknowledge it; 'pon me word, you must, Miss Mary."

Polly tore off her gaze from the snowy fields where the branches of the trees were making little zigzag paths in the moonlight, to fasten it on as much of his face as was visible between his cap and his high collar.

"And I really shouldn't think you would play with me," declared Mr. Bayley, nervously fingering the whip-handle, "I shouldn't, don't you know, because you are not the sort of girl to do that thing. 'Pon me word, you're not, Miss Mary."

"I? what do you mean?" cried poor Polly, growing more and more bewildered.

"Why I—I—of course you must know; 'pon me word, you must, Miss Mary, for it began five years ago, before you went abroad, don't you know?"

Polly sank back among her fur robes while he went on.

"And I've done what no other fellow would, I'm sure," he said incoherently, "in my place, kept constant, don't you know, to one idea. Been with other girls, of course, but only really made up my mind to marry you. 'Pon me word, I didn't, Miss Mary."

"And you've brought me out, away from the rest of the party, to tell me this," exclaimed Polly, springing forward to sit erect with flashing eyes. "How good of you, Mr. Bayley, to announce your intention to marry me."

"You can't blame me," cried Mr. Bayley in an injured way. "That cad of a Loughead means to speak soon—'pon me word, the fellow does. And I've never changed my mind about it since I made it up, even when you began to give music lessons."

"Oh, how extremely kind," cried Polly.

"Don't put it that way," he began deprecatingly. "I couldn't help it, don't you know, for I liked you awfully from the first, and always intended to marry you. You shall have everything in the world that you want, and go everywhere. And my family, you know, has an *entree* to any society that's worth anything."

"I wouldn't marry you," cried Polly stormily, "if you could give me all the gold in the world; and as for family," here she sat quite erect with shining eyes, "the Peppers have always been the loveliest people that ever lived—the very loveliest—oh"—she broke off suddenly, starting forward—"there's something on the road; see, Mr. Bayley!"

And spinning along, the horse now making up his mind to get to the depot in time, they both saw a big wagon out of which protruded two or three bags evidently containing apples and potatoes; one of the wheels determining to perform no more service for its master, was resting independently on the snowy thoroughfare, for horse and driver were gone.

"I beg your pardon," exclaimed Mr. Livingston Bayley suddenly, at sight of this, "for bringing you around here. But how was I to know of that beastly wreck?"

"We must get out," said Polly, springing off from her side of the sleigh, "and lead the horse around."

But this was not so easy a matter; for the farmer's wagon had stopped in the narrowest part of the road, either side shelving off, under its treacherous covering of snow. At last, after all sorts of ineffectual attempts on Mr. Bayley's part to induce the horse to stir a step, Polly desperately laid her hand on the bridle. "Let me try," she said. "There, you good creature," patting the horse's nose; "come, that's a dear old fellow," and they never knew quite how, but in the course of time, they were all on the other side of the wreck, and Mr. Livingston Bayley was helping her into the sleigh, and showering her with profuse apologies for the whole thing.

"Never mind," said Polly, as she saw his distress, "only never say such perfectly dreadful things to me again. And now, hurry just as fast as you can, please!"

And presently a swift turn brought the twinkling lights of the little station to view, and there was the entire party calling to them as they now spied their approach, to "Hurry up!" and there also was the train, holding its breath in curbed impatience to be off.

# CHAPTER V

# BAD NEWS

"Oh, Mamsie," cried Polly in dismay, "must Papa Fisher know?"

"Certainly," said Mrs. Fisher firmly, "your father must be told every thing."

"Dear me!" exclaimed Polly, turning off in dismay, "it seems so—so unfair to Mr. Bayley. Mightn't it be just as if he hadn't spoken, Mamsie?" She came back now to her mother's side, and looked anxiously into the black eyes.

"But he has spoken," said Mother Fisher, "and your father must be told. Why, Polly, that isn't like you, child, to want to keep anything from him," she added reproachfully.

"Oh! I don't—I couldn't ever in all this world keep anything from Father Fisher," declared Polly vehemently, "only," and the color flew in rosy waves over her face, "this doesn't seem like my secret, Mamsie. And Mr. Bayley would feel so badly to have it known," and her head drooped.

"Still it must be known by your father," said her mother firmly, "and I must tell Mr. King. Then it need go no further."

"Oh, Mamsie!" exclaimed Polly, in a sharp tone of distress, "you wouldn't ever in all this world tell Grandpapa!"

"I most certainly shall," declared Mrs. Fisher. "He ought to know everything that concerns you, Polly, and each one of you children. It is his right."

Polly sat down in the nearest chair and clasped her hands. "Grandpapa will show Mr. Bayley that he doesn't like it," she mourned, "and it will hurt his feelings."

Mrs. Fisher's lip curled. "No more do I like it," she said curtly. "In the first place to speak to you at all; and then to take such a way to do it; it wasn't a nice thing at all, child, for Mr. Bayley to do," here Mrs. Fisher walked to the window, her irritation getting the better of her, so that Polly might not see her face.

"But he didn't mean to speak then—that is"—began Polly.

"He should have spoken to your father or to Mr. King," said Mrs. Fisher, coming back to face Polly, "but I presume the young man didn't know any better, or at least, he didn't think, and that's enough to say about that. But as for not telling Mr. King about it, why, it isn't to be thought of for a minute. So I best have it over with at once." And with a reassuring smile at Polly she went out, and closed the door.

"Oh, dear me," cried poor Polly, left alone; and springing out of her chair, she began to pace the floor. "Now it will be perfectly dreadful for Mr. Bayley. Grandpapa will be very angry; he never liked him; and now he can't help showing what he feels. Oh! why did Mr. Bayley speak."

"Polly," called Jasper's voice, out in the hall.

For the first time in her life, she felt like running away from his call. "Oh! I can't go out; he'll guess something is the matter," she cried to herself.

"Polly?" and there was a rap at the door.

"Yes," said Polly from within.

"Can I see you a minute?"

Polly slowly opened the door, and tried to lift her brown eyes to his face.

"Oh, Polly," he pretended not to notice any thing amiss with her, "I came to tell you first; and you can help me to break it to father."

"Oh, what is it?" cried Polly, looking up quickly. "Oh, Jasper," as she saw that his face was drawn with the effort not to let her see the distress he was in.

He tried to cover up his anxiety, but she saw a yellow paper in his hand. "Oh, Jasper, you've a telegram," she cried breathlessly.

"Polly," said Jasper. He took her hand and held it firmly, "you will help father and me to bear it, I know."

"Oh, Jasper, I will," promised Polly, clinging to his hand. "Don't be afraid to tell me, Jasper."

"Listen; Marian has been thrown from her sleigh this morning; the horses ran," said Jasper hurriedly. "The telegram says 'Come.' She may be living, Polly; don't look so."

For the room grew suddenly so dark to her that she wavered and would have fallen had he not caught her. "I won't faint," she cried, "Jasper, don't be afraid. There, I'm all right. Now, oh, what can I do?"

"Could you go with me when I tell father?" asked Jasper. "I am so afraid I shall break it to him too sharply; and you know it won't do for him to be startled. If you could, Polly."

For the second time, everything seemed to turn black before her eyes, but Polly said bravely, "Yes, I'll go, Jasper." And presently, they hardly knew how, the two found themselves at old Mr. King's door.

There was a sound of voices within. "Oh, dear me!" exclaimed Polly, "I forgot Mamsie was here."

Jasper looked his surprise, but said nothing, and as they stood there irresolutely, Mrs. Fisher opened the door and came out.

"Why, Polly!" she exclaimed.

"Oh, Mrs. Fisher," cried Jasper, "we can't explain now, we must see father. But Polly will go and tell you," and in another minute they were both standing before Mr. King.

The old gentleman was walking up and down his apartment, fuming at every step. "The presumption of the fellow! How did he dare without speaking to me! Oh, eh, Polly"—and then he caught sight of Jasper, back of her.

"Father," began Jasper, "I've had a telegram from brother Mason."

"Oh, now what has he been doing?" cried Mr. King irritably. "I do wish Mason wouldn't be so abrupt in his movements. I suppose he is going abroad again. Well, let's hear."

Jasper tried to speak, but instead, looked at Polly.

"Dear Grandpapa," cried Polly, going unsteadily to the old gentleman's side, and taking his hand in both of hers. "Oh, we must tell you something very bad, and we don't know how to tell it, Grandpapa." She looked up piteously into his face.

Old Mr. King put forth his other hand, and seized the back of a chair to steady himself. "Tell me at once, Polly," he said hoarsely. "It isn't—Marian?" It was all he could do to utter the name.

"She is hurt," said Polly, going to the heart of the matter without delay, "but oh, Grandpapa, it may not be very badly, and they want Jasper to go on to New York."

Mr. King turned to Jasper. "Give me the telegram, my boy," he said through white lips; when it was all read, "Now tell Philip to pack me a portmanteau."

"Father," said Jasper, "you are not going?"

"No questions are to be asked, Jasper," said his father. "Be so good as to see that Philip packs quickly, and that you are ready. And now, Polly," the old gentleman turned to her, "I want to take you along, child, if your mother is willing. Will you go?"

"Oh, Grandpapa," cried Polly, "if I only may; oh, do take me."

"I don't want to go without you," said Mr. King. "There, run, child, and ask your mother if you may go. Send Phronsie to me; I must explain matters to her and bid her good-by."

Alexia and some of the other girls were hurrying in the east doorway of the King mansion, an hour later. "Oh, where's Polly, Mrs. Fisher?" cried Cathie Harrison.

***"We Don't Know How To Tell It, Grandpapa."***

"Polly has gone," said Mrs. Fisher, coming down the stairs. She looked as if she wanted to cry, but her hands held the basket of sewing as firmly as if no bad news had fallen upon the home.

"Gone?" cried all the girls. "Oh, Mrs. Fisher, where? Do tell us where Polly is?"

For answer Mrs. Fisher made them all go into the little reception room in an angle of the hall, where she told them the whole story.

"If that isn't perfectly dreadful," cried Alexia Rhys, throwing her muff into a chair, and herself on an ottoman. "Why, we were going to make up a theater party for to-morrow night. Mrs. Fisher, and now Polly is gone."

Her look of dismay was copied by every girl so exactly, that Mrs. Fisher had no relief in turning to any of the other four.

"And there is her Recital—what will she do about that?" cried Alexia, rushing on in her complaint. "Perhaps she'll give it up, after all," she added, brightening. "Now I most know she will, Mrs. Fisher," and she started up and began to pirouette around the room.

"Of course she has had to postpone it," said Mrs. Fisher, looking after her, "and she told Joel to write the notes to the pupils explaining matters. But never you fear, Alexia, that Polly will give up that Recital for good and all," she added, with a wise nod at her.

"Well, she must give it up for now anyway," said Alexia, coming to a pause to take breath, "that's some comfort. To think of Joe writing Polly's notes to the girls, oh, dear me!"

"Let us go and help him," proposed Cathie Harrison suddenly. "He must hate to do such poky work."

"Oh, dear me," began Alexia, taking up her little bag to look at the tiny watch in one corner. "We haven't the time. Yes—come on," she burst out incoherently; "where is he, Mrs. Fisher?"

"In the library, hard at work," said Mrs. Fisher, with a bright smile at them all.

"Come on, girls," said Alexia, rushing on. "Now that's what I admire Mrs. Fisher for," she said, when they were well in the hall, "she shows when she's not pleased, and when she likes what a body does, as well."

"I think she's just elegant," declared Cathie Harrison, who had privately done a good deal of worshiping at Mrs. Fisher's shrine.

"She's a dear," voted Alexia. "Well, do come on. Oh, Joe!" as they reached the library door.

Joel sat back of the writing table, a mass of Polly's note paper and envelopes sprawled before him, his head on his hands and his elbows on the table. Back of him paced Pickering Dodge with a worried expression of countenance.

"You do look so funny," burst out Alexia with a laugh; "doesn't he, girls?" to the bright bevy following her.

"I guess you would if you were in my place," growled Joel, scarcely giving them a glance. "Go away, Alexia; you can't get me into a scrape this morning—I've to dig at this."

"I don't want to get you into a scrape," cried Alexia, with a cold shoulder to Pickering, who had been claimed by the other girls, "we're going to help you."

"Is that so?" cried Joel radiantly; "then I say you're just jolly, Alexia," and he beamed at her.

"Yes, we want to help," echoed Cathie, drawing up a chair to the other side of the table. "Now do set us to work, Joel."

"Indeed and I will," he cried, spreading a clear place with a reckless hand.

"Take care," warned Alexia, "take care; you are spoiling all Polly's note paper. I wouldn't let you at my things, I can tell you, Joel Pepper!"

"As if I'd ever do this sort of thing for you, Alexia," threw back Joel.

"Well, do let us begin," begged Cathie, impatiently drumming on the table, as the other two girls and Pickering Dodge drew near.

"Yes, do," cried the girls, "and we'll toss those notes off in no time."

"I'll help you clear the table," cried Pickering; "do let me. I can't write those notes, but I can get the place ready;" and he began to pile the books on a chair. As he went around to Alexia's place she looked up and fixed her gaze past him, not noticing his attempt to speak.

"All right; if she wants to act like that, I'm willing," said Pickering to himself savagely and coolly going on with his work.

"Oh, dear me," groaned Cathie Harrison, "isn't it perfectly dreadful to have that dear sweet Mrs. Whitney hurt?"

"Ow!" exclaimed Joel.

"Do stop," cried Alexia with a nudge. "Haven't you any more sense, Cathie Harrison, than to speak of it?"

***"Now Do Set Us To Work, Joel"***

Cathie smothered a retort, and bit her lips to keep it back.

"Well, dear me, we are not working much," cried Alexia, pulling off her gloves; "how many notes have you to write, Joe?"

"Oh, a dozen, I believe," said Joel; "that is, counting this one."

"To whom is that?" asked Alexia, peering over his shoulder. "Oh, to Amy Loughead."

"Yes, I promised Polly this should go first. That Loughead girl was expecting her over this morning. Oh, she's a precious nuisance," grumbled Joel, dipping his pen in the ink.

"Well, then, I will write to Desiree Frye," said Alexia. "She was going to play a solo, Polly said, at the Recital. Oh, dear me, what shall I say?"

"Polly said tell them all what had happened, and that she should stay away as long as Aunty needed her, but she hoped to be home soon, and she would write them from New York."

"Oh, Joe, what a lot," exclaimed Alexia, leaving her pen poised in mid air.

"Cut it short, then," said Joel. "I don't care, only that's the sense of it."

"Oh, dear," began one of the girls, "I can't bear to write of the accident, and in the holidays, too."

Alexia made an uneasy gesture, scrawled two or three words, then threw down her pen and got out of her chair. "It's no use," she cried, running up to Pickering, who, his hands in his pockets, had his back to them all, and was looking out of the window. "I can't let myself do anything till I've said I'm sorry I was so cross," and she put out her hand.

"Eh?" exclaimed Pickering, whirling around in astonishment. "Oh, dear me!" and he pulled his right hand out of his pocket, and extended it to her.

"Mrs. Whitney has got hurt, and she was always sweet, and never said cross things, and oh, dear me!" cried Alexia incoherently, as he shook her hand violently.

"And I'm glad enough to have it made up," declared Pickering decidedly. "It's bad enough to have so much trouble in the world, without getting into fights with people you've known ever since you can remember."

"Trouble?" repeated Alexia wonderingly. "Oh, yes, Mrs. Whitney's accident, you mean; I know it's awful for all of us."

Pickering Dodge turned on his heel and walked off abruptly, and she ran back to her work with a final stare at him.

"I know now," she said to herself wisely, "and I've been mean enough to hurt him when he was bearing it. Oh, dear me, things are getting so mixed up!"

"Polly, you won't leave me, will you, till I get able to sit up?" cried Mrs. Whitney one day, a week after.

"No, Aunty, indeed I won't," declared Polly, leaning over to drop a kiss on the soft hair against the pillows.

Mrs. Whitney put up her hands to draw down the young face.

"Oh, Aunty!" exclaimed Polly in dismay, "be careful; you know doctor said you mustn't raise your arms."

"Well, just let me kiss you, dear, then," said Mrs. Whitney with a wan little smile. "Oh, Polly," when the kiss and two or three others had been dropped on the rosy cheek, "you are sure you can stay with me?"

"I'm sure I can, and I will," said Polly firmly. "Oh, Aunty, I shall be so glad to be with you; you can't think how glad."

She softly patted the pillows into the position Mrs. Whitney best liked, and then stood off a bit and beamed at her.

"It's dreadfully selfish in me to keep you," said Mrs. Whitney, "when you love your work so; and what will the music scholars do, Polly?"

"Oh, they are all right," said Polly gaily, "they're working like beavers. Indeed, Aunty, I believe they'll practice a great deal more than if I were home to be talking to them all the while."

"You are a dear blessed comfort, Polly," said Mrs. Whitney, turning on her pillow with a sigh of relief. "Now I do believe I shall get up very soon. But Jasper must go back; it won't do for him to stay away any longer from his business. Promise me, Polly, that you will make him see that he ought to go."

"I'll try, Aunty," said Polly, "and now that you are so much better, why, I do believe that Jasper will be willing to go."

"Oh, do make him," begged Mrs. Whitney, and then she tucked her hand under her cheek, and the first thing Polly knew she heard the slow, regular breathing that told she was asleep.

"Now that's just lovely," cried Polly softly, "and I will run and speak to Jasper this very minute, for he really ought to go back to his business."

But instead of doing this, she met a young girl, as she was running through the hall, who stopped her and asked, "Can I see Mr. King?"

"What!" cried Polly, astonished that the domestics had admitted any one, as it was against the orders.

"Oh, I am a relation," said the girl coolly, "and I told the man at the door that I should come in; and he said then I must wait, for I could not see Mr. King now, and he put me up in that little reception room, but I just walked out to meet the first person coming in the hall. Will you be so kind as to arrange it?"

She looked as if she fully expected to have her wish fulfilled, and her gaze wandered confidently around the picture-hung wall, until such time as Polly could answer.

"I'll see," said Polly, who couldn't help smiling, "what I can do for you; but you mustn't be disappointed if Grandpapa doesn't feel able to see you. He is very much occupied, you know, with his daughter's ill"—

"Oh, I understand," said the other girl, guilty of interrupting, "but he will see me, I know," and her light blue eyes were as calm as ever.

"Who shall I tell him wants to see him?" asked Polly, her own eyes wide at the stranger and her ways.

"Oh, you needn't tell him any name," said the girl carelessly.

"Then I certainly shall not tell him you wish to see him, unless I carry your name to him," Polly said quite firmly, and she looked steadily into the fair face before her.

"Oh, dear me," said the girl; "well, you may say I am Mr. Alexander Chatterton's daughter Charlotte."

Polly kept herself from starting as the name met her ear. "Very well," she said, "I will do what I can," moving off. "O, Grandpapa!"

For down the hall came Mr. King in velvet morning jacket and cap.

"Hoity-toity, I thought no one was to be admitted," he exclaimed, as he neared the door.

"Grandpapa," Polly endeavored to draw him off, but the young girl ran past her.

"Mr. King," she said quickly, "I am Charlotte Chatterton."

"The dickens you are!" exclaimed the old gentleman, looking her full in the face.

"Yes, sir; and my father is very ill." For a moment her voice trembled, but she quickly recovered herself. "It isn't money I want, Mr. King," and she threw her head back proudly, "but oh, will you come and see father?"

Mr. King looked at her again, then over at Polly. "Bring her in here," he said, pointing to the same little reception room that Charlotte had deserted, "I want you to stay, too, Polly," and the door closed upon them.

# CHAPTER VI

# OF MANY THINGS

"And father has asked her to go home when you and he go!" cried Jasper in irritation.

"Yes," said Polly; "oh, Jasper, never mind; I daresay it will be for the best; and I'm so sorry for Charlotte."

"She'll be no end of bother to you, I know," said Jasper. "And you must take her everywhere, Polly, and look out for her. What was father thinking of?" He could not conceal his annoyance, and Polly put aside her own dismayed feelings at the new programme, to help him into his usual serene mood.

"But think, Jasper, how she has never had any fun all her life, and now her father is sick."

"She'd much better stay and take care of him," declared Jasper.

"But he's sick because he has worried so, I do believe," Polly went on, "for you ought to have seen his face when we took Charlotte home, and Grandpapa talked with him, and asked him to let Charlotte pass the rest of the winter with us. Oh, I am glad, Jasper, for I do like Charlotte."

"The girl may be well enough," said Jasper shortly, "but she will bother you, nevertheless, Polly, I am afraid."

"Never mind," said Polly brightly, with a little pang at her heart for the nice times with the girls that now must be shared with another. "Grandpapa thought he ought to do it, I suppose, and that's enough."

"It does seem as if the Chattertons would never be done annoying us," said Jasper gloomily. "Now when we once get this girl fastened on us, there'll be an end to the hope of shaking her off."

"Perhaps we sha'n't want to," said Polly merrily, "for Charlotte may turn out perfectly lovely; I do believe she's going to." And then she remembered her promise to Mrs. Whitney, and she began: "Aunty is worrying about your staying away so long from your business, Jasper, and she wants you to go back."

A shade passed over his face. "I suppose I ought to go, Polly," he said, and he pulled a letter from his pocket and held it out to her, "I was going to show this to you, only the other matter came up."

Polly seized it with dread.

"We need your services very much" [the letter ran] "and cannot wait longer for your return. We are very sorry to be so imperative, but the rush of work at this time of the year, makes it necessary for all our force to be in place.

"Very sincerely

"DAVID MARLOWE."

"You see they are getting all the books planned out, and put in shape for the next year; and business just rushes," cried Jasper, with shining eyes, showing his eagerness to be in the midst of the bustle of manufacture.

"What, so early!" cried Polly, letting the letter drop. "Why, I thought you didn't do anything until spring, Jasper—about making the books, I mean."

He laughed. "The travelers go out on the road then," he said, "with almost all the books ready to sell."

"Out on the road?" repeated Polly in amaze. "Oh, what do you mean, Jasper?"

"Well, you see the business of selling is a good part of it done by salesmen, who travel with samples and take advance orders," said Jasper, finding it quite jolly to explain business intricacies to such an eager listener.

"Oh!" said Polly.

"And when I get back I shall be plunged at once into all the thick of the manufacturing work," he went on, straightening himself up; "Mr. Marlowe is as good as he can be, and he has waited now longer than he ought to."

"Oh, you must go, Jasper," cried Polly quickly; "at once, this very day," and her face glowed.

"If you think sister Marian is really well enough to spare me," he said, trying to restrain his impatience to be off.

"Yes—yes, I do," declared Polly. "Doctor Palfrey said this morning that all danger was over now from inflammation, and really it worries her dreadfully to think of your being here any longer. It really does hurt her, Jasper," repeated Polly emphatically.

"In that case I'm off, then, this afternoon," said Jasper, with a glad ring in his voice. "Polly, my work is the very grandest in all the world."

"Isn't it?" cried Polly, with kindling eyes; "just think—to make good books, Jasper, that will never stop, perhaps, being read. Oh, I wish I was a man and could help you."

"Polly?" he stopped a minute, looked down into her face, then turned off abruptly. "You are sure you won't bother yourself too much with Charlotte?" he said awkwardly coming back.

"Yes; don't worry, Jasper," said Polly, wondering at his unusual manner.

"All right; then as soon as I've seen father I'll throw my traps together and be off," declared Jasper, quite like the business man again.

But old Mr. King was not to hear about it just then, for when Jasper rapped at his door, it was to find that his father was fast asleep.

"See here, Jasper," said Mr. Whitney, happening along at this minute, "here's a nice piece of work. Percy declares that he shall be made miserable to go back to college to-morrow. His mother is able now for him to be settled at his studies; won't you run up and persuade him—that's a good fellow."

"I'm going back to my work to-night," cried Jasper, pulling out his watch, "that is, if father wakes up in time for me to take the train."

"Is that so? Good," cried Mr. Whitney. "Well, run along and tell Percy that, for the boy is so worried over his mother that he can't listen to reason."

So Jasper scaled the stairs to Percy's den.

"Well, old fellow, I thought I'd come up and let you know that I'm off to my work," announced Jasper, putting his head in the doorway.

"Eh!" cried Percy, "what's that?"

"Why, I'm off, I say; back to dig at the publishing business. Your mother doesn't want us fellows hanging around here any longer. It worries her to feel that we are idling."

"Is that so?" cried Percy. "How do you know?"

"Polly says so; she let me into the secret; says sister Marian requested me to go back."

"Did Polly really say so?" demanded Percy in astonishment.

"Yes, in good plain English. So I'm off."

"Well, if Polly really said that mamma wanted you to go, why, I'll get back to college as soon as I can," said Percy. "But if she should be worse?" He stopped short.

"They can send for you instantly; trust Polly for that," said Jasper. "But she won't be worse; not unless we worry her by not doing as she wishes. Well, good-by, I'm off."

"So am I," declared Percy, springing up to throw his clothes into traveling order. "All right, I'll take the train with you, Jappy."

"Now you see how much better I'm off," observed Van, coming in to perch on the edge of the bed while Percy was hurrying all sorts of garments into the trunk with a quick hand. "I tell you, Percy, I struck good luck when I chose father's business. Now I don't have to run like a dog at the beck of a lot of professors."

"Every one to his taste," said Percy, "and I can't bear father's business, for one."

"No, you'd rather sit up with your glasses stuck on your nose, and learn how to dole out the law; that's you, Percy. I say, I wouldn't try to keep the things on," with a laugh as he saw his brother's ineffectual efforts to pack, and yet give the attention to his eyeglasses that they seemed to demand.

"See here now, Van," cried Percy warmly, "if you cannot help, you can take yourself off. Goodness! I have left out my box of collars!"

"Here it is," cried Van, throwing it to him from the bed, where it had rolled off under a pile of underclothing. "Well, you don't know how the things make you look. And Polly doesn't like them a bit."

"How do you know?" demanded Percy, growing quite red, and desisting from his employment a minute.

"Oh, that's telling; I know she doesn't," replied Van provokingly.

For answer Van felt his arms seized, and before he knew it Percy was over him and holding him down so that he couldn't stir.

"Now how do you know that Polly doesn't like my eyeglasses?" he demanded.

"Ow—let me up!" cried Van.

"Tell on, then. How do you know she doesn't like them?"

"Because—Let me up, and I'll tell."

"No, tell now," said Percy, having hard work to keep Van from slipping out from under his hands.

"Boys," called Polly's voice.

"Oh dear me—she's coming!" exclaimed Percy, jumping to his feet, and releasing Van, who, red and shining, skipped to the door. "Come in, Polly."

"I thought I'd find you up here," said Polly in great satisfaction. "Percy, can't I do something for you? Jasper says you are going back to college right away."

"Yes, you can," said Percy, "take Van off; that would help me more than anything else you could do."

Polly looked at Van and shook her brown head so disapprovingly that he came out of his laugh.

"Oh, I'll be good, Polly," he promised.

"See that you are, then," she said. Then she went over to the trunk and looked in.

"Percy, may I take those things out and fold them over again?" she asked.

"Yes, if you want to," said Percy shamefacedly. "I suppose I have made a mess of them; but it's too hard work for you, Polly."

"I should like nothing better than to attack that trunk," declared Polly merrily. "Now, Van, you come and help me, that's a dear boy."

And in five minutes Polly and Van were busily working together; he putting in the things, while she neatly made them into piles, and Percy sorted and gave orders like a general.

"He does strut around so," said Van under his breath, "just see him now."

"Hush—oh, Van, how can you? and he's going back to college, and you won't see him for ever so many weeks."

Van swallowed something in his throat, and bent all his energies to settling the different articles in the trunk.

"Percy," said Polly presently in a lull, "I do just envy you for one thing."

"What for, pray?" asked Percy, settling his beloved eyeglasses for a better view of her.

"Why, you'll be with Joel and Davie," said Polly. "Oh, you don't know how I miss those boys!" She rested both hands on the trunk edge as she knelt before it.

***"Oh, You Don't Know How I Miss Those Boys!"***

"I wish you'd been our sister," said Van enviously, "then we'd have had good times always."

"Oh, I don't see much of Joel," said Percy. "Dave once in a while I run across, but Joel—dear me!"

"You don't see much of Joel," repeated Polly, her hands dropping suddenly in astonishment. "Why, Percy Whitney, why not, pray tell?"

"Why, Joel's awful good—got a streak of going into the prayer-meetings and that sort of thing," explained Percy, "and we call him Deacon Pepper in the class."

"He goes to prayer-meetings, and you call him Deacon Pepper," repeated Polly in amazement, while Van burst out into a fit of amusement.

"Yes," said Percy, "and he has a lot of old fogies always turning up that want help, and all such stuff, and I expect that he is going to be a minister."

He brought this out as something too dreadful to be spoken, and then fell back to see the effect of his words.

"Can you suppose it?" cried Polly under her breath, still kneeling on the floor, "oh, boys, can you?" looking from one to the other.

"Yes; I'm afraid it's true," said Percy, feeling that he ought to be thrashed for having told her, while Van laughed again.

"Oh—oh! it's too lovely. Dear, beautiful, old Joel!" cried Polly, springing suddenly to her feet; "just think how good he is, boys! Oh, it's too lovely to be true!"

Percy retreated a few steps hastily.

"And oh, how much better we ought to be," cried Polly in a rush of feeling. "Just think, with Joel doing such beautiful things, oh, how glad Mamsie will be! And he never told—Joel never told."

"And he'll just about kill me if you tell him I've let it out," said Percy abruptly. "Oh, dear me, how he'll pitch into me!" exclaimed Percy in alarm.

"I never shall speak of it," declared Polly in a rapture, "because Joel always hated to be praised for being good. But oh, how lovely it is!"

And then Grandpapa called, and she ran off on happy feet.

"Whew!" exclaimed Percy, with a look over at Van.

"I tell you what, if you want to get into Polly's good graces, you've just got to brush up on your catechism, and such things," remarked Van; "eyeglasses don't count."

Percy turned off uneasily.

"Nor suppers, and a bit of card-playing, eh, Percy?"

"Hold your tongue, will you?" cried his brother irritably.

"Nor swell clothes and a touch-me-if-you-dare manner," said Van mockingly, sticking his fingers in his vest pockets.

Percy made a lunge at him, then thought better of it.

"Leave me alone, can't you?" he said crossly.

Van opened his mouth to toss back a teasing reply, when Percy opened up on him. "I'd as soon take my chances with her, on the suppers and other things, as to have yours. What would Polly say to see you going for me like this, I'd like to know?"

It was now Van's turn to look uncomfortable, and he cast a glance at the door.

"Oh, she may come in," said Percy, bursting into a laugh, "then you'd be in a fine fix; and I wouldn't give a rush for the good opinion she'd have of you."

Van hung his head, took two or three steps to the door, then came back hurriedly.

"I cry 'Quits,' Percy," he said, and held out his hand.

"All right," said Percy, smoothing down his ruffled feelings, and putting out his hand too.

Van seized it, wrung it in good brotherly fashion, then raced over the stairs at a breakneck pace.

"Polly", he said, meeting her in the hall where she had just come from Mr. King's room, "I've been blackguarding Percy, and you ought to know it."

"Oh, Van!" cried Polly, stopping short in a sorry little way; "why, you've been so good ever since you both promised years ago that you wouldn't say bad things to each other."

"Oh, that was different," said Van recklessly; "but since he went to college, Percy has been a perfect snob Polly."

Polly said nothing, only looked at him in a way that cut him to the heart, as she moved off slowly.

"Aren't you going to say anything?" asked Van at last.

"I've nothing to say," replied Polly, and she disappeared into Mrs. Whitney's room and closed the door.

That evening Jasper and Percy, who went together for a good part of the way, had just driven to the station, when the bell rang and a housemaid presently laid before Polly a card, at sight of which all the color deserted her cheek. "Oh, I can't see him," she declared involuntarily.

"Who is it?" asked old Mr. King, laying down the evening paper.

"O, Grandpapa!" cried Polly, all in a tremor at the thought of his displeasure, "it does not matter. I can send word that I do not see any one now that Aunty is ill, and"—

"Polly, child," said the old gentleman, seriously displeased, "come and tell me at once who has called upon you."

So Polly, hardly knowing how, got out of her chair and silently laid the unwelcome card in his hand.

"Mr. Livingston Bayley," read the old gentleman.

"Humph! well, upon my word, this speaks well for the young man's perseverance. I'm very tired, but I see nothing for it but that I must respond to this;" and he threw aside the paper and got up to his feet.

"Grandpapa," begged Polly tremblingly at his elbow, "please don't let him feel badly."

"It isn't possible, Polly," cried Mr. King, looking down at her, "that you like this fellow—enough, I mean, to marry him?"

"O, Grandpapa!" exclaimed Polly in a tone of horror.

"Well, then, child, you must leave me to settle with him," said the old gentleman with dignity. "Don't worry; I sha'n't forget myself, nor what is due to a Bayley," with a short laugh. And then she heard him go into the drawing-room and close the door.

When he came back, which he did in the space of half an hour, his face was wreathed in smiles, and he chuckled now and then, as he sat down in his big chair and drew out his eyeglasses.

"Well, Polly, child, I don't believe he will trouble you in this way again, my dear," he said in a satisfied way, looking at her over the table. "He wanted to leave the question open; thought it impossible that you could refuse him utterly, and was willing to wait; and asked permission to send flowers, and all that sort of thing. But I made the young man see exactly how the matter stood, and that's all that need be said about it. It's done with now and forever." And then he took up his paper and began to read.

"Mamsie," said Phronsie, that very evening as she was getting ready for bed, and pausing in the doorway of her little room that led out of Mother Fisher's, "do you suppose we can bear it another day without Polly?"

"Why, yes, Phronsie," said Mother Fisher, giving another gentle rock to Baby's cradle, "of course we can, because we must. That isn't like you, dear, to want Polly back till Aunty has got through needing her."

Phronsie gave a sigh and thoughtfully drew her slippered foot over the pattern of the carpet. "It would be so very nice," she said, "if Aunty didn't need her."

"So it would," said her mother, "but it won't make Polly come any quicker to spend the time wishing for her. There, run to bed, child; you are half an hour late to-night."

Phronsie turned obediently into her own little room, then came back softly. "I want to give Baby, Polly's good-night kiss," she said.

"Very well, you may, dear," said Mrs. Fisher. So Phronsie bent over and set on Baby's dear little cheek, the kiss that could not go to Polly.

"If dear Grandpapa would only come home," and she sighed again.

"But just think how beautiful it is that Aunty was not hurt so much as the doctors feared," said her mother. "Oh, Phronsie, we can't ever be thankful enough for that."

"And now maybe God will let Grandpapa and Polly come back pretty soon," said Phronsie slowly, going off toward her own little room. And presently Mrs. Fisher heard her say, "Good-night, Mamsie dear, I'm in bed."

A rap at the door, and Jane put in her head, in response to Mrs. Fisher's "What is it?"

"Oh, is Dr. Fisher here?" asked Jane in a frightened way.

"No; he is downstairs in the library," said Mother Fisher. "What is the matter, Jane? Who wants him?"

"Oh, something dreadful is the matter with Helen Fargo, I'm afraid, ma'am," said Jane. "Griggs has just run over to say that the doctor must come quick."

*"And Please Make Dear Papa Give Her The Right Things."*

"Hush!" said Mrs. Fisher, pointing to Phronsie's wide-open door; but she was standing beside them in her little nightdress, and heard the next words plainly enough.

"Run down stairs, Jane," commanded Mother Fisher, "and tell the doctor what Griggs said; just as fast as you can, Jane."

And in another minute in rushed the little doctor, seized his medicine case, saying as he did so, "I sha'n't come back here, wife, if it is diphtheria, but go to my office and change my clothes. There's considerable of the disease around. Good-night, child." He stopped to kiss Phronsie, who lifted a pale, troubled face to his. "Don't worry; I guess Helen will be all right," and he dashed off again.

"Now, Phronsie, child," said Mrs. Fisher, "come to mother and let us talk it over a bit."

So Phronsie cuddled up in Mamsie's lap, and laid her sad little cheek where she had been so often comforted.

"Mamsie," she said at last, lifting her head, "I don't believe God will let Helen die, because you see she's the only child that Mrs. Fargo has. He couldn't, Mamsie."

"Phronsie, darling, God knows best," said Mrs. Fisher, holding her close.

"But he wouldn't ever do it, I know," said Phronsie confidently; "I'm going to ask Him not to, and tell Him over again about Helen's being the very only one that Mrs. Fargo has in all the world." So she slipped to the floor, and went into her own room again and closed the door. "Dear Jesus," she said, kneeling by her little white bed, "please don't take Helen away, because her mother has only just Helen. And please make dear papa give her the right things, so that she will live at home, and not go to Heaven yet. Amen."

Then she clambered into bed, and lay looking out across the moonlight, where the light from Helen Fargo's room twinkled through the fir-trees on the lawn.

# CHAPTER VII

# PHRONSIE

"I can't tell her," groaned Mrs. Pepper, the next morning, at sight of Phronsie's peaceful little face. "I never can say the word 'diphtheria' in all this world."

Phronsie laughed and played with Baby quite merrily, all such time as Miss Carruth, the governess, allowed her from the schoolroom that morning.

"Everything is beautiful, King dear," she would say on such little flying visits to the nursery. "Grandpapa and Polly, I do think, will be home pretty soon; and Helen is going to get well, because you know I asked God to let her, and he wouldn't ever, in all this world, take her away from her mother. He wouldn't, King," she added confidentially in Baby's small ear.

All day long the turreted Fargo mansion gleamed brightly in the glancing sunlight, giving no hint of the battle for a life going on within. Mrs. Fisher knew when her husband sent for the most celebrated doctor for throat diseases; knew when he came; and knew also when each hour those who were fighting the foe, were driven back baffled. And several times she attempted to tell Phronsie something of the shadow hanging over the little playmate's home. But Phronsie invariably put aside all her attempts with a gentle persistence, always saying, "He wouldn't, you know, Mamsie."

And at nightfall Helen had gone; and two white little hands were folded quietly across a young girl's breast.

No one told Phronsie that night; no one could. And she clambered into her little white bed, after saying her old prayer; then she lay in the moonlight again, watching Helen's house.

"The light is out, Mamsie," she called, "in Helen's room. But I suppose she is asleep." And presently Mrs. Fisher, stealing in, with unshed tears in her eyes, found her own child safe—folded in restful slumber, her hand tucked under her cheek.

But the next morning, when she must hear it!

"Phronsie," said Mrs. Fisher, "come here, dear." It was after breakfast, and Phronsie was running up into the school-room.

"Do you mean I am not to go to Miss Carruth?" asked Phronsie wonderingly, and fingering her books.

"Yes, dear. Oh, Phronsie"—Mrs. Fisher abruptly dropped her customary self-control, and held out her arms. "Come here, mother's baby; I've something bad to tell you, and you must help me, dear."

Phronsie came at once, with wide-open, astonished brown eyes, and climbed up into the good lap obediently.

"Phronsie," said Mrs. Fisher, swallowing the lump in her throat, and looking at the child fixedly, "you know Helen has been very sick."

"Yes, mamma," said Phronsie, still in a wonder.

"Well—and she suffered, dear, oh, so much!"

A look of pain stole over Phronsie's face, and Mrs. Fisher hastened to say, "But oh. Phronsie, she can't ever suffer any more, for—for—God has taken her home, Phronsie."

"Has Helen died?" asked Phronsie, in a sharp little voice, so unlike her own that Mrs. Pepper shivered and held her close.

"Oh, darling—how can I tell you? Yes, dear, God has taken her home to Heaven."

"And left Mrs. Fargo without any little girl?" asked Phronsie, in the same tone.

"My dear—yes—He knows what is best," said poor Mrs. Fisher.

The startled look on Phronsie's little face gave way to a grieved expression, that slowly settled on each feature.

"Let me get down, Mamsie," she said, quietly, and gently struggling to free herself.

"Oh, Phronsie, what are you going to do?" cried Mrs. Fisher. "Do sit with mother."

"I must think it out, Mamsie," said Phronsie, with grave decision, getting on her feet, and she went slowly up the stairs, and into her own room; then closed the door.

And all that day she said nothing; even when Mother Fisher begged her to come and talk it over with her, Phronsie would say, "I can't, Mamsie dear, it won't talk itself." But she was gentle and sweet with Baby, and never relaxed any effort for his amusement. And at last, when they were folding Helen away lovingly in flowers, from all who had loved her, Mrs. Fisher wrote in despair to Polly, telling her all about it, and adding, "You must come home, if only for a few days, or Phronsie will be sick."

"I shall go, too," declared old Mr. King, "for Marian can spare me now. Oh, that blessed child! And I can come back here with you, Polly, if necessary."

And Polly had nothing for it but to help him off, and Charlotte's father being ever so much better, she joined them; and as soon as it was a possible thing, there they were at home, and Thomas was driving them up at his best speed, to the carriage porch.

"Polly!" Phronsie gasped the word, and threw hungry little arms around Polly's neck.

"There, there, Pet," cried Polly cheerily, "you see we're all home. Here's Grandpapa!"

"Where's my girl?" cried old Mr. King hastily. "Here, Phronsie," and she was in his arms, while the tears rained down her cheeks.

"Bless me!" exclaimed the old gentleman, putting up his hand at the shower. "Well, that is a welcome home, Phronsie."

"Oh, Grandpapa, I didn't mean to!" said Phronsie, drawing back in dismay. "I do hope it hasn't hurt your coat."

"Never mind the coat, Phronsie," said Mr. King. "So you are glad to get us home, eh?"

Phronsie snuggled close to his side, while she clung to his hand without a word.

"Well, we mustn't forget Charlotte," cried Polly, darting back to a tall girl with light hair and very pale blue eyes, standing composedly in one corner of the hall, and watching the whole thing closely. "Mamsie, dear, here she is," taking her hand to draw her to Mrs. Fisher.

"Don't mind me," said Charlotte, perfectly at her ease. "You take care of the little girl," as Polly dragged her on.

Mrs. Fisher took a good long look at Charlotte Chatterton. Then she smiled, "I am glad to see you, Charlotte."

Charlotte took the firm fingers extended to her, and said, "Thank you," then turned off to look at Phronsie again.

And it wasn't till after dinner that Phronsie's trouble was touched upon. Then Polly drew her off to a quiet corner.

"Now, then, Phronsie," she said, gathering her up close in her arms, "tell me all about it, Pet. Just think," and Polly set warm kisses on the pale little cheek, "how long it is since you and I have had a good talk."

"I know it," said Phronsie wearily, and she drew a long sigh.

"Isn't it good that dear Aunty is so much better?" cried Polly cheerily, quite at a loss how to begin.

*Charlotte, Standing Composedly In One Corner Of The Hall.*

"Yes, Polly," said Phronsie, but she sighed again, and did not lift her eyes to Polly's face.

"If anything troubles you," at last broke out Polly desperately, "you'd feel better, Phronsie, to tell sister about it. I may not know how to say the right things, but I can maybe help a little."

Phronsie sat quite still, and folded and unfolded her hands in her lap. "Why did God take away Helen?" she asked suddenly, lifting her head. "Oh, Polly, it wasn't nice of him," she added, a strange look coming into her brown eyes.

"Oh, Phronsie!" exclaimed Polly, quite shocked, "don't, dear; that isn't like you, Pet. Why, God made us all, and he can do just as he likes, darling."

"But it isn't nice," repeated Phronsie deliberately, and quite firmly, "to take Helen now. Why doesn't He make another little girl then for Mrs. Fargo?" and she held Polly with her troubled eyes.

"Phronsie"—cried Polly; then she stopped abruptly. "Oh, what can I say? I don't know, dearie; it's just this way; we don't know why God does things. But we love him, and we feel it's right. Oh, Phronsie, don't look so. There, there," and she drew her close to her, in a loving, hungry clasp. "I told you I didn't think I could say the right things to you," she went on hurriedly, "but, Phronsie, I know God did just right in taking Helen to heaven. Just think how beautiful it must be there, and so many little children are there. And Helen is so happy. Oh, Phronsie, when I think of that, I am glad she is gone."

"Helen was happy here," said Phronsie decidedly. "And she never—never would want to leave her mother alone, to go off to a nicer place. Never, Polly."

Polly drew a long breath, and shut her lips. "But, Phronsie, don't you see," she cried presently, "it may be that Mrs. Fargo wouldn't ever want to go to Heaven unless Helen was there to meet her? It may be, Phronsie; and that would be very dreadful, you know. And God loved Mrs. Fargo so that he took Helen, and he is going to keep her happy every single minute while she is waiting and getting ready for her mother."

***Phronsie Went Over To The Window.***

Phronsie suddenly slipped down from Polly's lap. "Is that true?" she demanded.

"Yes, dear," said Polly, "I think it is, Phronsie," and her cheeks glowed. "Oh, can't you see how much nicer it is in God to make Mrs. Fargo happy for always with Helen, instead of just a little bit of a while down here?"

Phronsie went over to the window and looked up at the winter sky. "It is a long way off," she said, but the bitter tone had gone, and it was a grieved little voice that added, "and Mrs. Fargo can't see Helen."

"Phronsie," said Polly, hurrying over to her side, "perhaps God wants you to do some things for Mrs. Fargo—things, I mean, that Helen would have done."

"Why, I can't go over there," said Phronsie wonderingly. "Papa Fisher says I am not to go over there for ever and ever so long, Polly."

"Well, you can write her little notes and you can help her to see that God did just right in taking Helen away," said Polly; "and that would be the very best thing you could do, Phronsie, for Mrs. Fargo; the very loveliest thing in all this world."

"Would it?" asked Phronsie.

"Yes, dear."

"Then I'll do it; and perhaps God wants me to like Heaven better; does he, Polly, do you think?"

"I really and truly do, Phronsie," said Polly softly. Then she leaned over and threw both arms around Phronsie's neck. "Oh, Phronsie, can't you see—I never thought of it till now—but He has given you somebody else instead of Helen, to love and to do things for?"

Phronsie looked up wonderingly. "I don't know what you mean, Polly," she said.

"There's Charlotte," cried Polly, going on rapidly as she released Phronsie. "Oh, Phronsie, you can't think; it's been dreadfully hard and dull always for her at home, with those two stiff great-aunts pecking at her."

"Tell me about it," begged Phronsie, turning away from the window, and putting her hand in Polly's.

"Well, come over to our corner then." So the two ran back, Phronsie climbing into Polly's lap, while a look of contentment began to spread over her face.

"You see," began Polly, "Charlotte's mother has always been too ill to have nice times; she couldn't go out, you know, very much, nor keep the house, and so the two great-aunts came to live with them. Well, pretty soon they began to feel as if they owned the house, and Charlotte, and everybody in it."

"Oh dear!" exclaimed Phronsie, in distress.

"And Charlotte's father, Mr. Alexander Chatterton, couldn't stop it; and beside, he was away on business most of the time, and Charlotte didn't complain—oh, she behaved very nice about it; Phronsie, her father told Grandpapa all about it; and by and by her mother died, and then things got worse and worse; but Mr. Chatterton never knew half how bad it was. But when he was sick it all came out, and it worried him so that he got very bad indeed, and then he sent for Grandpapa—Charlotte couldn't stop him; he made her go. You see he was afraid he was going to die, and he couldn't bear to have things so very dreadful for Charlotte."

"And is he going to die?" broke in Phronsie excitedly.

"Oh no, indeed! he was almost well when we came away; it was only his worrying over Charlotte that made him so bad. Oh, you ought to have seen him, Phronsie, when Grandpapa offered to take Charlotte home with us for the winter. He was so happy he almost cried."

"I am so glad he was happy," cried Phronsie in great satisfaction, her cheeks flushing.

"And so now I think God gave Charlotte to you for a little while because you haven't Helen. I do, Phronsie, and you can make Charlotte glad while she is here, and help her to have a good time."

"Can I?" cried Phronsie, her cheeks growing a deep pink. "Oh, Polly, how? Charlotte is a big girl; how can I help her?"

"That's your secret to find out," said Polly merrily. "Well, come now," kissing her, "we must hurry back to Grandpapa, or he'll feel badly to have you gone so long."

"Polly," cried Phronsie, as they hurried over the stairs, "put your ear down, do."

"I can't till we get downstairs," laughed Polly, "or I'll tumble on my nose, I'm afraid. Well, here we are. Now then, what is it?" and she bent over to catch the soft words.

"I'm sorry," said Phronsie, her lips quite close to Polly's rosy cheek, "that I said God wasn't nice to take Helen away. Oh, I love him, Polly, I truly do."

"So you do," said Polly, with, a warm clasp. "Well, here's Grandpapa," as the library door opened, and Mr. King came out to meet them.

Polly, running over the stairs the next day to greet Alexia and some of the girls who were determined to make the most of her little visit at home, was met first by one of the maids with a letter.

"Oh, now," cried Alexia, catching sight of it, "I almost know that's to hurry you back, Polly. She sha'n't read it, girls." With that she made a feint of seizing the large white envelope.

***Alexia Coolly Read On, One Arm Around Polly.***

"Hands off from my property," cried Polly merrily, waving her off, and sitting down on the stair she tore the letter open.

Alexia worked her way along till she was able to sit down beside her, when she was guilty of looking over her shoulder.

"Oh, Alexia Rhys, how perfectly, dreadfully mean!" cried one of the other girls, wishing she could be in the same place.

Alexia turned a deaf ear, and coolly read on, one arm around Polly.

"Oh, girls—girls!" she suddenly screamed, and jumping up, nearly oversetting Polly, she raced over the remaining stairs to the bottom, where she danced up and down the wide hall, "Polly isn't going back—she isn't—she isn't," she kept declaring.

"What!" cried all the girls. "Oh, do stop, Alexia. What is it?"

Meantime Cathie Harrison ran up and quickly possessed herself of the vacated seat.

"Why, Mr. Whitney writes to say that Polly needn't go back—oh, how perfectly lovely in him!" cried Alexia, bringing up flushed and panting. "Oh, dear me, I can't breathe!"

"Oh! oh!" cried all the girls, clapping their hands.

"But that doesn't mean that I shall not go back," said Polly, looking up from her letter to peer through the stair-railing at them. "I think—yes, I really do think that I ought to go back."

"How nonsensical!" exclaimed Alexia impatiently. "If Mr. Whitney says you are not needed, isn't that enough? Beside he wrote it for Mrs. Whitney; I read it all."

"No, I don't think it is enough," answered Polly slowly, and turning the letter with perplexed fingers, "for I know dear Aunty only told him to write because she thought I ought to be at home."

"And so you ought," declared Alexia, very decidedly. "She's quite right about it, and now you're here, why, you've just got to stay. So there, Polly Pepper. Hasn't she, girls?"

"Yes, indeed," cried the girls.

Polly shook her brown head, as she still sat on her stair busily thinking.

"Here comes Mr. King," cried Cathie Harrison, suddenly craning her neck at the sound of the opening of a door above them. "Now I'm just going to ask him," and she sprang to her feet.

"Cathie—Cathie," begged Polly, springing up too.

"I just will," declared Cathie, obstinately scampering up over the stairs. "Oh, Mr. King, mayn't Polly stay home? Oh, do say yes, please!"

"Yes, do say yes, please," called all the other girls in the hall below.

"Hoity-toity!" exclaimed the old gentleman, well pleased at the onslaught. "Now then, what's the matter, pray tell?"

"I just won't have Cathie Harrison tell him," said Alexia, trying to run up over the stairs. "Let me by, Polly, do," she begged.

"No, indeed," cried Polly, spreading her arms. "It's bad enough to have one of you up there besieging Grandpapa."

"Then I'll run up the back stairs," cried Alexia, turning in a flash.

"Oh, yes, the back stairs!" exclaimed the other girls, following her. "Oh, do hurry! Polly's coming after us."

But speed as she might, Polly could not overtake the bevy, who, laughing and panting, stood before Mr. King a second ahead of her.

"A pretty good race," said the old gentleman, laughing heartily, "but against you from the first, Polly, my girl."

"Don't listen to them, Grandpapa dear," panted Polly.

"Mayn't she stay at home—mayn't she?"

"Hush, girls," begged Polly. "Oh, Grandpapa dear, don't listen to them. Aunty told Uncle Mason to write the letter, and you know"—

"Well, yes, I know all you would say, Polly. But I've also had a letter from Mason, and I was just going to show it to you." He pulled out of his vest pocket another envelope corresponding to the one in Polly's hand, which he waved at her.

"Oh, Grandpapa!" exclaimed Polly, quite aghast at his so easily going over to the enemy. With that, all the girls deserted the old gentleman, and swarmed around Polly.

"See here, now," commanded Mr. King, "every single one of you young things come back here this minute. Goodness me, Polly, I should think they'd be the death of you."

Polly didn't hear a word, for she was reading busily: "Marian says 'don't let Polly come back on any account. It worries me dreadfully to think of all that she is giving up; and I will be brave, and do without her. She must not come back.'"

Polly looked up to meet old Mr. King's eyes fixed keenly upon her.

"You see, Polly," he began, "I really don't dare after that to let you go back."

"Oh—oh—oh!" screamed all the girls.

"There, I told you so," exclaimed Alexia.

# CHAPTER VIII

# POLLY LOOKS OUT FOR CHARLOTTE

"Second floor—Room No. 3," said Buttons, then stood like an automaton to watch the tall young man scale the stair.

"He did 'em beautifully," he confided afterward to another bell-boy. "Mr. King himself can't get over them stairs better."

"Come in!" cried Jasper, in response to the rap.

"Halloo, old fellow!" cried Pickering Dodge, rushing in tumultuously. "Well, well, so this is your den," looking around the small room in surprise.

"Yes. Now this is good to see you!" exclaimed Jasper, joyfully leaping from his chair to seize Pickering's hand. "Well, what brought you? There's nothing wrong?" he asked, anxiously scanning Pickering's face.

"No—that is, everything's right; all except Polly."

"There isn't anything the matter with Polly?" Jasper turned quite white, scarcely speaking the words.

"No, she's all right, only"—Pickering turned impatiently off from the chair Jasper pulled forward with a hasty hand, and stalked to the other side of the little room. "She's—she's—well, she's so hard to come at nowadays. Everybody has a chance for a word with her but old friends. And now the Recital is in full blast."

Jasper drew a long breath, and began to get his color again. "Oh, yes—well, it's all going on well, the Recital, I mean, isn't it?" he asked.

"I believe so," said Pickering in a gloomy way. "The girls are wild over it; you can't hear anything else talked about at home. But," he broke off abruptly, "got a cigar, Jasper?" and he began to hunt the mantel among the few home-things spread around to enliven the hotel apartment.

"Haven't such an article," said Jasper.

"I forgot you don't smoke," said Pickering with a sigh. "Dear me! how will you bear trouble when it comes, old chap?" He came back to the table, and thrust his hands in his pockets, looking dismally at Jasper.

"I'm afraid a cigar wouldn't help me much," said Jasper, with a laugh; "but if you must have one, I can get it, eh?"

"Yes, I must," said Pickering in despair, "for I've something on my mind. Came over on purpose to get your help, and I can't do it without a weed."

"Very well," said Jasper, shoving the chair again toward Pickering. "Sit down, and I'll have one sent up," and he went over and touched the electric button on the wall.

"Yes, sir?" Buttons ran his head in the doorway, and stared at them without winking.

"A cigar for this gentleman," said Jasper, filliping a coin into the boy's hand.

"Is that the way you order cigars?" demanded Pickering, whirling around in his chair.

"Yes, when I order them at all," said Jasper, laughing; "a weed is a weed, I suppose."

"Indeed, and it is not, then," retorted Pickering. "I'll have none of your ordering. You needn't bring it up, boy; I'll go down to the office and pick some out for myself."

"All right, sir," said Buttons, putting down the coin on the table with a lingering finger.

"Keep it," said Jasper, with a smile.

"He's a gentleman," observed Buttons, on the way downstairs, Pickering treading his heels. "He ain't like the rest of 'em that boards here. They orders me around with a 'Here, you!' or a 'Hoi, there, boy!' They're gents; he's the whole word—a first-class gentleman, Mr. King is," he repeated.

"Now, then, for it," said Jasper, when at last the gleam of Pickering's cigar was steady and bright, "open your budget of news, old fellow," he added, with difficulty restraining his impatience.

"It ought not to be any news," declared Pickering, with extreme abruptness, "for I've never tried to conceal it. I love Polly."

Jasper started so suddenly his arm knocked from the table a slender crystal vase, that broke into a dozen pieces.

"Never mind," he said, at Pickering's dismayed exclamation, "go on."

Whew—puff! floated the rings of cigar smoke over Pickering's head. "And I can't stand it, and I won't, waiting any longer to tell her so. Why, man," he turned savagely now on Jasper, "I've loved her for years, and must I be bullied and badgered out of my rights by men who have only just been introduced to her—say?"

"Whom do you mean?" asked Jasper huskily, his fingers working over the table-cloth, under the pretense of pulling the creases straight.

"Why, that Loughead chap," said Pickering, bringing his hand down heavily on the table; "he has more sweet words from Polly Pepper in a week than I get in a month—and I such an old friend!"

"Polly is so anxious to help his sister," Jasper made out to say.

"Well, that's no reason why the fellow should hang around forever," declared Pickering angrily.

"Why, he's gone abroad!" exclaimed Jasper, "long ago."

"Ah, but he's coming back," said Pickering, with a sage nod, and knocking off the ashes from his cigar end.

"Is that so?" cried Jasper, in astonishment.

"Yes, 'tis," declared Pickering, nodding again, "and I don't like it. You know as well as I do," squaring around on Jasper, "that he don't care a rap about his sister's getting on; he's only thinking of Polly, and *I* love her."

Seeing that something was expected of him, Jasper made out to say, "You do?"

"Of course I do; and you know it, and every one knows it, or ought to; I haven't ever tried to conceal it," said Pickering proudly.

"How do you know that Loughead is coming back?" asked Jasper abruptly.

"How do I know? The best way in the world." Pickering moved uneasily in his chair. "Hibbard Crane had a letter yesterday; that's the reason I threw my traps together and started for you."

"For me?" cried Jasper, in surprise.

"Yes. You've got to help me. I can't stand it, waiting around any longer. It has almost killed me as it is." Pickering threw his head on the chair-back and took savage pulls at the cigar between his teeth.

"I help you?" cried Jasper, too astonished to do much more than to repeat the words. "How in all this world can I do anything in the matter?" he demanded, as soon as he could find his voice.

"Why, you can tell Polly how it is; you're her brother, or as good as one; and she'll see it from you. And you must hurry about it, too, for I expect that Loughead will turn up soon. He means mischief, he does."

"See here, Pick," cried Jasper, getting out of his chair hastily to face Pickering, "you don't know what you are asking. Why, I couldn't do it. The very idea; I never heard of such a thing! You—you must speak to Polly yourself."

"I can't," said Pickering, in a burst, and bringing up his head suddenly. "She won't give me the ghost of a chance. There's always those girls around her; and she's been away an age at Mrs. Whitney's. And everlastingly somebody is sick or getting hurt, and they won't have anybody but Polly. You know how it is yourself, Jasper," and he turned on him an injured countenance.

"Well, don't come to me," cried Jasper, beginning to pace the floor irritably. "I couldn't ever speak on such a subject to Polly. Beside it would be the very way to set her against you. It would any girl; can't you see it, Pick?" he added, brightening up.

"Girls are queer," observed Pickering shrewdly, "and the very thing you think they won't like, they take to amazingly. Oh, you go along, Jasper, and let her see how matters stand; how I feel, I mean."

"You will do your own speaking," said Jasper, in his most crusty fashion, and without turning his head.

"I did; that is, I tried to last night after I met Crane," began Pickering, in a shamefaced way, "but I couldn't get even a chance to see Polly."

"How's that?" asked Jasper, still marching up and down the floor; "wasn't she home?"

"Why, she sent Charlotte Chatterton down to see me," said Pickering, very much aggrieved, "and I hate that Chatterton girl."

"Why couldn't Polly see you?" went on Jasper, determined, since his assistance was asked, to go to the root of the matter.

"Oh, somebody in the establishment, I don't know who, had a finger-ache, I suppose," said Pickering, carelessly throwing away his cigar end and lighting a fresh one, "and wanted Polly. Never mind why; she couldn't come down, she sent word. So I gave up in despair. See here now, Jasper, you must help me out."

"I tell you I won't," declared Jasper, with rising irritation, "not in that way."

"You won't?"

"No, I won't. I can't, my dear fellow."

"Well, there's a great end of our friendship," exclaimed Pickering, red with anger, and he jumped to his feet. "Do you mean to say, Jasper King, that you won't do such a simple thing for me as to say a word to your sister Polly, when I tell you it's all up with me if you don't speak that word—say?"

"You oughtn't to ask such a thing; it's despicable in you," cried Jasper, aghast to find his anger rising at each word. "And if you insist in making such a request when I tell you that I cannot speak to Polly for you, why, I shall be forced to repeat what I said at first, that I won't have anything to do with it."

"Do you mean it," Pickering put himself in front of Jasper's advancing strides, "that you will not speak to Polly for me?"

"I do."

"I tell you," declared Pickering, now quite beside himself, "it's absolutely necessary for me to have your word with her, Jasper King."

"And I tell you I can't give that word," said Jasper. Then he stopped short, and looked into Pickering's face. "I'm sorry, old chap," and he put out his hand.

Pickering knocked it aside in a towering passion. "You needn't 'old chap' me," he cried. "And there's an end to our friendship, King." He seized his hat and dashed out of the room.

"Miss Salisbury!" Alexia Rhys, in real distress, threw herself against her old teacher, who was hurrying through the long school-room.

"Well, what is it?" asked Miss Salisbury, settling her glasses for a look at her former pupil. "You mustn't hinder me; I'm on my way to the recitation room," and her hand made a movement toward her watch.

"Oh, don't think of time, Miss Salisbury!" begged Alexia, just as familiarly as in the old days, "when Polly Pepper needs to be looked out for."

"If Polly Pepper needs me in any way, why, I must stop," said the principal of the "Young Ladies' Select Boarding and Day School," "but I don't see how she can need me, Alexia," she added in perplexity, "Polly is fully capable of taking care of herself."

"Oh, no, she isn't," cried Alexia abruptly. "Beg your pardon, but Polly is a dear, sweet, dreadful idiot. Oh dear me! what do you suppose, Miss Salisbury, she has gone and done?"

"I am quite at a loss to guess," said Miss Salisbury calmly, "and I must say, Alexia, I am very much pained by your failure to profit by my instructions. To think that one of my young ladies, especially one on whom I have spent so much care and attention as yourself, should be so careless in speech and manner, as you are constantly. 'Gone and done'—oh, Alexia!" she exclaimed in a grieved way.

"Oh, I know," cried Alexia imperturbably, "you did your best, dear Miss Salisbury, and it isn't your fault that I'm not fine. But oh, don't waste the time, please, over me, when I want to tell you about Polly."

"What is it about Polly?" demanded Miss Salisbury, fingering her watch-chain nervously. "Really, Alexia, I think Polly would do very well if you didn't try so hard to take possession of her. I quite pity her," she added frankly.

Alexia burst into a laugh. "It's the only way to catch a glimpse of her. Miss Salisbury," she cried, "for everybody is trying to take possession of Polly Pepper. And now—oh, it's getting perfectly dreadful!"

Miss Salisbury took an impatient step forward.

"Oh, Miss Salisbury," cried Alexia in alarm, "wait just a minute, do, dear Miss Salisbury," she cried, throwing her arms around her, thereby endangering the glasses set upon the fine Roman nose, "there can't any one help in this but just you."

"It is very wrong," said Miss Salisbury, yet yielding to the embrace, "for me to stay and listen to you in this way, but—but I've always been fond of you, Alexia, and"—

"I know it," cried Alexia penitently, "you've just been a dear, always, Miss Salisbury, to me. If you hadn't, why, I don't know what I should have done, for I had nobody but aunt," with a little pathetic sniff, "to look after me."

"My dear Alexia," cried Miss Salisbury, quite softened, "don't feel so. You are very dear to me. You always were," patting her hand. "And so what is it that you want to tell me now? Pray be quick, dear."

"Well, then, will you promise to make Polly Pepper do what she ought to, Miss Salisbury?" cried Alexia, quite enchanted with her success thus far.

Miss Salisbury turned a puzzled face at her. "Will I make Polly Pepper do as she ought to?" she repeated. "My dear Alexia, what a strange request. Polly Pepper is always doing as she ought."

"Well, Polly is just hateful to herself," declared Alexia, "and if it wasn't for us girls, she'd—oh, dear me! I don't know what would happen. What do you suppose, Miss Salisbury, she's gone and—oh dear, I didn't mean to—but what do you suppose Polly has just done?"

Before Miss Salisbury could reply, Alexia rushed on frantically. "If you'll believe me, Polly has gone and asked that Charlotte Chatterton to sing at her Recital; just think of that!" exclaimed Alexia, quite gone at the enormity of such a blunder.

"Why, doesn't Charlotte Chatterton sing well?" asked Miss Salisbury, in surprise.

"Oh, frightfully well," said Alexia, "that's just the trouble. And now Polly's Recital will all be part of that Chatterton girl's glory. And it was to be so swell!" And Alexia sank into a chair, and waved back and forth in grief.

"Swell! Oh, Alexia," exclaimed Miss Salisbury in consternation.

"Oh, do excuse me," mumbled Alexia, "but Polly really has spoiled that elegant Recital. It won't be all Polly's, now. Oh, dear me!"

Miss Salisbury drew a long breath. "I'm very glad Polly has asked Miss Chatterton to sing," she said at last. "It was the right thing to do."

"Very glad that Polly has asked that Chatterton girl to sing?" almost shrieked Alexia, starting out of her chair.

"Yes," said Miss Salisbury decidedly. "Very glad indeed, Alexia."

***"My Dear Alexia," Cried Miss Salisbury, Quite Softened, "Don't Feel So."***

"And now you won't make Polly see that Charlotte Chatterton ought not to be stuck into that Recital?" cried Alexia wildly. "Oh, dear me! and you are the only one that can bring Polly to her senses—oh, dear me!"

"Certainly not," said Miss Salisbury, with a little dignified laugh. "The Recital is Polly's, and she knows best how to manage it."

"Well, we won't applaud, we girls won't," declared Alexia, stiffening up, "when that Charlotte Chatterton sings; but we'll all just look the other way—every single one of us."

"Alexia Rhys!" slowly ejaculated Miss Salisbury in real sorrow.

"Well, we can't; it wouldn't be right," gasped Alexia. "Don't look so, Miss Salisbury. Oh, dear me, why will Polly act so! Oh, dear me! I wish Charlotte Chatterton was in the Red Sea."

Miss Salisbury gathered herself up in quiet disapproval; and with a parting look prepared to leave the room.

"Oh, Miss Salisbury," cried Alexia, flying after her, to pluck her gown, "do turn around. Oh, dear me!" and she began to cry as hard as she could.

"When you have come to your better self, Alexia, I will talk with you," said Miss Salisbury distinctly, and she went out, and closed the door.

"Did she say she would—did she—did she?" cried a group of the "old girls," as Miss Salisbury's present scholars called Polly and her set, as they came tiptoeing in. "Why, where are you, Alexia?"

"Here," said a dismal voice from the depths of a corner easy chair. They all rushed at her.

"I've had an awful time with her," sobbed Alexia, her face buried in her handkerchief, "and I suppose it really will kill me, girls."

"Nonsense!" cried one or two. "Well, what did she say about making Polly listen to reason?"

"Oh, dreadful—dreadful!" groaned Alexia gustily. "You can't think!"

"You don't mean to say that she approves, after all that Polly Pepper has worked over that old Recital, to"—

—"Have some one else come in and grab the glory?" finished another voice.

"Oh, dear—dear!" groaned Alexia in between. "And Miss Salisbury would kill you, Clem, if she heard you say 'grab.'"

"Well, do tell us, what did Miss Salisbury say?" demanded another girl impatiently.

"She said it was right for Polly to ask Charlotte Chatterton to sing, and she was glad she was going to do it."

"Oh, horrors!" exclaimed the group in dismal chorus.

"The idea! as much as she loves Polly Pepper!" cried Sally Moore.

"And I hate the word 'right,'" exploded Alexia, whirling her handkerchief around her fingers. "Now! It's poked at one everlastingly. I think it's just sweet to be wicked."

"Oh, Alexia Rhys!"

"Well, just a little bit wicked," said Alexia.

Cathie Harrison shook back the waves of light hair on her brow. "Girls," she began hesitatingly. But no one would listen; the laments were going on so fast over Polly and her doings.

"It *is* right!" cried Cathie at last, after many ineffectual attempt to be heard. "Do stop, girls, making such a noise," she added impatiently.

"That's a great way to preach," said Clem, laughing, "lose your temper to begin with, Cathie."

"I didn't—that is, I'm sorry," said Cathie. "But, anyway, I want to say I ought to have been ashamed to act so about that Chatterton girl. Where should I have been if Polly Pepper hadn't taken me up?"

She looked down the long aisle to a seat in the corner. "There's where I sat," pointing to it, "and you all know it, for a whole week, and I thought I should die; I did," tragically, "without any one speaking to me. And one day Polly Pepper came up and asked wouldn't I come to her house to the Bee you were all going to get up to fit out that horrible old poor white family down South. And I wanted to get up and scream, I was so glad."

"Cathie Harrison," exclaimed Alexia, springing to her feet defiantly, "what do you want to bring back those dreadful old times for! You are the most uncomfortable person I ever saw."

"You needn't mind it now, Alexia," cried Cathie, rushing at her, "for you've been too lovely for anything ever since—you dear!"

"I lovely? oh, girls, did you hear?" cried Alexia, sinking into her chair again, quite overcome. "She said I was lovely—oh, dear me!"

"And so you are," repeated Cathie stoutly; "just as nice and sweet and lovely to me as you can be. So!" throwing her long arms around Alexia.

"I didn't want to be; Polly made me," said Alexia.

"I know it; but I don't care. You are nice now, any way."

"And I suppose we must be nice to that Chatterton girl now, if she does break up our fun," said Alexia with a sigh, getting out of her chair. "Come on, girls; let us go and tell Polly it's just heavenly that Charlotte is to sing."

# CHAPTER IX

# POLLY'S RECITAL

Charlotte Chatterton stood back of the portiere pulling a refractory button of her glove into place, as a gay group precipitated themselves into the dressing-room of The Exeter.

"Now remember, girls," cried Alexia, rushing at the toilet table to bestow frantic twitches at the fluffy waves of hair over her forehead, "that we must applaud the very minute that she gets through singing. Oh dear me, just look at my bangs; they are perfect frights. Hateful things!" with another pull at the offending locks.

"It's a swell house," exclaimed one of the girls delightedly.

"Just let Miss Salisbury catch you saying 'swell,'" warned Alexia. "Take care now, Sally Moore, this is a very proper and select occasion."

"Well, do let some of us have that glass a minute," retorted Sally, "and mend your manners before you take occasion to correct my speech."

"My bangs are worse than yours, Sally," cried another girl, crowding up; "do let me get one corner of that glass," trying to achieve a view of her head over Alexia's shoulder.

Alexia calmly picked at the fluffy bunch of hair on her brow, giving it a little quirk before she said, "Don't fight, girls; it quite spoils one's looks; I never do when I'm dressed up."

"Of course not," said Sally Moore, "for you get everything you want without fighting."

"The idea!" exclaimed Alexia, with an injured expression, "when I never have my own way. Why, I give up and give up the whole time to somebody. Well, never mind; let's talk about the Recital. Oh, it's going to be quite elegant for Polly Pepper. There's a regular society cram in the Hall."

"Well, I don't think 'society cram' is a bit better than a 'swell affair,'" said Clem Forsythe, slipping out of her opera cloak.

"Nor I either," cried three or four voices.

"Oh, I don't object to 'swell affair' myself," said Alexia; "I have used the words on more than one occasion, unless my memory is treacherous. I only wanted to spare Miss Salisbury's nerves."

"Pity you didn't give more attention to Miss Salisbury's nerves five or six years ago," said Sally. "Do get away from that glass."

"It's no time to talk about me now," observed Alexia. "All our minds should be on Polly, and her Recital. Girls, *did* you see Jack Loughead down at the door?"

"Didn't we?" cried the girls.

"He's as handsome as a picture, isn't he?" cried Alexia, with another little pull at her rebellious hair.

"Isn't he?" hummed the girls.

"Well, he won't look at you, for all your fussing over those bangs," said Sally vindictively.

"Did you suppose I thought he would?" cried Alexia coolly. "Why, it's Polly Pepper, everybody knows, that brings him here."

"What's become of Mr. Bayley?" asked one of the girls suddenly.

"Hush—sh! you mustn't ask," cried Alexia mysteriously, and turning away from the mirror, with a lingering movement; "there, it looks shockingly, but it is as good as I can fix it."

"Your hair always does look perfectly horrid," declared Sally Moore, deftly slipping into the vacated place.

"Well, do tell all you know about Mr. Bayley and Polly," begged the girl who had raised the question, "I'm just dying to know."

"Alexia Rhys doesn't know a thing more than we do, Frances," said Clem, "only she pretends she's in the secret."

"I was down at Dunraven at the Christmas splurge," said Alexia, "and you were not, Clem. That's all I shall say," and she leisurely disposed herself in a big chair, and began to draw on her gloves, with the air of one who could reveal volumes were she so disposed.

"Polly wouldn't ever send him off," said one of the girls, "I don't believe. Why, he's horribly rich; and just think of marrying into the Bayley family—oh my!"

"I should think the shock of being asked to enter that family, would kill any girl, to begin with," said Clem. "Why, he goes back to William the Conqueror, doesn't he? And there's an earl in the family, and I don't know what else. And then beside, there's his mother; the idea of sitting opposite to her at the table every single day—oh dear me! I know I should drop my knife and fork and things, from pure fright."

"I'm sure I don't see why anybody is proud to have his family go back all the time," said Alexia Rhys; "for my part I should want to start things forward a little myself."

"Well, who does know anything about it, why Mr. Bayley has gone off suddenly?" demanded Frances.

"No one knows," said Clem.

Alexia hummed a tune provokingly.

"We all guess, and it's easy enough to guess the truth; but Polly won't ever let it out, so that's all there is about it."

"Well, now, girls," said Alexia suddenly, "we must remember what we promised each other."

"What do you mean?" asked Frances; "I didn't promise anything to anybody."

"You weren't with us when we promised, my dear," answered Alexia, "and I'll rise and explain. You see we don't any of us like that Charlotte Chatterton; not a single one of us. She's a perfect stick, I think."

"So do I," said another girl; "this is the way she walks." Thereupon followed a representation given to the life, of Charlotte Chatterton's method of getting her long figure over the ground, which brought subdued peals of laughter from the girls looking on.

"And she has no more feeling than an oyster," pursued Alexia, when she had recovered her breath, "or she might see that Polly was just giving up all her fun and ours too, by dragging her into everything that is going on."

"I know it," said the girls.

"And I'm so sick of her taking in everything so as a matter of course," observed Alexia; "oh! she's quite an old sponge."

"It's bad enough to be called an oyster, without having old sponge fastened to one," said Sally Moore, coming away from the mirror, thereby occasioning another rush for that useful dressing-room appointment.

"Well, she is both of those very things," declared Alexia, "nevertheless we must applaud her dreadfully when she's finished singing. That's what we promised each other, Frances. It will please Polly, you know."

"You better hurry, or you will lose your seats," announced a friendly voice in the doorway, which had the effect to send the whole bevy out as precipitately as they had hurried in.

When she was quite sure that no one remained, Charlotte Chatterton shook herself free from the friendly portiere-folds, and stepped to the center of the deserted room.

"I'll not sing one note!" she declared, standing tall, "not one single note!" Just then, in ran Amy Loughead.

"Oh dear, and oh dear!"

"What is the matter?" asked Charlotte, not moving.

"Oh, I'm so frightened," gasped Amy, shivering from head to foot, "there are so many people in there, oh—oh! I can't play!" beating her hands together in terror.

"You must," said Charlotte unsympathizingly.

"I can't—I can't. Oh, I shall die! The hall is full, and they keep coming in. Oh—Miss Pepper!"

For Polly, in her soft white gown, was coming quickly into the dressing-room.

"Your hands are just as cold as ice," said Polly, gathering up Amy's shaking little palms into her own. "There now, we'll see if we can't coax them into playing order," rubbing them between her own warm ones.

"Oh, I can feel all those people's eyes staring through me," cried Amy, huddling up against Polly.

"You mustn't think of their eyes, child," laughed Polly. But there was a little white line around her mouth. Just then a messenger came in with a note.

"Any answer?" asked Polly. "Oh, stay; I would better read it before you go." And she tore it open.

"I am so sorry that I cannot keep my engagement to play the duet with Miss Porter, but the doctor has just been here, and he says I must not go out. I should have written this morning that I had a sore throat, but I thought I could manage to go. I'm so sorry—oh, Miss Pepper, I'm so sorry!

"JULIA ANDERSON."

***"I'll Not Sing A Note!"***

The note fell to Polly's lap, and for a minute she could not speak. "There is no answer," at last she said to the messenger.

"Oh, Miss Pepper, what is it?" cried Amy Loughead, brought out of her own fright, by the dread of a new trouble.

"Julia Anderson is sick and cannot be here," said Polly.

"Oh, dear! and she was going to play with Miss Porter. What will you do?" cried Amy in consternation.

"Why, I shall have to take her place," said Polly, forcing herself to speak.

"Oh, dear—dear!" exclaimed Amy, trying not to burst into tears. "Everything is just as bad and horrid as it can be. Oh, dear, dear, and I can't play; I should disgrace you!"

"Oh, no, no, Amy," said Polly, trying to smile, "that you'll never do." She threw the note on the floor now, and began to rub the cold little hands again.

"But—but, I'm so frightened," gasped Amy.

Charlotte Chatterton walked to the window.

"I may be a stick, and an oyster, and an old sponge, and everybody wish me out of the way, but I'm not such a villain as to bother her now by telling her I won't sing. If they only won't applaud!" She shut her teeth tightly, and turned back again.

"I wouldn't, Miss Loughead," she began. But her voice sounded cold and unsympathetic, and Amy clung to Polly tighter than ever.

Ben now looked in. "Come, Polly," he said. "You really ought to be out here, and it's almost three o'clock."

Amy gave a gasp. "What shall I do?"

"You may stay in here, if you really wish," said Polly in a low voice, Charlotte Chatterton looking on with all her eyes, "and I will excuse you."

"And will—will you be disappointed in me?" Amy brought out the question shamefacedly.

"Very much," said Polly.

"And will you never try me again—and never give me music lessons?" asked Amy fearfully.

"I do not seem to teach you successfully," said Polly very slowly, "so it would be no use to continue the lessons." And she put aside the clinging hands. "You may stay here, Amy; I am coming, Ben," looking over at him.

"I'll play," cried Amy Loughead desperately. "I'd rather, oh, dear me, if they were bears and gorillas looking on—and I just know I shall die—but I'd rather, Miss Pepper, than to have you give me up."

Charlotte Chatterton drew a long breath.

"What's the matter?" asked Ben in dismay.

"Miss Loughead was a little scared, I believe," said Charlotte, with a touch of scorn in her manner.

Ben gave an uneasy exclamation. "Everything seems to be all right now," he said, in a relieved way, looking off at Polly and Amy.

"Oh, yes; a scare don't amount to much if one has a mind to put it down," said Charlotte.

"I should think you'd be scared," said Ben, looking at her admiringly, "to stand up and sing before all those people. But I suppose you never are; you don't seem to mind things like the rest of us."

Charlotte shrugged her shoulders, but said nothing.

"We are all ready," said Polly cheerfully coming up with Amy. "Oh, Charlotte, you are such a comfort," she found time to whisper.

Charlotte clasped her hands tightly together so that an ominous rent appeared in one of her pretty gloves. "I'll sing," she kept saying to herself all the way out to the platform, "oh, I'll sing—I'll sing." And later on, while looking down into the eyes of the girls waiting to applaud, "I'll sing—I'll sing," she had to declare to herself till her name was announced.

As the last note died away, "Who is that girl?" went around the hall. Charlotte Chatterton had made a sensation.

Alexia Rhys, angry at the effect of the song, still clapped steadily together her soft-gloved hands, looking at Polly with the air of a martyr all the while.

"Charlotte—oh, I'm glad!" whispered Polly radiantly, "they want you to sing again," trying to pull her forward, as the storm of applause went on.

"I'll not sing!" cried Charlotte passionately. "Never! Don't ask it, Polly."

"Why, Charlotte!" implored Polly, astonished at the passion in the girl usually so cold and indifferent. Still the applause continued, Polly's set keeping at it like veterans.

Ben ran up the platform steps with shining eyes. "Grandpapa requests Charlotte to sing again," he whispered to Polly.

"There, you hear, Charlotte." said Polly. "Grandpapa wishes it."

"Very well," said Charlotte, resuming her ordinary manner, and looking as if it really made no difference to her whether she sang or was quiet, she walked to her place.

Polly slipped back of the piano, and began the accompaniment, and again Charlotte's singing carried all by storm.

Polly, looking down into Jasper's face, saw him smile over to his father, and nod in a pleased surprise; and she was aghast to feel a faint little wish begin to grow in her heart, that Charlotte Chatterton had not been asked to sing.

"Of course Jasper is surprised, as he has never heard her sing," said Polly to herself, "and her voice is so beautiful in this big hall, oh, it's so very beautiful!" as Charlotte came back, apparently not hearing the expressions of delight that rang over the concert-room.

"That Chatterton girl will be all the rage now," whispered Alexia savagely to Clem who sat next to her. "Look at Mrs. Cabot. She has her 'I'll-take-you-up-and-patronize-you air' on, and I know she's making up her mind to give Charlotte a musicale."

Other people also, scattered here and there in the hall, were making up their minds to introduce Miss Chatterton to their friends; as a girl with such a wonderful voice, it would be quite worth one's while to bring out.

Polly, by this time, explaining to the audience, the failure of Miss Anderson to take her part in the duet, caught little ends of the whispers going on beneath her, such as "Perfectly exquisite." "Most wonderful range." "Shall certainly ask her to sing." And again she saw Jasper's beaming face, while Ben took no pains to conceal his delight. And she sat down to the piano mechanically, and began in a dazed way to help Miss Porter through with the duet that was to have been one of the finest things on the carefully prepared programme.

*"For Shame, Polly, If The Little Brown House Teachings Are Forgotten Like This"*

Suddenly, in the midst of a slow movement, Polly glanced down and caught her mother's eye.

"Polly," it said, just as plainly as if Mrs. Fisher had spoken, "is this my girl? For shame, if the Little Brown House teachings are forgotten like this."

Polly straightened up, sent Mamsie down a bright smile that made Mrs. Fisher nod, and flash back one in return, then bent all her energies to making that duet speak its message through the concert-room. People who had rather languished in their chairs, now gathered themselves up with fresh interest, and clapped their hands at the brilliant passages, and exclaimed over the ability of the music teacher who could change an apparent failure to such a glorious success. Everybody said it was wonderful; and when the duet was over, the house rang with the charming noise by which the gratified friends tried to express their delight. But Polly saw only Mamsie's eyes, filled with joy.

Meantime, Charlotte Chatterton had hurried out to the dressing-room, tossing on her walking things with a quick hand; and held fast for a minute as she crept out into the broad passage, by the duet now in full progress, she went softly down the stairs.

When it was all over, everybody crowded around Polly.

"Oh, Miss Pepper, your Recital is lovely! oh, how beautifully Miss Chatterton sang!" and,

"Oh, Miss Pepper, I am delighted with your pupils' progress; and what an exquisite voice Miss Chatterton has!"

And then it was, "Oh, it must have been so hard, Miss Pepper, for you to excuse Miss Anderson at the last minute; and we can't thank you enough for letting us hear Miss Chatterton sing."

"Oh, I shall fly crazy to hear them go on," cried Alexia to a little bunch of girls back of the crowd; "will nothing stop them?" wringing her hands angrily together. "It's all Chatterton, Chatterton now; and after Polly's magnificent playing too. Oh dear me, I knew it would be so!"

Polly turned, with a happy face, to pull Charlotte forward to hear the kind things. "Why, where"—

"Oh, she's gone home," answered Alexia, stepping forward hastily—"Hasn't she, girls?" appealing to them. "She must have; she went out like a shot. Don't, Polly, how can you?" she begged, turning back to twitch Polly's arm, "you've done enough, I should think."

"What did she run off for?" cried Jasper, scaling the platform steps. Polly glanced quickly up into his beaming face.

"Oh, Jasper, she has gone home—I couldn't help it," and her face fell.

He looked annoyed. "Never mind, Polly," he said, his brow clearing, "father wanted to introduce her to some friends, that's all. Well, and wasn't it a grand success, though!" and he beamed at her.

"Yes," said Polly, settling Amy's music with an unsteady hand.

"And Charlotte really surprised us all," he went on gaily. "Why, Polly, who would think that we have—or you rather, for you have done it all—the honor to bring out a nightingale! Here, let me do that for you." He was fairly bubbling over with delight, and as he essayed to take the music out of Polly's hand, he laughed again. "Dear me, how stupid I am," as a piece fluttered to the floor.

"And didn't Amy do nicely?" asked Polly beginning to feel a bit tired now.

"Yes, indeed," assented Jasper enthusiastically, as he recovered the piece. "Just splendidly! I didn't know she had so much music in her. Oh, here comes a horde of congratulations, Polly." He threw her the brightest of smiles as he moved to make way for a group of friends hurrying up to shower Polly with compliments, and every one had something delightful to add of Charlotte Chatterton's singing.

"Jasper couldn't help but be happy over Charlotte's singing," said Polly to herself, and looking after him, "it's so beautiful," as they came up.

"Where are you going, Polly?" called Alexia at last, when it was all over, and the janitor was closing the big outer door, as Polly ran ahead of the girls and down the long steps of The Exeter.

***Polly Turned And Waved Her Music-roll At Them]***

Polly turned and waved her music-roll at them for a reply.

"Now somebody is going to carry her off," grumbled Alexia; "hurry up, girls, let's see who it is." So they ran as lightly as Polly herself, after her, down the steps, only in time to see old Mr. King help her into the carriage with Mrs. Fisher and Phronsie, and drive rapidly off.

"Whatever in the world is the matter?" cried Alexia, running up to Jasper who was watching them speed away.

"Why, Polly thinks Charlotte is sick," explained Jasper, "because she went home before the Recital was out."

"Stuff and nonsense!" exclaimed Alexia angrily. "What is the matter with Polly, Jasper? She grows worse and worse. Why can't she let Charlotte Chatterton alone, pray tell. I, for one, should think mischief enough had been done by that girl."

"You should think mischief enough had been done by Charlotte?" repeated Jasper in astonishment. "I must say, Alexia, that I fail to understand you."

"To hear people praise to the very skies that Chatterton girl," cried Alexia in a passion—she was actually stamping her foot now—"oh, oh! why don't some of you say something?" she cried, appealing suddenly to the girls. "You all feel as I do about Polly's pushing forward that girl; and there you stand and make me do all the talking."

Jasper looked grave at once. "There is no occasion for any one to exert herself to talk over this," he said. "It is Polly's affair, and hers alone." He raised his hat to her, and to the rest of the group, and walked off.

# CHAPTER X

# PHRONSIE HAS A PLAN

Phronsie was the first to reach Charlotte's door.

"Charlotte?" she called softly through the keyhole. There was no answer, and after one or two ineffectual attempts, Phronsie turned fearfully away.

"I do believe something is in the room with Charlotte," she said, as Polly came running up the stairs. Then she sat down on the top step and clasped her hands. "I heard it raging up and down."

"Oh, no, Phronsie," said Polly reassuringly, "there couldn't be anything in there with Charlotte. I'll try," and she laid a quick hand on the knob. "Oh, Charlotte, do open the door; you are worrying us all so," called Polly imploringly.

Charlotte flung wide the door. Two red spots burned on her cheeks, and her pale blue eyes snapped. But when she saw Polly, she said, "I'm sorry I frightened you, but I'm best alone."

"Isn't there really anything in here with you, Charlotte?" asked Phronsie, getting off from her stair, to peer past Polly. "Oh, I'm sure I heard it raging up and down."

"That was I," said Charlotte; "I was the wild beast, Phronsie."

"Oh, dear," breathed Phronsie.

"And oh!" exclaimed Polly.

"Charlotte," said Phronsie, coming in to slip her hand into Charlotte's, "it was just beautiful when you sang; I thought it was birds when you went clear up into the air. I did really, Charlotte."

"Oh, don't!" begged Charlotte, looking over at Polly.

"Come down to dinner, Charlotte," said Polly quickly. "Really you must, else I am afraid Grandpapa will be up here after you."

"I don't want any dinner," said Charlotte, drawing back.

"Indeed, but you must come down," said Polly firmly, holding out her hand. "Come, Charlotte."

"Let me smooth your hair," begged Phronsie, standing on tiptoe; "do bend down just a very little, please. There, that's it," patting Charlotte's head with both hands; "now you look very nice; you really do—doesn't she, Polly."

"Yes, indeed," said Polly cheerily, "just as fine as can be. There, they are coming after us," as quick footsteps sounded in the hall below. "Hurry, Charlotte, do. We're coming, boys," she called.

They had just finished dinner, when a note was handed Polly. It ran thus:

"Do, dear Polly, run over to-morrow morning early. I want to consult you in regard to asking Miss Chatterton to sing at my next 'At Home.' I should be charmed to have her favor us.

"Felicia A. Cabot."

"The very thing!" exclaimed Jasper, with only a thought for Polly's pleasure, when Polly had cried, "How nice of Mrs. Cabot!" "Don't you say so, father?" he added.

"Assuredly," said old Mr. King with great satisfaction in Polly's pleasure, and at her success in drawing Charlotte out. And then he thought no more about it, and the bell ringing and Mr. Alstyne coming in, he went off into the library for a quiet chat.

And after this, there were no more quiet days for Charlotte Chatterton. Everybody who was musical, wanted to revel in her voice; and everybody who wasn't, wanted the same thing because it was so talked about. So she was asked to sing at musicales and receptions without end, until Alexia exclaimed at last, "They are all raving, stark-mad over her, and it's all Polly's own fault, the whole of it."

Phronsie laid down the note she was writing to Mrs. Fargo, a fortnight later, and said to herself, "I would better do it now, I think," and going out, she went deliberately to old Mr. King's room, and rapped at the door.

"Come in!" called the old gentleman, "come in! Oh, bless me, it's you, Phronsie!" in pleased surprise.

"Yes, Grandpapa," said Phronsie, coming in and shutting the door carefully, "I came on purpose to see you all alone."

"So you did, dear," said Mr. King, highly gratified, and pushing away his writing table, he held out his hand. "Now, then, Phronsie, you are never going to be too big, you know, to sit on my knee, so hop up now."

"Oh, no, Grandpapa," cried Phronsie in a rapture, "I could never be too big for that," so she perched up as of old on his knee, then she folded her hands and looked gravely in his face.

"Well, my dear, what is it?" asked the old gentleman presently, "you've come to tell me something, I suppose."

"Yes, Grandpapa, I have," said Phronsie decidedly, "and it is most important too, Grandpapa, and oh, I do wish it so much," and she clasped her hands tighter and sighed.

"Well, then, Phronsie, if you want it, I suppose it must be," said Mr. King, quite as a matter of course. "But first, child, tell me what it is," and he stroked her yellow hair.

"Grandpapa," asked Phronsie suddenly, "how much money did Mrs. Chatterton say I was to have?"

"Oh, bless me!" exclaimed Mr. King, with a start. "Why, what makes you ask such a question? Oh, she left you everything she had, Phronsie; a couple of millions or so it is; why?"

"Grandpapa," asked Phronsie, looking intently at him, "isn't Charlotte very, very poor?"

"Charlotte poor?" repeated the old gentleman. "Why, no, not exactly; her father isn't rich, but Charlotte, I think, may do very well, especially as I intend to keep her here for a while, and then I shall never let her suffer, Phronsie; never, indeed."

"Grandpapa," said Phronsie, "wasn't Mrs. Chatterton aunt to Charlotte?"

"Yes; that is, to Charlotte's father," corrected Mr. King. "But what of that, child, pray? What have you got into your head, Phronsie?"

"If Mrs. Chatterton was aunt to Charlotte," persisted Phronsie slowly, "it seems as if Charlotte ought to have some of the money. It really does, Grandpapa."

"But Cousin Eunice didn't think so, else she'd have left it to Charlotte," said Mr. King abruptly, "and she did choose to leave it to you. So there's an end of it, Phronsie. I didn't want you to have it, but the thing was fixed, and I couldn't help myself. And neither can we do anything now, but take matters as they are."

"I do think," said Phronsie, without taking her eyes from his face, "that maybe Mrs. Chatterton is sorry now, and wishes that she had left some money to Charlotte. Don't you suppose so, Grandpapa?" and one hand stole up to his neck.

"Maybe," said the old gentleman, with a short laugh, "and I shouldn't wonder if Cousin Eunice was sorry over a few other things too, Phronsie."

"Wouldn't it make her very glad if I gave Charlotte some of the money?" Phronsie's red lips were very close to his ear now, "oh, I do want to so much; you can't think, Grandpapa, how much!"

For answer, Mr. King set her down hastily on the floor, and took two or three turns up and down the room. Phronsie stood a moment quite still where he left her, then she ran up to him and slipped her hand within his.

"Oh, I do so wish I might," she said, "there's so much for a little girl like me. It would be so nice to have Charlotte have some with me."

Still no answer. So Phronsie went up and down silently by his side for a few more turns. Then she spoke again. "Does it make you sorry, Grandpapa dear, to have me want Charlotte to have the money with me?" she asked timidly.

"No, no, child," answered Mr. King hastily, "and yet I don't know what to say. I don't feel that it would be right for you to give any of your money to her."

"Right?" cried Phronsie, opening her brown eyes very wide. "Why, isn't the money my very own, Grandpapa?"

"Yes, yes, of course; but you are too young to judge of such things," said the old gentleman decidedly, "as the giving away of property and all that."

"Oh, Grandpapa!" exclaimed Phronsie, in gentle reproach, and standing very tall. "Why, I am thirteen."

"And when you get to be ten years older, you might blame me," said Mr. King, "and I can't say but what you'd have reason if I let you do such a thing as to give away any money to Charlotte."

"Blame you? Why, Grandpapa, I couldn't." Phronsie drew a long breath, then threw herself convulsively into his arms, her face working hard in her efforts not to cry. But it was no use, and Mr. King caught her in time to see the quick drops roll down Phronsie's cheek and to feel them fall on his hand.

"Oh, dear me!" he cried in great distress, "there, there, child, you shall give away the whole if you wish; I've enough for you without it—only don't cry, Phronsie. You may do anything you like, dear. There," mopping up her wet little face with his handkerchief, "now that's a good child; Phronsie, you are not going to cry, of course not. There, do smile a bit; that's my girl now," as a faint light stole into Phronsie's eyes. "I didn't mean you'd really blame me, only"—

"I couldn't," still said Phronsie, and it looked as if the shower were about to fall again.

"I know, child; you think your old Grandpapa does just about right," said Mr. King soothingly, and highly gratified.

"He's ever and always right," said Phronsie, still not moving.

"Bless you, child," cried the old gentleman, much moved, "I wish I could say I believed what you say. But many things in my life might have been bettered."

"Oh, no, Grandpapa," protested Phronsie in a tone of horror, "they couldn't have been better. Don't, Grandpapa, don't!" she caught him around the neck imploringly.

"Well, I won't, child," promised Mr. King, holding her close. "And now, Phronsie, I'll tell you; I'll think of all this that you and I have talked over, and I'll let you know by and by what you ought to do about it, and you mustn't say anything about it to anybody, not to a single soul, child. It shall be just a secret between you and me."

"I won't, Grandpapa," said Phronsie obediently, and patting his broad back with her soft hand.

"And, meantime," said Mr. King, quite satisfied, "why, Charlotte is having pretty good times, I think. Polly is looking out for that."

"Polly is making her have beautiful times," said Phronsie happily, "oh, very beautiful times indeed, Grandpapa."

"I expect she's an awful nuisance," the old gentleman broke out suddenly.

"Oh, Grandpapa!" exclaimed Phronsie, breaking away from him to look into his face.

"Well, well, perhaps I shouldn't say quite that," said Mr. King, correcting himself. "But, well, now, Phronsie, you run back to your play, child, and I'll set to work at once to think out this matter."

"I was writing a note to Mrs. Fargo," said Phronsie, putting up her lips for a kiss. "You are sure you won't make your head ache thinking about it, Grandpapa?" she asked anxiously.

"Sure as I can be, Phronsie," said old Mr. King, smiling. "Good-by, dear."

"See here, Pickering," Mr. Cabot threw wide the door of his private office with a nervous hand. "It is time I had a good talk with you. Come in; I never get one nowadays."

"Can't stop, Uncle," said Pickering hastily. "Besides, what would be the use, you never see anything encouraging about me or my career. And I believe I am going to the dogs."

"Indeed you are not, Pickering," cried Mr. Cabot quickly, the color rising to his cheek. "There, there, my sister's boy shall never say that. But come in, come in." He laid hold of Pickering's arm and gently forced him into the little room.

Not to be ungracious, the young man threw himself into a chair. "Well, what is it, Uncle? Do out with it; I'm in no mood for a lecture, though, this morning."

"I'm not going to lecture you, my boy," said Mr. Cabot, closing the door, then going to the mantel to lean one elbow on it, a favorite attitude of his, while he scanned his nephew. "But something worse than common has come to you. Can I help in any way?"

"No, no, don't ask me," ejaculated Pickering, striking his knee with one glove, and turning apprehensively in his chair. "Oh, hang it, Uncle, why can't you let me alone?"

"I've seen this thing, whatever it is, coming upon you for sometime," said Mr. Cabot, too nervous to notice the entreaty in Pickering's voice and manner, "and I cannot wait any longer to find out the trouble. It's my right, Pickering; you have no father to see to you, and I've always wanted to have the best success be yours." He turned away his head now, a break coming in his voice.

***"I'm Not Going To Lecture You."]***

"You have, Uncle, you have," assented Pickering, brought out a trifle from his distress, "but then I'm not equal to the strain my relatives put upon me. Not worth it, either," he added, relapsing into his gloom. Then he shoved his chair so that he could not look his uncle in the face, and bent a steady glance out of the window.

Mr. Cabot gave a nervous start that carried him away from the mantel a step or two. But when he was there, he felt so much worse, that he soon got back into the old position.

"I don't see, Pickering," he resumed, "why you shouldn't get along. You're through college."

"Which is a wonder," interpolated Pickering.

"Well, I can't say but that I was a good deal disturbed at one time," said Mr. Cabot frankly; "but never mind that now, you are through," and he heaved a sigh of relief, "and nicely established with Van Metre and Cartwright. It's the best law firm in the town, Pickering." Mr. Cabot brought his elbow off from the mantel enough to smite his palms together smartly in enthusiasm. "I got you in there."

"I know you did, Uncle," said Pickering; "you've done everything that's good. Only I repeat I'm not worth it," and he drummed on the chair-arm.

"For Heaven's sake, Pickering!" cried his uncle, darting in front of the chair and its restless occupant, "don't say that again. It's enough to make a man go to the bad, to lose hope. What have you been doing lately? Do you gamble?"

"What do you take me for?" demanded Pickering, starting to his feet with flashing eyes, and throwing open his top-coat as if the weight oppressed him. "I've been a lazy dog all my life, and a good-for-naught; but I hope I've not sunk to that."

"Oh, nothing, nothing—I'm sure I didn't mean," cried Mr. Cabot, starting back suddenly in astonishment. "Dear me, Pickering," taking off his eyeglasses to blow his nose, "you needn't pick me up so violently. I've been much worried about you," settling his glasses again for another look at his nephew. "And I can't tolerate any thoughts I cannot speak."

"I should think not," retorted Pickering shortly; "the trouble is in having the thoughts."

"And I am very much relieved to find that my fears are groundless—that you've been about nothing that my sister or I should be ashamed of," and he picked up courage to step forward gingerly and pat the young man on the shoulder. "You are in trouble, though, and I insist on knowing what it is."

Pickering dropped suddenly beneath his uncle's hand, into the nearest chair.

# CHAPTER XI

# THINGS ARE GETTING MIXED

"How can you ask me, Uncle?" cried Pickering passionately.

"Because I will know." Mr. Cabot was quite determined.

"Well, then, if you must have it, it's—it's Polly Pepper." Pickering could get no further.

"It's Polly Pepper!" ejaculated Mr. Cabot. Then a light broke over his face, and he laughed aloud, he was so pleased. "You mean, you are in love with Polly Pepper?"

"As if everybody didn't know it?" cried Pickering hotly. "Don't pretend, Uncle, that you are surprised;" he was really disrespectful now in manner. "Oh, beg pardon, sir," recovering himself.

"Never mind," said Mr. Cabot indulgently, "you are over-wrought this morning. My boy," and he came over and clapped his nephew on the back approvingly, "that's the best thing you ever told me; you make me very happy, and"—

"Hold, Uncle," cried Pickering, darting away from the hand, "don't go so fast. You are taking too much for granted."

Mr. Cabot for answer, bestowed another rap, this time on Pickering's arm, indulging all the while in the broadest of smiles.

Just then some one knocked at the door, and in response to Mr. Cabot's unwilling "Come in," Ben's head appeared. "Beg pardon, Mr. Cabot, but Mr. Van Metre wants you out here."

Pickering lunged past Ben. "Don't stop me," he cried crossly, in response to Ben's "Well, old fellow."

Ben stared after him with puzzled eyes as he shot down the long store; and all that afternoon he could not get Pickering and his strange ways out of his mind, and on the edge of the twilight, jumping out of his car at the corner nearest home, he buttoned up his coat and rushed on, regardless that Billy Harlowe was making frantic endeavors to overtake him.

"What's got into the old chap," said Ben to himself, pushing on doggedly with the air of a man who has thoughts of his own to think out. "I declare, if I should know Pickering Dodge lately; I can't tell where to find him."

***"Don't Stop Me," Cried Pickering Crossly.***

And with no light on his puzzle, Ben turned into the stone gateway, and strode up to the east porch to let himself in as usual, with his latch key. As he was fitting it absently, all the while his mind more intent on Pickering and his changed demeanor than on his own affairs, he heard a little rustling noise that made him turn his head to see a tall figure spring down the veranda floor in haste to gain the quickest angle.

"Charlotte, why, what are you doing out here?" exclaimed Ben, leaving his key in the lock to look at her.

"Don't speak!" begged Charlotte hastily, and coming up to him. "Somebody will hear you. I came out here to walk up and down—I shall die in that house; and I am going home to-morrow." She nervously twisted her handkerchief around her fingers, and Ben still looking at her closely, saw that she had been crying.

"Charlotte, what are you talking about?" he cried, opening his honest blue eyes wide at her. "Why, I thought you had ever so much sense, and that you were way ahead of other girls, except Polly," he added, quite as a matter of course.

"Don't!" cried Charlotte, wincing, and, "but I shall go home to-morrow."

"Look here," Ben took out his key and tucked it into his pocket, then faced Charlotte, "take a turn up and down, Charlotte; you'll pull out of your bad fit; you're homesick." Ben's honest face glowed with pity as he looked at her.

"I'm—I'm everything," said Charlotte desperately. "O, Ben, you can't think," she seized his arm, "Polly is just having a dreadful time because I'm here."

"See here, now," said Ben, taking the hand on his arm in a strong grip, as if it were Polly's, "don't you go to getting such an idea into your head, Charlotte."

"I can't help it," said Charlotte; "it was put there," she added bitterly.

Ben gave a start of surprise. "Well, you are not the sort of girl to believe such stuff, any way," he said.

Charlotte pulled away her hand. "I'm going home," she declared flatly.

"Indeed you are not," said Ben, quite as decidedly.

"O, yes, I am."

"We'll see;" he nodded at her. "Take my advice, Charlotte, and don't make a muff of yourself.

"It's very easy for you to talk," cried Charlotte, a little pink spot of anger rising on either cheek, "you have everybody to love you, and to be glad you are here; very easy, indeed!"

With that, she walked off, swinging her gown disdainfully after her.

"Whew!" ejaculated Ben, "well, I must say I'm surprised at you, Charlotte. I didn't suppose you could be jealous."

"Jealous?" Charlotte flamed around at him. "O, Ben Pepper, what do you mean?"

"You are just as jealous as you can be," said Ben honestly, "absolutely green."

"I'd have you to know I never was jealous in my life," said Charlotte, quite pale now, and standing very still.

"You don't know it, but you are," said Ben imperturbably; "when people begin to talk about other folks being loved and happy and all that, they're always jealous. Why in the world don't you think how everybody is loving you and wanting to make you happy?" It was quite a long speech for Ben, and he was overcome with astonishment at himself for having made it.

*"I'm Going Home." Declared Charlotte.*

"Because they are not," said Charlotte bitterly, "at least, they can't love me, if they do try to make me happy."

"Stuff and nonsense!" exclaimed Ben.

"And Polly"—then Charlotte pulled herself up.

"Well, what about Polly?" demanded Ben.

"Oh, nothing." Charlotte twisted uneasily, and shut her lips tightly together.

"If you think my sister Polly doesn't love you and want to make you happy, there's no use in my talking to you," said Ben, in a displeased way.

"I didn't say so," cried Charlotte quickly. "Oh, don't go. You are the only one who can help me," as he made a movement toward the door. "I never told anybody else, and they don't guess."

"And it's a pity that they should now," said Ben. "I tell you, Charlotte, if you never say anything like this again, I'll believe that you're the girl I thought you, with plenty of sense, and all that. There, give us your hand. Hurry up, now; here comes Phronsie."

Charlotte slowly laid her hand in Ben's big palm, as Phronsie opened the oaken door, and peered out into the darkness.

"I can't think what makes Ben so late," she said softly to herself.

"I'm going into the other door," said Charlotte, springing off down the veranda.

"Halloo, Pet!" Ben rushed into the hall, and seized Phronsie for a good hug.

"O, Ben, you're so late!" cried Phronsie.

"Well, I'm here now," said Ben comfortably.

"You can't think what has happened," said Phronsie, with a delightful air of mystery.

"To be sure I can't; but you are going to tell me," declared Ben with assurance.

"O, Bensie, I'd so much rather you would guess," said Phronsie, clasping her hands.

"Well, then, you have a new cat," said Ben at a hazard, while he disposed of his coat and hat.

"O, Ben," cried Phronsie in reproach, "why, I've given up having new cats; indeed I have."

"Since when?" asked Ben.

"Why, last week. I really have. I'm not going to get any more," said Phronsie.

Ben shouted. At the sound of his voice, somebody called over the stairs, "O, Ben, are you home? Come up here."

"Come on, Pet," cried Ben, "we're wanted," seizing Phronsie, and hurrying off to the stairs.

"I did so want to tell you myself," mourned Phronsie on the way.

"Then you shall." Ben set her on the floor suddenly. "I'll come up in a minute or so," he called. "There now, Phronsie, we'll have the wonderful news. Out with it, child."

"I don't suppose you ever could guess," said Phronsie, pausing a moment, "I really don't, Ben, because this is something you never would think of."

"No, I'm quite sure I should never guess in all the world," said Ben decidedly, "so let us have it."

"Grandpapa has promised to give us a surprise party," announced Phronsie, with careful scrutiny to see the effect of her news.

"A surprise party? Goodness me!" exploded Ben, "what do you mean, Phronsie?"

"A surprise party to go and see Jasper; and we are to start to-morrow. Now, Ben!" and Phronsie, her news all out, beamed up into his face.

"Oh, so it's Jasper's surprise party," cried Ben.

"Yes, and it's ours too; because you see we didn't any of us think Grandpapa was going to do it," said Phronsie.

"Well, it's my surprise party, too," said Ben lugubriously, "for I'm astonished; and beside I'm left out in the cold."

"O, Ben, can't you go?" cried Phronsie, her face falling instantly.

"No, Pet; wait till you get to be a business man and you'll see that surprise parties can't be indulged in very often."

"Won't Mr. Cabot let you go?" asked Phronsie, with an anxious droop of the head. "O, I think he will; truly I do."

"I sha'n't ask him," said Ben; "I'm sure of that."

"But Grandpapa will," said Phronsie, her face changing.

"No, no, Pet; you mustn't say anything about that. I'd rather stick to the business. There, come on; they're wild, I suppose, upstairs, to tell the news."

Just then some one called Phronsie. "Oh, dear," she sighed involuntarily, as Ben sped over the stairs without her.

"I thought you were never coming home, Ben," said Polly, meeting him in the upper hall. "Oh, we've such a fine thing to tell you!"

"I'm going to guess," said Ben wisely.

"Oh, you never can," declared Polly; "never in all this world. Don't try."

"Can't I, though? Give me a chance. You are to have a surprise party, and go to see Jasper. There!"

"How did you guess?" cried Polly in wide-eyed astonishment.

Ben burst into a hearty laugh. "Well, I met Phronsie, if you must know."

"Of course," laughed Polly; "how stupid in me! Well, was ever anything so fine in all this world?" and she danced down the hall, and came back flushed and panting.

"And Grandpapa has written to tell Mr. Cabot how it is, and to ask for a day or two off for you," she said, with a little pat on his back.

"O, Polly!" exclaimed Ben, in dismay, "Grandpapa shouldn't—I mean, I ought not to go. I'd really rather not."

"Well, Grandpapa says that you are working too hard, Bensie, and it's quite true," Polly gave him another pat, this time a motherly one; "and so you are going."

But Ben shook his head.

"And we start to-morrow," ran on Polly, "and Jasper doesn't know a word about our coming; and we are going to stay at the hotel two or three days." And here Phronsie ran eagerly up the stairs.

"And it's going to be lovely, and not rain any of the time; and we are to take Jasper a box full of everything," she announced in great excitement. "We began to pack it the very minute that Grandpapa told us we were to go."

"That's fine! Well, I'll drop something into that box," said Ben.

"Of course," said Polly, in great satisfaction.

"And Jasper wouldn't like it not to have something of Ben's in it," said Phronsie.

"Well, now, Bensie, run down after dinner and ask Pickering Dodge to go. That's a good boy." Polly patted the broad back coaxingly this time.

Ben's face fell. "How do you know that Grandpapa would like to have him along?" he asked abruptly.

"As if I'd ask you to invite him," cried Polly, "unless Grandpapa had said he could go. The very idea, Ben!"

"Well, something is the matter with Pick," confessed Ben unwillingly, "and I don't want to ask him."

"Something the matter with Pickering?" repeated Polly in dismay. "O, Ben, is he sick?"

"No," said Ben bluntly, "but he's cross."

"O, Ben, then something very bad must have happened," said Polly, "for Pickering is almost never cross."

"Well, I don't know what to make of him," said Ben; "he's been queer for a week now, more or less, and to-day he wouldn't speak to me; just shot off telling me to let him alone;" and Ben rapidly laid before Polly the little scene of the morning in the store.

"Now, Ben," said Polly, when it was all over, "I know really that something dreadful is the matter with Pickering, and I shall send him a note to come here to-night. He must tell us what it is. I'm going to write it now." And Polly sped off to her room, followed by Phronsie.

Ben went slowly down the hall to get ready for dinner. "I don't know how it is," he said, "but everything seems to be getting mixed up in this house, and all our good, quiet times gone. And now what can Charlotte have heard to make her want to go home?"

And all the time during dinner, Ben kept up a steady thinking, until Polly, looking across the table, caught his eye.

"Don't worry," her smile said, "I've sent a note to Pickering, and we'll find out what the trouble is."

Ben sat straight in his chair, and nodded back at her. "I can't tell her now that Pick is not what I'm stewing over," he said to himself, "and I can't tell her any time, either, for Charlotte has heard something that makes her think Polly is bothered by her being here. I must just fuss at it myself till I straighten it out."

So when Pickering Dodge, with a radiant face at being sent for by Polly's own hand, ran lightly up the steps of the King mansion, about an hour later, Ben hurried off to find Charlotte Chatterton.

"I can't come down," called Charlotte from the upper hall, "I'm tired; good-night."

"So am I tired," declared Ben, "but I'm going to talk to you, Charlotte," he added, decidedly.

"No; I don't want to talk," said Charlotte, shaking her head. "Good-night. Thank you, Ben," she added a bit pleasanter, "but I'm not going down."

"Indeed you are!" said Ben obstinately. "I'm not going to stir from this spot," he struck his hand on the stair railing, "until you are down here. Come, Charlotte."

"No," began Charlotte, but the next moment she was on the stairs, saying as she went slowly down, "I don't want to talk, Ben. There isn't anything to say."

"Now that's something like," observed Ben cheerfully, as she reached his side. "Come in here, do, Charlotte," leading the way into Mother Fisher's little sewing-room.

"But I'm not going to talk," reiterated Charlotte, following him in.

"You are going to talk enough so that I can know how to get this ridiculous idea out of your head," said Ben, as he closed the door on them both.

Mr. Cabot hurried into his wife's room, his face lighted with great satisfaction. "Well, Felicia," he said, "I believe I needn't worry about that boy any more."

"Who, Pickering?" asked Mrs. Cabot, with a last little touch to the lace at her throat.

"Of course Pickering. Well, he's in better hands than mine. Oh, I'm so glad to be rid of him;" and he threw himself into an easy chair and beamed at her.

"What in the world do you mean, Mr. Cabot?" demanded his wife. "You haven't had another fuss with Pickering? Oh, I'm quite sure he'll do well in the Law, if you'll only have patience a little longer."

"Nonsense, Felicia," said Mr. Cabot, "as if I'd get him out of that office, when it was such a piece of work to fasten him in there. Well, to make a long story short, he loves Polly Pepper. Think of that, Felicia!" And Mr. Cabot, in his joy, got out of the chair and began to rush up and down the room, rubbing his hands together in glee.

"O, Mr. Cabot—Mr. Cabot," cried his wife, flying after him, "you don't mean to say that Pickering and Polly are betrothed? Was ever anything so lovely! Oh! never mind about dinner; I couldn't eat a mouthful. I must go right around there, and get my arms around that dear girl. Tell Biggs to put the horses in at once."

"Stop just one moment, Felicia, for Heaven's sake!" cried Mr. Cabot, putting himself in front of her; "that's just like a woman; only hear the first word, and off she goes!"

"Do order the carriage," begged Mrs. Cabot, with dancing eyes. "I can't wait an instant, but I must tell Polly how glad we are. And of course you'll come too, Mr. Cabot. Oh, dear, it's such blessed news!"

"I didn't say they were engaged," began Mr. Cabot frantically, "I—I"—

"Didn't say that Polly and Pickering were engaged?" repeated Mrs. Cabot. "Well, what did you say, Mr. Cabot?"

"I said he loved her," said Mr. Cabot. "O, Felicia, it's the making of the boy," he added jubilantly.

Mrs. Cabot sank into her husband's deserted chair, unable to find a word.

# CHAPTER XII

# POLLY TRIES TO DO WHAT IS RIGHT

"O, Pickering!" Polly actually ran into the drawing-room with outstretched hands. "Why did Jencks put you in here?"

"I asked to come in here," said Pickering. "I don't want to see a lot of people to-night; I only want you, Polly."

"But Mamsie could help you—she'd know the right thing to say to you," said Polly.

"No, no!" cried Pickering in alarm, and edging off into a corner. "Do sit down, Polly, I—I want to talk to you."

So Polly sat down, her eyes fastened on his face, and wishing all the while that Mamsie would come in.

"I don't wonder you think I'm in a bad way," began Pickering nervously; "it was awfully good in you to send for me, Polly, awfully."

"Why, I couldn't help it," said Polly. "You know it's just like having one of the boys in trouble, to have you worried, Pickering."

"Yes, yes," said Pickering, "I know."

"Well, I want to tell you something," began Polly radiantly, thinking it better to cheer him up a bit with her news before getting at the root of his trouble. "Do you know that Grandpapa is going to take us all to-morrow to see Jasper? It's to be a surprise party."

"Ah," said Pickering, all his gladness gone.

"Yes; and Grandpapa wants you to go with us, Pickering," Polly went on.

"Oh, dear me—I can't—can't possibly!" exclaimed Pickering, in a tone of horror. "Don't ask me, Polly. Anything but that."

"O, yes, you can," laughed Polly, determined to get him out of his strange mood. "Why, Pickering, we don't want to go without you. It would spoil all our fun."

"Well, I can't go," cried Pickering, in an agony at being misunderstood. "I'd do anything in the world you ask, Polly, but that."

"Why not, you ridiculous boy?" asked Polly, quite as if it were Joel who was before her.

"Because Jasper and I don't speak to each other," Pickering bolted out; "we had a fight."

***"What Do You Say?" Cried Polly.***

Polly sprang to her feet. "What do you say?" she cried.

"It's beastly, I know," declared Pickering, his face aflame, "but, Polly, if you knew—I really couldn't help it; Jasper was"—

"Don't tell me that it was any of Jasper's doings," cried Polly vehemently, clasping her hands tightly together, so afraid she might say something to make the matter worse. "I know, Pickering, it was quite your own fault if you won't speak."

"O, Polly!" exclaimed Pickering, the hot blood all over his face, "don't say that; please don't."

"I must; because I know it is the truth," said Polly uncompromisingly. "If it isn't, why, then come with us to-morrow, Pickering," and her brow cleared.

"I can't, Polly, I can't possibly," cried Pickering in distress; "ask me anything but that, and I'll do it."

"This is the only thing that you ought to do," said Polly coldly. "O, Pickering, suppose that anything should happen so that you never could speak!" she added reproachfully.

"I'm sure I don't want to speak to a man when I've broken friendship with him," said Pickering sullenly. "What is there to talk about, I'd like to know?"

"If you've broken friendship with Jasper, I'm quite, quite sure it is your own fault," hotly declared Polly again; "Jasper never turned away from a friend in his life." And Polly broke off suddenly and walked down the long room, aghast to find how angry she was at each step.

"Don't you turn away from me, Polly," begged Pickering in such a piteous tone that Polly felt little twinges of remorse, and in a minute she was by his side again.

"I didn't mean to be cross," she said quickly, "but you mustn't say such things, Pickering."

"I must tell you the truth," said Pickering doggedly, "and that is that I've broken friendship with Jasper, and I can't speak to him."

"Pickering," said Polly, whirling abruptly to get a good look at his face, "you must speak to Jasper," and she drew a long breath.

"I tell you I can't," said Pickering, his face paling with the effort to control himself.

"Then," said Polly, very deliberately, yet with a glow of determination, "you can't speak to me; so good-night, Pickering," and she ran out of the room.

Pickering stared after her a moment in a dazed way, then picked up his hat, and darted out of the house, shutting the door hard behind him.

Polly, hurrying over the stairs to her own room, kept saying to herself over and over, "Oh! how could I have said that—how could I? when I want to help him—and now I have made everything worse."

"Polly," called Mrs. Fisher, as Polly sped by her door, "you are going to take the noon train, you know, to-morrow, Mr. King says; so you can pack in the morning easily."

"I'm not going, Mamsie; that is—I hope we are not any of us going," said Polly incoherently, as she tried to hurry by.

"Not going! Polly, child, what do you mean?" cried Mrs. Fisher aghast.

"O, Mamsie, don't ask me," begged Polly, having hard work to keep the tears back. "Do forgive me, but need I tell?" and Polly stopped and clung to the knob of the door.

"No, Polly, if you cannot tell mother your trouble willingly, I will not ask it, child." And Mrs. Fisher turned off, and began to busy herself over her work.

Polly, quite broken down by this, deserted her door-knob, and rushed into the bedroom.

"O, Mamsie, it's about—about other people, and I didn't know as I ought to tell. Need I?" cried Polly imploringly, seizing her mother's gown just as Phronsie would.

"No more had you a right to tell, Polly," said her mother, "if that is the case," and she turned a cheerful face toward her; "I can trust my girl, that she won't keep anything that is her own, away from me. There, there;" and she smoothed Polly's brown hair with her hand. "How I used to be always telling you to brush your hair, and now how nice it looks, Polly," she added approvingly.

"It's the same fly-away hair now," said Polly, throwing back her rebellious locks with an impatient toss of the head. "Oh! how I do wish I had smooth hair like Charlotte's."

"Fly-away hair, when it's taken care of as it ought to be," observed Mrs. Fisher, "is one thing, and when it's all sixes and sevens because a girl doesn't have time to brush it, is another. Your hair is all right now, Polly, There, go, child;" and she dismissed her with a final loving pat. "I can trust you, and when your worry gets too big for you, why, bring it to mother."

So Polly, up in her own room at last, crept into a corner, and there went over every word, bitterly lamenting what she had done. At last she could endure it no longer, and she sprang up. "I'll write a note to Pickering and say I am sorry," she cried to herself. "Maybe Ben will take it to him. O, dear! I forgot; Ben is vexed with him; but perhaps he will leave it at the door. Any way, I'll ask him."

So Polly scribbled down hastily:

Dear Pickering:

I am so sorry I said those words to you; I don't see how I came to. Do forget them, and forgive Polly.

"Ben, Ben!" Polly ran over the stairs, nervously twirling the little note. "O, dear me, where are you, Ben?"

"Here," called Ben, "in Mamsie's sewing-room."

"Oh! I beg your pardon," exclaimed Polly, throwing wide the door on the tete-a-tete Ben was having with Charlotte.

"Come in, Polly," cried Ben, his blue eyes glowing with welcome. "That's all right; you don't interrupt us. Charlotte and I were having a bit of a talk, but we're through. Now what's the matter?" with a good look at Polly's face.

"O, Ben, if you could," began Polly fearfully, "it's only this," waving the note with trembling fingers. "Now do say you will take this note to Pickering Dodge."

"Why, I thought you sent him a note before dinner," said Ben in surprise.

"So I did; and he came," said Polly, her head drooping in a shamefaced way, "and I was cross to him."

"O, Polly, you cross to him!" exclaimed Ben; "as if I'd believe that!" while Charlotte stared at her with wide eyes.

"I truly was," confessed Polly. "There, don't stop, Ben, to talk about it, please, but do take this note," thrusting it at him.

But Ben shook his head. "I thought I told you, Polly, that Pick don't want to speak to me. How in the world can I go at him?" At this Charlotte stared worse than ever.

"You needn't go in the house," said Polly, "just leave it at the door. Ah, do, Ben;" she went up to him and coaxingly patted his cheek.

"All right, as long as you don't want me to bore him," said Ben, slowly getting out of his chair. "Here, give us your note, Polly. Of course you'll make me do as you say."

"You're just as splendid as you can be," cried Polly joyfully. "There, now, Bensie," pushing the note into his hand, "do hurry, that's a good boy."

And in a quarter of an hour, Ben rushed in, meeting Polly in the hall, kis face aglow, and eyes shining. "Here, Polly, catch it," tossing her a note; "that's from Pick."

"Why, did you see him?" asked Polly, in amazement.

"Yes; couldn't help it—he was rushing out the door like a whirlwind, and we came together on the steps," said Ben, with a burst of laughter at the remembrance, "and we spoke before we meant to; couldn't help it, you know; just ran into each other—and he read your note, and then he flew into the house, and was gone a moment or two, and came back mumbling it was all his fault, and he'd written; that you'd understand, or something of that sort, and he gave me this note to carry back; and I guess Pick is all right, Polly." Ben drew a long breath of relief after he got through; he was so unaccustomed to long speeches.

Polly tore open her note, and stooped to read it by the dancing flames of the hall fire.

To show that I forgive you, Polly, I'll go to-morrow with you all to see Jasper.

PICKERING.

"Won't Jasper be surprised?" Phronsie kept exclaiming over and over, when they were once fairly in the cars; much to old Mr. King's delight, who never tired of congratulating himself on planning the outing. "Grandpapa dear, I do think it was, oh! so lovely in you to take us all."

"Well, Jasper has been working hard lately," said the old gentleman, "and it will be no end of good to him even if it doesn't agree with you, my pet," pinching Phronsie's ear.

"Oh, but it does agree with me," said Phronsie in great satisfaction, "very much, indeed, Grandpapa."

"So it seems," said the old gentleman. "Well, now, Phronsie," glancing around at the rest of his party, "everything is moving on well, and I believe I'll take a bit of a nap; that is, if that youngster," with a nod toward the end of the car, "will allow me to."

"I don't believe that baby will cry any more," said Phronsie, with a hopeful glance whence the disturbing sounds came, "he can't, Grandpapa; he's cried so much. Now do lean your head back; I'm going to put this rug under it;" and Phronsie began to pull out a traveling blanket from the roll.

Polly, across the car aisle, laid down her book, and clambered out her seat. "Let me take baby," she said, coming up unsteadily to the pale little woman who was endeavoring to pacify a stout, red-cheeked boy a year old, just beginning on a fresh series of roars.

An old gentleman in the seat back, laid down the paper he had been trying to read, to see the fresh attempts on the small disturber.

"He'll tire you out, Miss," said the pale little woman deprecatingly. "There, there, Johnny, do be still," with an uneasy pull at Johnny's red skirt.

"Indeed he won't," laughed Polly merrily. Hearing this, Johnny stopped beating the window in the vain effort to get out, and deliberately looked Polly over. "I like babies," added Polly, "and if you'll let me," to the little mother, "I'm going to play with this one." And without waiting for an answer, she sat down in the end of the seat, and held out her hands alluringly to Johnny.

"Young lady, there are babies and babies," observed the old gentleman solemnly, and leaning over the back of the seat, he regarded Polly over his spectacles with pitying eyes, "and I'd advise you to have nothing to do with this particular one."

But Johnny was already scrambling all over Polly's traveling gown, and she was laughing at him. And presently the pale little woman was stretched comfortably on the opposite seat, her eyes closed restfully.

"Well done!" cried the old gentleman; "I'll read my paper while the calm spell lasts;" as the train rumbled on, the sound only broken by Johnny's delighted little gurgles, as Polly played "Rabbit and Fox" for his delectation.

Phronsie looked down the intervening space, and heaved a sigh at Polly's employment.

"Don't worry; I like it," telegraphed Polly, nodding away to her. So Phronsie turned again to her watch, lest Grandpapa's head should slip from the blanket pillow in a sudden lurch of the cars.

"I'd help her if I knew how," Charlotte, several seats off, groaned to herself, "but that lump of a baby would only roar at me. Dear, dear, am I never to be any good to Polly?"

She leaned her troubled face against the window-side, her chin resting on her hand, and gave herself up to the old thoughts. "What did Ben say?" she cried suddenly, flying away from the window so abruptly that she involuntarily glanced around to be quite sure that none of her fellow-passengers were laughing at her. "'You may be sure, Charlotte, if you keep on the lookout, there will a time come for you to help Polly.' That's what he said, and I'll hold fast to it."

On and on the train rumbled. The little mother woke up with a new light in her eyes, and a pink color on her cheeks. "I haven't had such a sleep in weeks," she said gratefully. Then she leaned forward.

"I'll take Johnny now," she said; "you must be so tired."

But Johnny roared out "No," and beat her off with small fists and feet.

"He's going to sleep," said Polly, looking down at him snuggled up tightly within her arm, his heavy eyelids slowly drooping, "then I'll put him down on the seat, and tuck him up for a good long nap."

At the word "sleep" Johnny screamed out, "No, no!" and thrust his fat knuckles into his eyes, while he tried to sit up straight in Polly's lap.

"There, there," cried Polly soothingly, "now fly back, little bird, into your nest."

Johnny showed all the small white teeth he possessed, in a gleeful laugh, and burrowed deeper than before within the kind arm as he tried to play "Bo-peep" with her.

"You see," said Polly, to the little mother's worried look; "he'll soon be off in Nodland," she added softly.

"I've never had any one be so good to me," said Johnny's mother brokenly, "as you, Miss."

"Is Johnny your only little boy?" asked Polly, to stop the flow of gratitude.

"Yes, Miss; I've buried four children."

"Oh!" exclaimed Polly, quite hushed.

The little mother wiped away the tears from her eyes, and looked out of the window, steadily fixing her gaze on the distant landscape. And the train sped on.

"But the worst is, the father is gone." She turned again to Polly, then glanced down at her black dress. "Johnny and me have no one now."

"Don't try to tell me," cried Polly involuntarily, "if it pains you."

She would have taken the thin hand in hers, but Johnny's uneasy breathing showed him still contesting every inch of progress the "children's sandman" was making toward him, and she didn't dare to move.

"It does me good," said the little woman, "somehow, I must tell you, Miss. And now I'm going to Fall River. Somebody told me I'd get work there in the Print Mills. You see, I haven't any father nor mother, nor anybody belonging to Johnny's father nor me."

"Are you sure of getting work when you reach Fall River?" asked Polly, feeling all the thrill of a great lonely world, for two such little helpless beings to be cast adrift in it.

"No'm," said the little woman; "but it's a big mill, they say, and has to have lots of women in it, and there must be a place for me. I do think that times are going to be good now for Johnny and me, and"—

A crash like that when the lightning begins on deadly work; a surging, helpless tossing from side to side, when the hands strike blindly out on either side for something to cling to; a sudden fall, down, down, to unknown depths; a confused medley of shouts, and one long shuddering scream.

"Oh! what"—began Polly, holding to Johnny through it all. And then she knew no more.

# CHAPTER XIII

# THE ACCIDENT

A roaring sound close to her ear made Polly start, and open her eyes. Johnny's fat arms were clutched around her neck so tightly she could scarcely breathe, while he was screaming as hard as he could.

—"is the matter?" cried Polly, finishing her sentence.

A pair of strong arms were lifting her up, and pulling her from beneath something, she could not tell what, that was lying heavily over her, while Johnny rolled off like a ball.

"O, Ben!" cried Polly gratefully, as the arms carried her off. And then she saw the face above her: "Why, Pickering!"

"Are you hurt anywhere?" gasped Pickering, speaking the words with difficulty.

"What is it?" cried Polly, in a dazed way.

"There's been an accident," said Pickering. "Oh, Polly, say you're not hurt!" as he set her carefully down.

"An accident!" exclaimed Polly, and she sprang to her feet and glanced wildly around. "Pickering—where—where"—she couldn't ask "are Phronsie and Ben and Grandpapa?"

But Pickering cried at once, "All right—every single one. Here comes Phronsie, and Ben too."

And Phronsie running up, with streaming hair and white cheeks, threw glad arms around her neck. "Oh, Polly, are you hurt?" And Ben seized her, but at that she winced; and her left arm fell heavily to her side.

"Where's Baby?" cried Polly, trying to cover up the expression of pain; "do somebody look after him."

"Charlotte has him," said Phronsie, looking off to a grassy bank by the railroad track, where Charlotte Chatterton sat with Johnny in her lap.

Polly followed the glance, then off to the broken car, one end of which lay in ruins across the rails, and to the crowds of people running to the scene, in the midst of which was the fearful hush that proclaimed death.

"Oh! do come and help," called Polly, and before they knew it, she was dashing off, and running over the grass, up to the track. "There was a woman—Johnny's mother," she cried, pushing her way into the crowd, Phronsie and Ben and Pickering close behind—"in the seat opposite me."

Two or three men were picking up a still figure they had just pried out from the ruins of the car-end, dropped helplessly on its side, just as it fell when the fatal blow came. "Let me see her," said Polly hoarsely. They turned the face obediently; there was a long, terrible gash on the forehead that showed death to have come instantly to Johnny's mother, and that "good times" had already begun for her, and her weary feet were safely at rest in the Heavenly Home.

Polly drew a long breath, and bending suddenly dropped a kiss on the peaceful cheek; then she drew out her handkerchief, and softly laid it over the dead face. "Take her to that farmhouse." She pointed to a large white house off in the fields. "I will go there—but I must help here first."

***"Oh, Polly, Are You Hurt?"***

"Yes, Miss," said the men obediently, moving off with their burden.

"Polly—Polly, come away," begged Pickering and Ben.

"Grandpapa is sitting on the bank over there," pointed Phronsie, with a beseeching finger. "Oh, do go to him, Polly; I'll stay and help the poor people."

"And no one was hurt," said Ben quickly, "only in this end of the car. See, Polly, everybody is out," pointing past the crowd into the car, to the vacant seats.

"There was an old gentleman in the seat back of me," cried Polly, in distress. "Hasn't any one seen him?" running up and down the track; "an old gentleman with a black velvet cap"—amid shouts of "Keep out—the car is taking fire. Don't go near it."

A little tongue of flame shooting from one of the windows at the further end of the car proclaimed this fact, without the words.

"Has no one seen him?" called Polly, in a voice so clear and piercing that it rose above the babel of the crowd, and the groans of one or two injured people drawn out from the ruin, and lying on the bank, waiting the surgeon's arrival. "Then he must be in the car. Oh, Ben—come, we must get him out!" and she sprang back toward the broken car end.

"Keep back, Polly!" commanded Ben, and "I shall go," cried Pickering Dodge. But Polly ran too, and clambered with them, over the crushed car seats and window frames of the ruin.

"He's not here," cried Ben, while the hot flame seemed to be sweeping with cruel haste, down to catch them.

"Look—oh, he must be!" cried Polly wildly, peering into the ruin. "Oh, Ben, I see a hand!"

But a rough grasp on her shoulder seized her as the words left her mouth. "Come out of here, Miss, or you'll be killed," and Polly was being borne off by rescuers who had seen her rush with the two young men, in amongst the ruin. "I tell you," cried Polly, struggling to get free, "there is an old gentleman buried in there; I saw his hand."

"Everybody is out, Miss," and they carried her off. But Ben and Pickering were already in a race with the flames, for the possession of the old gentleman, whose body, after the car seat was removed, could plainly be seen.

"There's the axe," cried Ben hoarsely, pointing to it, where it had fallen near to Pickering.

Pickering measured the approach of the flames with a careful eye. "He is probably dead," he said to Ben. "Shall we?"

"Hand the axe," cried Ben. Already the car was at a stifling heat, and the roar of the flames grew perilously near. Would no one come to help them? Must they die like animals in a trap? Well, the work was to be done. Two—three ringing blows breaking away a heavy beam, quick, agile pulling up of the broken window frame, and in the very teeth of the flames, young arms bore out the old body.

A great shout burst from the crowd as they staggered forth with their burden. Pickering had only strength to look around for Polly, before he dropped on the grass.

And when he looked up, the tears were raining on his face.

"O, Pickering!" cried Polly. "Now there isn't anything more to long for. You are all right?"

Pickering lifted his head feebly, and glanced around. The walls of the "spare room" at the farm-house, gay in large flowered paper, met his eyes. "Why, where am I?" he began.

"At good Farmer Higby's," said Polly. And then he saw that her arm was in a sling. "That's nothing," she finished, meeting his look, "it's all fixed as good as can be, and has nothing to do but get well—has it, Ben?"

Ben popped up his head from the depths of the easy chair, where he had crouched, afraid lest Pickering should revive and see him too suddenly.

"How are you, old fellow?" he now cried, advancing toward the bed. "There, don't try to speak," hurriedly, "everything is all right. Wait till you are better."

"How long have I been here?" asked Pickering, looking at Polly's arm.

"Only a day," said Polly, "and now you must have something to eat," starting toward the door.

"I couldn't eat a mouthful," said Pickering, shutting his mouth and turning on the pillow.

"Indeed you will," declared Polly, hurrying on. "The doctor said as soon as you could talk, you must have something to eat; and I shall tell Mrs. Higby to bring it up." So she disappeared.

"Goodness me! have I had the doctor?" asked Pickering, turning back to look after her.

"Yes," said Ben. Then he tried to turn the conversation. But Pickering broke in. "Did Polly break her arm at—at the first?" he asked, holding his breath for the answer.

"Yes," said Ben, "don't talk about it," with a gasp—"Polly says that she is so glad it isn't her right arm," he added, with an attempt at cheerfulness. "And the doctor promises it will be all right soon. It's lucky there is a good one here."

Pickering groaned. "It's a pity I wasn't in the old fellow's place, Ben," he said, "for I've got to tell Polly how I wanted to leave him, and I'd rather die than see her face."

"See here," cried Ben, "if you say one word to Polly about it, I'll pitch you out of the window, sick as you are."

"Pitch ahead, then," said Pickering, "for I shall tell Polly."

"Not to-day, any way. Now promise," said Ben resolutely.

"Well—but I shall tell her sometime," said Pickering. "I'd rather she knew it—but I wish we could have saved him."

"He's in the other room," said Ben suddenly.

"Poor old thing—to die like that."

"Die? He's as well as a fish," said Ben; "sitting up in an easy chair, and to my certain knowledge, eating dried herrings and cheese at this very minute."

"He's eating dried herrings and cheese!" repeated Pickering, nearly skipping out of bed. "Why, wasn't he dead when we brought him out?"

"No, only stunned. There, do get back," said Ben, pushing Pickering well under the blankets again, "the doctor says on no account are you to get up until he came. Do keep still; he'll be here presently," with a glance at Mrs. Higby's chimney clock.

"The doctor—who cares for him!" cried Pickering, nevertheless he scrambled back again, and allowed Ben to tuck him in tightly. And presently in came Polly, and after her, a bright apple-cheeked woman bearing a tray, on which steamed a bowl of gruel.

And in less time than it takes to tell it, Pickering was bolstered up against his pillows, and obediently opening his mouth at the right times to admit of the spoonfuls Polly held out to him.

***Old Mr. King Drew Up His Chair To Oversee It All.***

And Phronsie came in and perched on the foot of the four-poster, gravely watching it all. And old Mr. King followed, drawing up the easy chair to the bedside, where he could oversee the whole thing. And before it was over, the door opened, and a young man, with a professional air, looked in and said in great satisfaction, "That's good," coming up to the bed and putting out his hand to Pickering.

"Here's the doctor," cried old Mr. King, with a flourish of his palm. "Well, Doctor Bryce, your patient is doing pretty well, I think."

"I should say so," answered the doctor, with a keen glance at Pickering. "O, he's all right. How is the arm?" to Polly.

"Let me feed Pickering, do," begged Phronsie, slipping from the bed, "while Doctor looks at your arm, Polly."

"I can wait," said the doctor, moving down to the foot of the four-poster, where he stood looking at the feeding process, "and I can go in and see Mr. Loughead meanwhile."

Pickering dodged the spoon, nearly in his mouth. "Who?" he cried.

"Dear me," cried Polly, trying to save the gruel drops from falling on Mrs. Higby's crazy quilt, "how you frightened me, Pickering."

"Who did he say?" demanded Pickering, as Dr. Bryce went out.

"Pickering," said Polly, with shining eyes, "who do you think you and Ben saved so bravely? Jack Loughead's uncle, who has just got here from Australia, and he's"—

Pickering gave a groan and turned on his pillow. "Don't give me any more, Polly," he said, putting up his hand.

Polly set the spoon in the gruel bowl, with a disappointed air.

"Never mind," said the young doctor, coming back again, "he's eaten enough. Now may I see your arm?" He turned to Polly gently. "We must go in the other room for that," with a nod at Pickering.

A thrill went over Phronsie, which she tried her best to conceal, and she turned quite pale. Polly smiled at her as she went over toward the door, followed by the doctor, old Mr. King and Ben. Pickering Dodge clenched his hand under the bedclothes, and looked after them, then steadfastly gazed at the large flowers blooming with reckless abandon up and down over the dark-green wall-paper.

"Phronsie," said Polly, hearing her footsteps joining the others out in the hall, "will you go in and see how Charlotte is getting on with Johnny? Do, dear," she whispered in Phronsie's ear, as she gained her side.

"I'd rather stay with you, Polly," said Phronsie wistfully, "and hold your other hand."

"But I do so want you to help Charlotte," said Polly beseechingly. "Will you, Phronsie?" and she set a kiss on Phronsie's pale cheek.

"I will, Polly," said Phronsie, with a sigh. But she looked back as she went slowly along to the opposite end of the hall. "Please don't hurt Polly," she said imploringly to the doctor.

"I won't, little girl," he replied, "any more than I can help."

"Seems's if I sha'n't ever get over the shock," she said to herself, looking off to the railroad track, shining in the morning sunlight. "To look up from my sewing and see—la! and 'twas the first time I ever sat down to that rag-rug since I had to drop it and run over and take care of Simon, when they brought me word he was 'most cut to pieces in the mowing machine. My senses! I'm afraid to finish the thing."

"I want to get out in the woods and holler," she declared; "seems's if then I'd feel better. To look up, expecting to see the cars coming along real lively and pleasant, just as they always do so sociable-like when I'm sewing, and then—oh, dear me!" she wrung her fat hands together, "there, all of a sudden, were two of 'em bumping together, one end smashed into kindling wood, and t'other end sticking up straight in the air. Oh! my senses, I don't wonder I thought I was going crazy, and that I let the rug fly and jumped into the middle of the floor, till I heard the screaming, and I run to help, and there was that poor soul they were bringing here, and she dead as a stone. Oh, dear, dear!"

Mrs. Higby turned away so that she could not see the shining railroad track, and looked off over the meadow, while a happier expression came over her features. "I'm awful tickled this house is big," she said, with a good degree of comfort, "so's Jotham and me could take 'em in. Now I'm glad we didn't sell last spring, when Mary Ann was married, and move down to the village. Seems's if Providence was in it. Gracious, see that man running here! I hope there ain't anything else happened!" and with her old flutter upon her, Mrs. Higby turned to meet a young man advancing to the door-stone, with more speed than was ordinarily exhibited by the natives of Brierly.

"Is this Mr. Jotham Higby's house?" asked the stranger. And although he was very pale and evidently troubled, he touched his hat, and waited for her answer.

"Yes," said Mrs. Higby; "what do you want? Do excuse me," all in the same breath, "but I'm all upset; there was an awful railroad accident along here yesterday. You haven't come to tell of anything else bad, have you?" And she was sharper than ever.

"No," said the young man, "my friends are here; you took them in so kindly. Do show me the way to them." He was quite imperative now, moving over the flat stone, and into the square entry like one accustomed to being obeyed. "Which way?" he asked, glancing up the stairs.

"Oh, my!" exclaimed Mrs. Higby, "excuse me, sir; the rooms upstairs"—nodding like a mandarin in the direction named, "any of 'em—all of 'em; they've got 'em all; you can't make a miss."

The young man was already opening the door of the room where Dr. Bryce was examining Polly's arm, old Mr. King and Ben looking on anxiously.

Polly saw him first. "Oh, Jasper!" she cried, with a sudden start.

"Take care!" exclaimed Dr. Bryce, looking off from the bandages he was nicely adjusting, to bestow a keen glance on Jasper.

Jasper gave one hand to his father in passing, but went straight to Polly's side, and laid his other hand on her shoulder.

"It's all right, Jasper," said Polly, seeing he couldn't speak. "Doctor says my arm is doing beautifully."

"Well, well," said old Mr. King, trying to speak cheerfully, but only succeeding in a nervous effort, "this isn't just the most successful way to give you a surprise party, Jasper, but it's the best we could do. And we had to send you a telegram, for fear you'd see it in the papers. So you thought you'd come on and see for yourself, eh?" as Jasper showed no inclination to talk.

"Yes," said Jasper, still confining himself to monosyllables.

"And that's the sensible thing to do," said Ben, with a grateful look at Jasper, "than to wait till we are able to move on—Pickering and all."

"Is Pickering Dodge with you?" exclaimed Jasper, quickly.

Polly turned in her chair, and looked into his eyes. "Yes; Pickering came with us expressly to see you, Jasper." Then without waiting for an answer, "He is in the next room; do go and see him."

"Very well," said Jasper, "I'll be back in a moment or two, father," going out.

Pickering Dodge still lay, gazing at the sprawling flowers on the wall, and doing his best not to count them. The door opened suddenly. "Well, well, old fellow." Jasper came up to the bedside with the air of one who had been in the habit of running in every little while. "It's good to see you again, Pick," he added, affectionately, laying his hand, that good right hand, on the nervous one playing with the coverlids.

"Of course you couldn't do what I asked, Jasper; no one could," said Pickering, rolling over to look at him. "And I was a fool to ask it."

"But I might have been kinder," said Jasper, compressing his lips; "forget that, Pick."

"Don't say any more," said Pickering, his face flushing, "and I know it's all up with me, any way, Jasper." And he turned pale again. "We pulled an old fellow out of the wreck, at least Ben did the most of it—Polly wanted us to; and who do you suppose he is? Why, Jack Loughead's uncle. Of course *he*'ll be here soon, and it's easy to see the end."

At that, Pickering bolted up in bed to a sitting position, and clutched at the collar of his morning jacket with savage fingers.

"Don't, Pick," begged Jasper, in an unsteady voice.

"I'm going to get up," declared Pickering deliberately. "Clear out, Jasper," with a forbidding gesture, "or I'll pitch into you."

"You'll lie down," said Jasper decidedly; "there, get in again," with a gentle push on Pickering's long legs. "Aren't you ashamed of yourself, though, to act like this!" trying to speak playfully.

Pickering scrambled back into bed, fuming every instant. "To lie like a log here, while that fellow dashes around carrying everything before him—it's—it's—abominable and atrocious! Let me out, I say!" And he dashed toward the edge of the bed, nearly knocking Jasper over.

"Hold on, there," cried Jasper, pinning down the clothes with a firm hand, "don't you see"—while Pickering struggled to toss them back "Take care, you'll tear this quilt!—that I'll help you on to your feet all in good time? And if you behave yourself, you'll be around, and a match for any Jack Loughead under the heavens. There, now, will you be still?"

"Send that dunce of a doctor to me as soon as you can," said Pickering, rolling back suddenly once more, into the hollow made in the center of the four-poster. "Dear me, he's sweet on Polly too!" he groaned under the clothes.

"Whew!" exclaimed Jasper, pulling out his handkerchief to wipe his forehead. "I won't agree to hold you in bed again, Pick. I'll send the doctor," he added, going out, "but you see that you don't lose your head while I'm gone."

"I'll promise nothing," said Pickering softly to himself, the moment the door closed, and slipping neatly out of bed, he tiptoed over and turned the key in the lock. "There," snapping his fingers in the air, "as if I'd have that idiot of a doctor around me." Then he proceeded to dress himself very rapidly, but with painstaking care.

"I'm all right," and he gave himself a final shake; "that doctor would have made a fool of me and kept me in bed, like enough, for a week. And with that Jack Loughead here!" He gave a swift glance into the cracked looking-glass hanging over the high shelf, and with another pull at his necktie-end, unlocked the door and went out.

"Halloo!"

"Oh, beg pardon!" A long figure that had just scaled the stairs, came suddenly up against Pickering, stalking along the narrow hall.

"How d'ye do?" said Pickering quite jauntily, and extending the tips of his fingers; "just got here, I take it, Loughead?"

"Yes," returned Jack Loughead. Pickering was made no more steady in his mind, nor on his feet, by seeing the other's evident uneasiness, but he covered it up by a careless "Well, I suppose you have come to look up your uncle, hey?"

"Yes, oh, yes," said Jack, "of course, my uncle. Well, were any of the others hurt?"

"Yes; one woman was killed." Pickering could not trust himself to mention Polly's broken arm yet.

Jack Loughead's face carried the proper amount of sympathy. "No one of your party was hurt, I believe?" he said quickly.

"Oh, look us over, and see for yourself," said Pickering, beginning to feel faintish, and as if he would like to sit down. And then the door at the end of the hall was opened, and out came all the others and the doctor, who was saying, "I'll just step in and look at the young man, though he's doing well enough—oh, my gracious!"

"Thank you, I am doing well enough," said Pickering, with his best society manner on, and extending his hand, "much obliged, I'm sure; what I should have done without you, I don't know, of course; send in your bill, and I shall be only too happy to make it all right."

Jack Loughead rushed up to Polly. "No one told me—is your arm—" he couldn't say "broken," being quite beyond control of himself.

"How are you, Mr. Loughead?" said old Mr. King rather stiffly, at being overlooked, and putting out his courtly old hand.

"Oh, beg pardon." Jack mumbled something about being an awkward fellow at the best, and extended a shaking hand.

"You are anxious to see your uncle, of course," continued the old gentleman, leading off down the hall, "this way, Mr. Loughead."

"Of course, yes, indeed," stammered Jack Loughead, having nothing to do but to follow.

# CHAPTER XIV

# JOEL

Joel threw down his books in an uneasy way. "I must give it up; there's no other way," he exclaimed.

"Halloo, Joe!"

"You here?" cried Joel, whirling in surprise. "Come out of your hole, Dave," peering into the niche between the book-shelves and the bed. "What are you prowling in there for?"

"Oh! my cuff-button rolled in here somewhere," said David, emerging crab-wise, and lifting a red face. "Give us a hand, Joe, and help pull out the bed. Plague on this room for being such a box! There!" with an impatient shove.

Joel burst into a fit of laughter, and then stared; it was such an unusual thing to see a frown on David's placid face. "What's come over you, any way? Stand out of the way; I'll have this bed over there in a jiffy," rolling it into the center of the small room as he spoke.

David sprang to one side lightly. "Whew! what a dust you kick up," he cried, snapping his clothes gingerly.

"So you are in your best toggery," exclaimed Joel, standing straight, his labors over the bed being completed.

"Yes, I'm going to the Parrotts' to dinner," said David, hurrying off for the whisk broom to remove the last speck of dust from his dress suit. "Of course you've forgotten it, Joe, though I don't suppose you'd go, any way."

"No, I wouldn't go, any way," said Joel, tossing back his black locks from his forehead. "You forget, Dave, it's the Association night."

David let another little frown settle on his face. "No, I didn't forget that, Joe, but I do wish you'd think it possible to take a Thursday evening off once in a while for the sake of your friends, if for no other reason."

"Well, I can't," said Joel, getting down on all-fours to hunt for the button, "so don't let's go over old arguments. Where in time is that thing? oh"—and he came up bright and shining to his feet, holding the button between his thumb and finger. "My compliments to you," presenting it to David. "There, stick it in before it gets lost again, and hurry off; you look pretty as a pink."

"Stop your nonsense, Joe," cried David sharply, who hated being reminded of his girlish beauty. "Well, I'll make the usual excuses for you. Good-by," and not forgetting to pick up his walking stick with his hat, he ran off on his way to the florist's for the *boutonniere* that must go on before he presented himself at the Parrotts' dinner party.

Joel shoved back the bed into position with one long thrust that would have been a godsend to a lagging boat crew; then dashed to the table and sat down, doggedly throwing open the first book that came to hand.

"I'd rather chop wood," he exclaimed in the old way, leaning his head on his hands. "Whew! weren't those good days, though, in the little brown house, when we had all outdoors to work in!" He dropped his arms to pinch the muscles of one with his other fingers. "Isn't that beautiful?" he said affectionately. Then he swung them over his head, tilting back his chair restfully.

"What did Mamsie say?" he cried, bringing the chair down with a remorseful thud. "'I'd work myself to skin and bone but I'd go through creditably.' Here goes!"

And by the time that Davie was handing in Miss Lulu Parrott to dinner Joel clapped together his last book, threw on his hat, and rushed out to a hasty supper at Commons, *en route* to the Christian Association meeting.

Little Perkins ran up to him at the close of the meeting. "Stop a bit. Pepper, do," he begged; "Johnson's gone back to his cups, and we can't do anything with him."

A cloud fell over Joel's face. "Where is he?" he asked.

"Oh, in the little room back. He won't show his face here, and yet he can't keep away, he says. You must get your hand on him, Pepper," and Little Perkins hurried off.

Joel dashed into the "little room back." "How d'ye, Johnson?" putting out his hand "Come out for a walk, do; why, this room is stifling."

"I can't," said Johnson miserably; "you don't know, Mr. Pepper, I've been drinking, or you wouldn't ask me."

"Nonsense—but I would, though," said Joel sharply. "Come out, I say, Johnson; it's enough to make you drink again to stay in such a room."

Johnson not getting out of his chair, Joel went in and laid hold of his arm. "It's no use, Johnson," he said, "I can't talk to you here; it's too hot and close. And I do want a walk, so let's have it together. There, button up your coat," as they were well out in the hall, and Johnson flung his hat on his head with a reckless hand.

As they hurried down the steps they ran against a crowd of college boys. Johnson shrank up miserably against the stone fence, and tried to look as small as possible. Glances of recognition passed, and Joel spoke to right and left as the boys went by. But a few hisses, low and insistent, were all he got.

"Do let me go," begged Johnson, still hugging the fence, "you can't save me; and they hate you enough for such work."

"Come on!" roared Joel at him, and plucking him off from the fence with a determined hand.

"It's time we went for him," said one of the college boys, with a backward glance at Joel and his companion, "the Deacon is absolutely insulting. The idea of his speaking to us."

"Let's have it over to-night," said another. "What do you say?" to the others.

"Where's Davina?" asked another.

"Oh, Pink-and-White is out dining," said the first voice. "My pretty little girl is safe at the Parrotts'."

"Sure?"

"As a gun. Met him with a posy in his button-hole, and sweet as a little bud himself, and he told me so."

"All right. He'll stay away late, then; the Parrotts always have music or a dance after their dinners. Come on." The last speaker rolled up his sleeves, and boxed imaginary rounds in a scientific manner in the air.

"Agreed?" the tall fellow who proposed it looked over the whole crew. "Do you all want to have it done to-night?" as they came to a standstill on the pavement.

"Yes—yes."

"Hush—that cop is looking. Move on, will you? Now, not a man of you backs out, you understand; if he does, he gets worse than the Deacon will. All right."

*"We're all such jolly good fellows,*
*We're all such jolly good fellows"*—

Everybody smiled who passed them singing their way down town.

"It always does me good to hear those students sing. They're so happy, and so affectionate toward each other," said one lady, hanging on her escort's arm.

He, being a college man, said rapturously, "Oh yes!"

Joel, back in his own room, threw himself in his easy chair, first turning down the gas. "Just so much less of a bill for Grandpapa. Our debt is rolling up fast enough without burning up the money. Dear me, if Johnson drinks after this, I shall be in despair." He threw up his long legs, and rested them on the mantel, while he thrust his hands in his pockets, to think the better.

A knock at the door. "Come in!" called Joel, not looking around, till a rushing sound of feet trying to step carefully, called him out of himself.

"Now—now!" Two or three swifter than the others, darted for the chair, but Joel was not in it. On the other side of it, looking at them, his hands out of his pockets, he stood, saying, "What do you want?"

"Oh, come, Pepper, it's no use," said a tall fellow, wiry and agile, "too many against you in this little call. Come along," and he advanced on Joel.

"You come along yourself, Dobbs," said Joel pleasantly, and holding up a fist that looked hard to begin with, "and you'll get this; that's all."

***"You come along yourself, Dobbs," said Joel pleasantly.***

"Come on, fellows!" Dobbs looked back and winked to the others. "Now!" there was a shoulder-to-shoulder rush; a wild tangle of arms, followed by a wilder tangle of legs, and Joel was through the ranks, his black eyes blazing, and tossing his black hair from his forehead.

"Do you want some more?" he cried, flirting his fists in the air, "or will you leave my room?"

"Lock the door!" "Get up, Bingley," and, "Stop your roaring." "No, we'll give it to you now, and no mistake." "If you won't come quietly, you shall some way, Deacon."

These were some of the smothered cries.

"Now!" and there was another blind rush; this time, over Bingley, who didn't heed the invitation to get up.

Joel, watching his chance to reach the door, had no time before they were on him, and he heard the key click in the lock.

"It's for Mamsie now, sure—and for Polly!" he said, setting his teeth hard. On they came. But Joel, in rushing through as before, was so mindful of stepping over Bingley carefully, that it lost him an instant; and a grasp firm as iron, was on his arm. The others rallied, and closed around him.

"Unhand me!" yelled Joel, beating them off. But he might as well have fought tigers, unless he could knock off, with cruel aim, the one hanging to his arm. It was no time to mince matters, and Joel, only careful to avoid the face, struck a terrible blow that felled Dobbs flat.

"Now will you go?" roared Joel, aghast at what he had done, yet swinging his arms with deadly intent on either side, "or, do you want some more?"

There lay two valiant fellows on the floor. The rest drew off and looked at them.

"You'll pay for this, Deacon," they declared under their breath.

"I suppose so," said Joel, still swinging his arms for practice; "probably you'll wait for me with kindly intent some dark night behind a tree, as you know I don't carry a pistol. Why don't you have it out now? Come on if you want to."

But no one seemed to want to.

"There'll be a row over this," said one or two, consulting together; "as long as those thin-skinned fellows don't get up," pointing to the floor, "we must wait." Suddenly the door was unlocked, and the whole crew stampeded.

"See here," cried Joel, bounding after them, "come back and take care of your two men."

But the crew disappeared.

Bingley lifted his head feebly.

"Just like Dobbs," he said, "get us into a scrape, and then cut."

"Hush—don't say anything," said Joel, rushing frantically back, "I think he's dead—oh, Bingley, I'm sorry I hurt you too."

He was rapidly pouring water into the basin, and dashing it into Dobbs' unconscious face. "I must go for the doctor," he groaned. "Bingley, he can't be dead—do say he isn't!" in a flood of remorse.

Bingley managed to roll over and look at his late leader. "He looks like it," he said; "I shouldn't think you'd be sorry, Pepper."

"Oh!" groaned Joel, quite horror-stricken, and dashing the water with a reckless hand, feeling like a murderer all the time.

"Bingley, could you manage to do this?" at last he cried in despair. "I must run for a doctor, there's not a minute to lose."

"I wouldn't go for any doctor," advised Bingley cautiously; "see; his eyelids are moving—this row will be all over town if you do."

But Joel was flying off. "Come back!" called Bingley, "I vow he's all right; he's opened his eyes, Pepper."

Joel turned; saw for himself that Dobbs was really looking at him, and that his lips moved as if he wanted to say something.

"What is it, Dobbs?" cried Joel, throwing himself down on his knees by Dobbs' side.

"Let him alone, and help me up," said Bingley crossly, "I'm hurt a great deal more. He's tough as a boiled owl. Give us a hand, Pepper."

But Joel had his ear down to Dobbs' mouth.

"Where are the fellows?" asked Dobbs in a whisper.

"Gone," answered Joel, briefly.

"Gone—and left me here like a dog?" said Dobbs.

"Yes," said Joel.

"They couldn't wait, my friend," observed Bingley sarcastically, "for people of such trifling consequence, as you and I."

"The deuce! you here, Bingley?" exclaimed Dobbs, in his natural voice, and trying to get his head up.

"Oh, you are coming to, are you?" said Bingley carelessly. "Well, Dobbs, I think you better get on your feet, and help me out, since Pepper won't; for I vow I can't stir."

"Oh, I'll help you," declared Joel, getting up to run over and put his hands under Bingley's arms, paling as he exclaimed, "I didn't mean to hurt you so, Bingley, on my honor I didn't."

"And you didn't," said Bingley, wincing with the pain, as Joel slowly drew him to his feet; "it wasn't your stinger of a blow, Pepper, but some of those dastardly cads stepped all over me; I could feel them hoofing me. There, set me in that chair, and I'll draw a long breath if I can."

"Now, I shall go for a doctor," declared Joel, setting Bingley within the easy-chair, and making a second dash for the door.

"I tell you, you will not," cried Bingley, from his chair. "Wait a minute, till I see where I'm hurt. I'm coming out of it better than I thought. Come back, Pepper."

"Really?" Joel drew off from the door, and looked at him.

"Yes; go and take care of Dobbs; he was only shamming," said Bingley, leaning his head comfortably on the chair-back. Dobbs already was on his feet, and slowly standing quite straight.

"Sure you don't want any help?" asked Joel, putting out his hand.

"Thanks, no," said Dobbs scornfully, not looking at the hand, but making for the door.

"Let him alone, Pepper," advised Bingley; "a mean, low-lived chap like that isn't hurt; you couldn't kill him," as Joel looked out anxiously to watch Dobbs' progress along the hall, at last following him along a bit.

"He's in his own room, thank fortune," exclaimed Joel, coming back, "and I suppose I can't do any more. But oh, I do wish, Bingley, it hadn't happened."

Joel leaned his elbow on the mantel, and looked down at the easy-chair and its occupant.

"Perhaps you'd rather be lying there," said Bingley, pointing to the floor, "instead, with a flopper under your ear, like the nasty one you gave me, Pepper."

"I am so sorry for that, too," cried Joel, in a fresh burst of remorse.

"I got no more, I presume, than was good for me," said Bingley, feeling the bump under his ear. "And don't you worry, Pepper, for your mind must be toned up to meet those fellows. They'll be at some neat little game to pay you up for this, you may rest assured."

"I suppose so," said Joel indifferently. "Well, now are you sure I can't do anything for you, Bingley?"

"Sure as a gun," said Bingley decidedly; "I'm getting quite limbered out; so I'll go, for I know my room is better than my company, Pepper," and he dragged himself stiffly out of his chair.

"Don't go," said Joel hospitably; "stay as long as you want to; I should be glad to have you."

Bingley turned a pair of bright eyes on him. "Thank you," he said, "but Davina will be in soon, and things will have to be explained a little, and I'm not quite up to it to-night. No, I must go," moving to the door; "I don't feel like making a pretty speech, Pepper," he said, hesitating a bit, "or I'd express something of what's on my mind. But I think you understand."

"If you want to do me a favor," said Joel steadily, "you'll stop calling David, Davina. It makes him fearfully mad, and I don't wonder."

"He's so pretty," said Bingley, with a smile, and wincing at the same time, "we can't help it. It's a pity to spoil that lovely name."

"But you must," declared Joel, growing savage; "I tell you, it just ruins college life for Dave, and he's so bright, and leads his class, I don't see how you can."

"Oh, we're awfully proud of him," said Bingley, leaning heavily on the table, "of course, and trot him out behind his back for praises and all that, but when it comes to giving up that sweet name—that's another thing," he added regretfully. "However, I'll do it, and make the other fellows, if I can."

"Good for you!" cried Joel gratefully. "Good-night, Bingley; sure you don't want any help to your room?"

"Sure," declared Bingley, going out unsteadily and shutting the door.

Joel threw himself on his knees by the side of the easy-chair, and burrowed his head deep within it. "Oh, if I only had Mamsie's lap to lay it in," he groaned, "and Mamsie's hands to go over it."

"Joe—Joe!" David flung wide the door, "where are you?" he cried.

Joel sprang to his feet.

"Here's a telegram," said David, waving a yellow sheet at him. "I just met the boy bringing it up. The folks were going to see Jasper—on a surprise party; something happened to the cars, and Polly has her arm broken—but that's all," delivered David, aghast at Joel's face.

"Polly? oh, not Polly?" cried Joel, putting up both hands, and feeling the room turn around with him.

"Yes, Polly," said David; "don't look so, Joe," he begged, feeling his own cheeks getting white, "it's only broken—it can't be bad, for we are not to go, Grandpapa says; see," shaking the telegram at him.

"But I shall go—we both must," declared Joel passionately, beginning to rush for his hat behind the door; "the idea—Polly hurt, and we not to go! Come on, Dave, we can catch the midnight train," looking at his watch.

"But if it makes Polly worse," said David doubtfully.

Joel's hand carrying the hat to his head, wavered, and he finally tossed the head-gear into the nearest corner. "I suppose you are right, Dave," he said helplessly, and sinking into a chair.

## CHAPTER XV

# THE FARMHOUSE HOSPITAL

Jack Loughead marched into his uncle's room. "Well—well—well," exclaimed the old gentleman with a prolonged look, and sitting straight in his chair. "So this really is you, Jack? I must say, I am surprised."

"Surprised?" echoed Jack, getting his uncle's hands in both of his. "Why, Uncle, I cabled Crane Brothers just as soon as I got your letter, that I was coming."

"This is the first thing I've heard of it," said old Mr. Loughead. "Well, how did you track me here, for goodness' sake?"

"Why, I saw an account of your accident in the New York paper as soon as I landed," said Jack.

"Oh! confound those papers," exclaimed his uncle ungratefully. "Well, I came near being done for, Jack," he added. "In fact, I was left in the wreck."

Jack shuddered.

"But that little girl there," pointing toward the next room, where the talking seemed to be going on busily, "insisted that I was buried in the smash-up, so they tell me, and she made them come and look for me. None too soon, I take it, by all accounts." The old gentleman placidly tore off two or three grapes from the bunch in the basketful, put at his elbow, and ate them leisurely.

"Phronsie is a good child," said Jack Loughead, with feeling, "and an observing one, too."

"Phronsie? Who's talking of Phronsie?" cried his uncle, pushing back the fruit-basket. "It was the other one—Polly; she wouldn't let them give over till they pulled me out. So the two young men tell me; very well-meaning chaps, too, they are, Jack."

"You said it was a little girl," Jack managed to remark.

"Well, and so she is," said old Mr. Loughead obstinately, "and a nice little thing, too, I should say."

"Miss Pepper is twenty years old," said his nephew suddenly. Then he was sorry he had spoken.

"Nonsense! not a day over fifteen," contradicted the old gentleman flatly. "And I must say, Jack, you've been pretty expert, considering the time spent in this house, in taking the census."

"Oh! I knew her before," said Jack, angry to find himself stammering over what ought to be a simple account enough.

"Hem—hem!" exclaimed the old gentleman, bestowing a keen scrutiny on his nephew. "Well, never mind," he said at last; "now, let's to business."

"Are you strong enough?" asked Jack, in duty bound, yet longing to get the talk into safe business channels.

"Strong enough?" repeated the old gentleman, in a dudgeon, "I'm really better than I was before the shake-up. I'm going home tomorrow, I'd have you to know, Jack."

"You would better not move too soon," said his nephew involuntarily. Then he added hastily, "At least, take the doctor's advice."

"Hem—hem!" said his uncle again, with a shrewd smile, as he helped himself to a second bunch of grapes.

"Well, now, as to that matter you sent me over to London about," began Jack, nervously plunging into business.

"Draw up that chair, and put your mind on the matter, and we'll go over it," interrupted old Mr. Loughead, discarding the grape-bunch suddenly, and assuming his commercial expression at once.

So Jack drew up his chair, as bidden; and presently the financial head of the Bradbury & Graeme Company, and the enterprising young member who was the principal part of "Company," were apparently lost to all else in the world, but their own concerns.

Meantime, Pickering Dodge was having a truly dreadful time of it.

The doctor, washing his hands of such a troublesome patient, had just run downstairs, jumped into his little old gig in displeasure, and was now half across a rut worn in the open meadow, dignified by the name of the "Short Road."

"Do go to bed," implored Ben, studying Pickering's pale face.

"Hoh, hoh!" Pickering made out to exclaim, "if I couldn't say anything original, I wouldn't talk. You're only an echo to that miserable little donkey of a medical man."

"But you really ought to go back to bed," Ben insisted.

"Really ought?" repeated Pickering, in high disdain; "as if I'd put myself again under that quack's thumb. No, sir!" and snapping his fingers derisively at Ben, he straightened up jauntily on his somewhat uncertain feet. "All I want is a little air," stumbling off to the window.

***"I'll help you; I'm strong," said Charlotte.***

"Well, I'm going to tell Phronsie that my arm is all right," said Polly, hurrying off; "beside I want to see Johnny"—

"It's time for me to look after that young man, too," said old Mr. King, following her; "I haven't heard him roar to-day. Come on, Jasper; you must see Johnny."

As they disappeared, Ben ran over to Pickering, and was aghast to find that the face laid against the window-casing was deathly white, and that all his shaking of the broad shoulders could not make Pickering open his eyes.

"Jasper," called Ben, in despair.

"Hush!" Some one came hurrying up. "Don't call Jasper; then Polly will know. Let me help."

Ben looked up. "O, Charlotte! that's good. Pick's done up. Call Mrs. Higby, will you? we must get him to bed."

"I'll help you; I'm strong." Charlotte held out her long arms.

Ben looked them over approvingly. "You're right," he said; "it's better not to stir Mrs. Higby up. There, easy now, Charlotte; put your hands under there. You are sure it won't hurt you?"

"Sure as I can be," said Charlotte, steadily moving off in pace with Ben, as they carried Pickering between them.

"Excuse me!" Ben rushed in without knocking upon the Bradbury & Graeme Company. "Do you mind"—to Jack—"I'm awfully sorry to ask it, but I can't leave him. Will you run to the doctor's and fetch him? Mrs. Higby, the landlady downstairs, you know, will tell you where to find him." Ben was all out of breath when he got through, and stood looking at young Loughead.

"What's the doctor wanted for?" cried Company, springing to his feet, and seizing his hat from the table. "Why, of course I'll go—delighted to be of use—who for?"

"Pickering Dodge—got up too soon—keeled over," said Ben briefly. "I've got to stay with him—he's in bed—and we don't want Grandpapa or Polly to know."

But Jack Loughead after the first word, was half over the stairs.

"See here," cried old Mr. Loughead suddenly, as Ben was rushing out, "can't I see your sister? I'm horribly lonesome," turning in his chair; "that is, if her arm will let her come," he added, as a second thought struck him. "Don't ask her if you think she's in pain."

"Doctor has fixed Polly's arm," said Ben, "and I know she'll like to come in and sit with you. It's a shame," and his honest face flamed with regret, "I had to ask such a favor as"—

"Tut, tut! go along with you," commanded the old gentleman imperatively, "and send Polly here; then I'll make by the operation," and he began to chuckle with pleasure.

So Ben ran off, and presently Polly, her arm in a sling, came hurrying in.

"Bless my soul," cried the old gentleman, "if your cheeks aren't as rosy as if you had two good arms, and this was an every-day sort of excursion for pleasure."

"It's so nice," said Polly, sitting down on one of Mrs. Higby's spare-room ottomans, on which that lady had worked a remarkable cat in blue worsted reposing on a bit of green sward, "to think that everybody is getting on so well," and she hugged her lame arm rapturously.

"Hem—hem! I should say so," breathed old Mr. Loughead, regarding her closely. "Where have they buried that woman?" he demanded suddenly.

Polly started. "Out in the meadow," she said softly. "Mrs. Higby wanted it here instead of in the churchyard. It is under a beautiful oak-tree, Mr. Loughead, and Mr. Higby is going to make a fence around it, and Grandpapa is to put"—

"Up the stone, I suppose you mean," interrupted the old gentleman. "Well, and when that's done, why, what can be said upon it, pray tell? You don't know a thing about it—who in Christendom the woman was—not a thing."

"Johnny's mother," said Polly sorrowfully, the corners of her mouth drooping; "that's going to be on it, and Grandpapa is to have the letters cut, telling about the accident; and Mrs. Higby hopes that sometime somebody

***"So Nice, Everybody Is Getting On So Well," Said Polly***

will come to inquire about it. But I don't believe anybody ever will come in all this world," added Polly softly, "because there is no one left who belongs to Johnny," and she told the story the pale little mother had just finished when the car went over.

Old Mr. Loughead "hemmed," and exclaimed impatiently, and fidgeted in his chair, all through the recital. When it was over, and Polly sat quite still, "What are you going to do with that horrible boy?" he asked sharply. "Almshouse, I suppose, eh?"

"O, no!" declared Polly, in horror. "Phronsie is going to take him into the Home."

"Phronsie is going to take that little rat into her home?" cried old Mr. Loughead in disgust. "You don't know what you are talking of. I shall speak to Mr. King."

"Johnny is just a dear," cried Polly, having great difficulty not to spring from her chair, and turn her back on the old gentleman, then and there.

"But into your home," repeated old Mr. Loughead, his disgust gaining on him with each word; "it's monstrous—it's"—

"Oh! I didn't mean our home," explained Polly, obliged to interrupt him, he was becoming so furious. "Johnny is going down to Dunraven, to the Children's Home," and then she began on the story of Phronsie's company of children, and how they lived, and who they were, with many little side stories of this small creature, who was "too cunning for anything," and that funny little boy, till the old gentleman sat helplessly listening in abject silence. And the latch was lifted, and young Mr. Loughead put his head in the doorway, looking as if he had finished a long tramp.

"Come in, Jack," said his uncle, finding his tongue. "We've a whole orphan asylum in here, and I don't know what all; every charity you ever heard of, rolled into one. Do come in, and see if you can make head or tail to it."

"Oh! Mr. Loughead knows all about it," cried Polly brightly, while her cheeks glowed, "for he went down to Dunraven with us at Christmas, and he showed the children stereopticon pictures, and told them such nice stories of places that he had seen."

"He—my Jack!" exploded the old gentleman, starting forward and pointing to his nephew. "Great Caesar! he never did such a thing in his life."

"Ah!" said Polly, shaking her brown head, while she looked only at the old gentleman, "you ought to have seen, sir, how happy the children were that day."

"My Jack went to an orphan asylum to show pictures to the children!" reiterated the old gentleman, unable to grasp another idea.

"Do be still, Uncle," begged his tall nephew, jogging his elbow.

"Here—here's Polly!" cried Jasper's voice. And at the same moment in sped little Dr. Fisher, his glasses shining with determination, as he gazed all over the room for Polly.

"My dear, dear child," he cried, as he spied her.

And "Papa Fisher!" joyfully from Polly, as she sprang from Mrs. Higby's ottoman, and precipitated herself into the little doctor's arms.

"Softly, softly, child," he warned; "you'll hurt it," tenderly covering the poor arm with his right hand, while he fumbled in his pocket with the other, for his handkerchief. "Dear me!" and he blew his nose violently. "Yes; well, you're sure you're all right except this?" and he held Polly at arm's length and scanned her closely.

"I am all right if you will only tell me that Mamsie is well, and isn't worried about us," said Polly, an anxious little pucker coming on her forehead.

"Your mother is as bright as a button," declared Father Fisher emphatically.

"Come, come!" ejaculated Mr. King, appearing in the doorway; "this isn't just the way to take possession of Mr. Loughead's apartment. Jasper, I don't see what you were thinking of. Come, Fisher, my room is next; this way."

Polly blushed red as a rose as old Mr. Loughead said briskly, "Oh! I sent for her to cheer me up, and now, I wish you'd all stay."

"Beg pardon for this inroad," said little Doctor Fisher, going up to the old gentleman's chair and offering his hand. "Well, well, Loughead," to Jack, "this is a surprise party all round!"

"No inroad at all, at least a pleasant one," old Mr. Loughead kept saying, while Polly ran up to Jasper:

"Did Pickering's uncle come with Papa Fisher?"

"No," said Jasper, with his eyes on Jack Loughead, "the Doctor was all alone, Polly."

And then the door of Pickering's room opened, and out came Dr. Bryce, with bad news written all over his face.

"I fear brain fever," he said to Dr. Fisher after the introduction was over, making the two physicians acquainted. "Come," and the door of Pickering's room closed on them both.

And twilight settled down on the old square white house, and on the new-made grave under the oak in the meadow; and Brierly people, by twos and threes, came to inquire for "the sick young man," going away with saddened faces. And a messenger from the telegraph office drove up just as Mr. Higby was pulling on the boots to his tired feet for a long walk to the village, handing in the message:

Mrs. Cabot and I will take the midnight train.

RICHARD A. CABOT,

***Then Phronsie Glanced Back Again, And Softly Jogged The Cradle.***

And then there was nothing more to do, only to wait for the coming of Pickering's uncle and aunt.

And the next day Pickering's calls were incessant for "Polly, Polly," sometimes upbraiding her as the brown eyes were fastened piteously on his wild face; and then begging her to just smile at him and remember how he had loved her all these years. "And now I am going to die," he would cry.

"O, Polly! Polly!" Mrs. Cabot would wring her hands and beg at such times, a world of entreaty in her voice. And then old Mr. King would interfere, carrying Polly off, and declaring it was beyond all reason for her to be so annoyed.

And Phronsie would climb up on the bed and lay her cool little hand gently on the hot forehead. Then the sick boy's cries would drop into unintelligible murmurs, while his fingers picked aimlessly at the coverlet.

"There! he is better," Phronsie would say softly to the watchers by the bed, "and I guess he is going to sleep."

But the quiet only ushered in worse ravings when Pickering lived over once more the horror of the train-wrecking, and then it took many strong arms to hold him in his bed. "Come on, Ben," he would shout, struggling hard; "leave him alone—we shall be caught—the fire! the fire!" until his strength died away, and he sank to a deathly stupor.

Phronsie sat down to write a letter to Mrs. Fargo. One like it was dropped every morning into the basket set on Mrs. Higby's front entry table, ready for the neighbor's boy to take to the village post-office.

DEAR MRS. FARGO:

[wrote Phronsie, looking off from the wooden cradle that Mrs. Higby had dragged down from its cobwebby corner under the garret eaves, with the remark, "I guess Johnny'll sleep well; all the Higbys since the first one, has been rocked in it."] I must tell you that dear Pickering isn't any better. [Then she glanced back again, and softly jogged the cradle, as Johnny turned over with a long sigh.] And Papa Fisher and the other doctor don't think he is going to get well. And Mrs. Cabot cries all the time, and Polly cries sometimes too. And we don't know what to do. But I guess God will take care of us. And Charlotte is going to take Johnny down to the Dunraven Home in a day or two. She says she can, though I know she don't like babies, especially boy-babies; she said so once. And so he will be happy. And that's all I can write to-day, Mrs. Fargo, because every minute I'm afraid Polly will want me.

FROM PHRONSIE.

And just the very minute when Phronsie was dotting the "i" in her name. Mrs. Higby came toiling up the stairs, holding her gingham gown well away from her feet.

"Say!" she cried in a loud whisper, and pausing midway to wave a large square envelope at Phronsie, curled up on the hall window-seat.

Phronsie got down very softly, and tiptoed over to the stair-railing to grasp the letter Mrs. Higby thrust between the bars, going back to her old post, to open it carefully.

DEAR PHRONSIE:

I think God meant that I was to have Johnny for my very own. So won't you give him to me, dear? Let Charlotte bring him soon, please, for my heart is hungry for a baby to hold. I will make him happy all my life, Phronsie, so I know you will give him to

HELEN'S MOTHER.

# CHAPTER XVI

# ON THE BORDERLAND

Phronsie came into the Higby kitchen, her hands full of wind-blossoms and nodding trilliums.

"Pickering will like these," she said to herself in great satisfaction, and surveying her torn frock with composure, "for they are the very first, Mrs. Higby," addressing that individual standing over by the sink in the corner. "Please may I wash my hands? I had to go clear far down by the brook to get them."

But Mrs. Higby, instead of answering, threw her brown-checked apron high over her head.

Phronsie stood quite still.

"Why do you put your apron there, Mrs. Higby?" she asked at last. "And you do not answer me at all," she added in gentle reproach.

"Land!" exclaimed Mrs. Higby, in a voice spent with feeling, "I couldn't, 'cause I was afraid I sh'd burst out crying, and I didn't want you to see my face. O, dear! he's had a poor spell since you went out flowerin' for him, and your pa and Dr. Bryce say he's dyin'. O, dear!"

Down came the apron, showing Mrs. Higby's eyelids very red and swollen.

Phronsie still stood holding her flowers, a breathing-space, then turned and went quickly to the back stairs.

"Sh! don't go," called Mrs. Higby in a loud whisper after her; "it's dreadful for a little girl like you to see any one die. Do come back."

"They will want me," said Phronsie gravely, and going up carefully without another word. When she reached Pickering's door, she paused a moment and looked in.

"I don't believe it is as Mrs. Higby said," she thought, drawing a long breath, a faint smile coming to her face as she went gently in.

But old Mr. King put up his hand as he turned in his chair, at the foot of the bed, and Phronsie saw that his face was white and drawn. And Dr. Bryce turned also, looking off a minute from the watch that he held, as if he were going to bid her go away.

***"Why Do You Put Youk Apkon Up There?" Asked Phronsik Is Gentle Reproach.***

"Phronsie," said Grandpapa, holding out both arms hungrily.

Phronsie hurried to him, a gathering fear at her heart, and getting into his lap, laid her cheek against his.

"Oh! my dear, you oughtn't to be here—you are too young," said Mr. King brokenly, yet holding her close.

"I am not afraid, Grandpapa," said Phronsie, her mouth to his ear, "and I think Pickering would like me to be here. I brought him some flowers." She moved the hand holding the bunch, so that the old gentleman could see it. "He likes wild flowers, and I promised to get the first ones I could."

"O, dear!" groaned old Mr. King, not trusting himself to look.

"May I lay them down by him?" whispered Phronsie.

"Yes, yes, child," said the old gentleman, allowing her to slip to the floor. The group around the bedside parted to let her pass, and then Phronsie saw Polly. Mrs. Cabot was holding Polly's well hand, while her head was on Polly's shoulder.

"Grandpapa said I might," said Phronsie softly to the two, and pointing to her flowers.

"Yes, dear."

It was Polly who answered; Mrs. Cabot was crying so hard she could not speak a word.

Phronsie's little heart seemed to stop beating as she reached the bedside. She had not thought that she would be afraid, but it was so different to be standing there looking down upon the pillow where Pickering lay so still and white, and with closed eyes, looking as if he had already gone away from them. She glanced up in a startled way and saw Dr. Fisher at the head of the bed; he was holding Pickering's wrist. "Yes," he motioned, "put them down."

So Phronsie laid down her blossoms near the poor white face, and stole back quickly, only breathing freely when she was as close to Polly as she could creep, without hurting the broken arm.

"I'm dying—I'm not afraid," suddenly said Pickering's white lips. Dr. Fisher sprang and put a spoonful of stimulant to them, while Mrs. Cabot buried her face yet deeper on Polly's shoulder, her husband turning on his heel, to pace the floor and groan. "Polly, Polly!" called Pickering quite distinctly, in a tone of anguish.

"O, Polly, Polly! he's dying—go to him do!" Mrs. Cabot tore her hand out of Polly's, almost pushing her from the chair. "Quick, dear!"

Polly put Phronsie aside, and stepped softly to the bedside; Pickering's eyes eagerly watched for her face.

He smiled up at her, "Polly," and tried to raise his hand.

She laid her warm, soft palm on the cold one lying on the coverlid. He clasped his thin fingers convulsively around it.

"I am here, Pickering," said Polly, unable to find voice for anything else.

"Don't—ever—leave me," she could just make out the words, bending close to catch them.

"I never will," said Polly quietly.

A sudden gleam came into his face, and he tried to smile, grasping her hand tighter as his eyes closed.

"It has come," said Dr. Fisher in a low voice to Mr. Cabot; "tell your wife," and he bent a professional ear over the white face on the pillow, while

Dr. Bryce hurried forward; then brought his head up quickly, a peculiar light in the sharp eyes back of the spectacles. "He is sleeping!"

Polly was sitting, a half-hour by the bedside, Pickering's thin fingers still tightly grasping her hand. They had made her comfortable in an easy chair, Jasper bringing one of Mrs. Higby's biggest cushions for her to lean her head against. He now stood at the side of her chair, Phronsie curled up on the floor at her feet.

"Don't stay." Polly's lips seemed to frame the words rather than speak them, looking up at him.

He shook his head, resting his hand on the back of the chair. Polly tried to smile up a bit of comfort into his eyes. "Jasper loved Pickering so," she said to herself, "that he cannot leave him; but oh! he looks so dreadfully, I wish he would go and rest," and she began to have a worried look at once.

"What is it?" asked Jasper, catching the look at once, and bending to whisper in her ear.

"You will be sick if you do not go and rest," whispered back Polly.

"I cannot—don't ask it." Jasper brought the words out sharply, with just a bitter tone to them.

"He thinks it is strange that I ask it; he is so fond of Pickering," said Polly to herself. "And now I have grieved him—O, dear!"

"I won't leave Pickering," she said, lifting her brown eyes quickly.

A spasm came over Jasper's face, and his brow contracted.

"Don't," he begged, and Polly could feel that the hand resting on the back of the chair grasped it so tightly that it shook beneath her.

"I ought to have remembered that Jasper couldn't leave him; he loves him so," mourned Polly. "Oh! why did I speak?"

In the room at the end of the hall Mrs. Cabot was excitedly walking the floor, twisting her handkerchief between her nervous fingers, and talking unrestrainedly to Charlotte Chatterton.

"I do believe this will melt Polly's heart," she cried. "Oh! it must, it must! Don't you think it must, Miss Chatterton?"

"I don't know what you mean," said Charlotte Chatterton in a collected manner, as she bent over the cradle to tuck the shawl over Johnny's legs where he had kicked it off in his sleep.

"Oh! you know quite well what I mean, Miss Chatterton," declared Mrs. Cabot, in her distress losing her habitually polite manner. "Why, everybody knows that Pickering has loved Polly since they were boy and girl together."

Not knowing what was expected of her, Charlotte Chatterton wisely kept silent.

"And now, why, it's just a Providence, I do believe—that is, if he gets well—that brought all this about, for of course Polly must be touched by it. She must!" brought up Mrs. Cabot quite jubilantly.

And this time she waited for Charlotte to speak, at last exclaiming, "Don't you see it must be so?"

"I think love goes where it is sent," said Charlotte slowly.

"Sent? Well, that is just it. Isn't it sent here?" cried Mrs. Cabot impatiently.

"I don't know," said Charlotte. Then she said distinctly, "I know love is very different from pity"—

"Of course it is—but then, sometimes it isn't," said Mrs. Cabot nervously. "Well, any way, Polly has almost as good as promised to marry Pickering," she finished triumphantly—"so—and you are very cruel to talk to me in this way, Miss Chatterton."

Charlotte Chatterton turned away from Johnny and faced Mrs. Cabot. "You don't mean to say you think Polly would feel bound by what she said when we all thought he was dying?"

"I do, certainly—knowing Polly as I do—if Pickering took it so. And I am quite sure he will say so when he gets well; quite sure. Polly isn't a girl to break her word," added Mrs. Cabot confidently.

"Then I'm sure Providence hasn't had anything to do with this," said Charlotte shortly, "and Polly shall never be tormented into thinking it her duty either," and she turned off to pick up a new gown "in the works" for Johnny.

"What you think duty, Miss Chatterton, wouldn't be Polly Pepper's idea of duty in the least," said Mrs. Cabot, getting back into the refuge of her society manner again, now that her confidence in Polly grew every moment, "so we will talk no more about it if you please," she added icily, as she went toward the door. "Only mark my words, my dear boy and that dear girl will be engaged, and quite the appropriate match it will be too, and please every one."

"You must go back, my boy," said old Mr. King two days later. "It's just knocking you up to stay," studying Jasper's face keenly. "Goodness me! I should think you'd fallen off a dozen pounds. Upon my word I should, my boy," he repeated with great concern.

"Never mind me, father," said Jasper a trifle impatiently, "and as to my work, Mr. Marlowe will give me a few more days. He's goodness itself. I shall telegraph him this morning for an extension."

"You will do nothing of the kind," declared Mr. King testily. "What can you do here, pray tell, by staying? You would be quite a muff in a few more days, Jasper," he added, "you are so down-hearted now. No, I insist that you go now."

"Very well," said Jasper quite stiffly, "I will take myself off by the afternoon train, then, father, since I am in the way."

"How you talk, Jasper!" cried his father in astonishment. "You know quite well that I am only thinking of your own good. What's got into you—but I suppose this confounded hospital we're in, has made you lose your head."

"Thank you, father," said Jasper, recovering himself by a great effort, "for putting it so, and I beg you to forgive me for my hasty words." He came up to the old gentleman and put out his hand quickly, "Do forgive me, father."

"Forgive you? Of course I will, though I don't know when you've spoken to me like that, Jasper," said his father, not yet able to shake himself free from his bewilderment. "Well, well, that's enough to say about that," seeing Jasper's face, "and now get back to your work, my boy, as soon as you can, and you'll thank me for sending you off. And as soon as Pickering Dodge is able to be moved home, why, the rest of us will finish our trip, and give you that surprise party—eh, Jasper?" and Mr. King tried to laugh in the old way, but it was pretty hard work.

"Well, now, Polly," said Dr. Fisher, a week after as he held her at arm's length, and brought his spectacles to bear upon her face, "remember what I say, child; you are to take care of yourself, and let Mrs. Cabot look out for things. It will do the woman good to have something to do," he added, dropping his voice. "I don't like to carry home your face, child; it won't do; you're getting tired out, and your mother will be sure to find it out. I really ought to stay and take care of you," and the little doctor began to look troubled at once.

"Indeed, Papa Fisher," cried Polly, brightening up, "you will do nothing of the kind. Why, my arm is doing famously. You know you said you never saw a broken arm behave so well in all your life."

"It isn't your arm, Polly, that worries me," said Father Fisher; "that's first-rate, and I shouldn't wonder if it turned out better perhaps for breaking, but it's something different, and it quite puzzles me; you look so down-hearted, child."

"Do I?" said Polly, standing quite straight, and rubbing her forehead with her well hand; "there, now, I will get the puckers and wrinkles out. There, Papa Fisher, are they all gone?" She smiled as cheerily as ever, but the little man shook his head, then took off his spectacles, wiped them, and set them back on his nose.

"No; it won't do; you can't make your old father believe but what you've something on your mind, Polly. I think I shall have to send your mother down here," he said suddenly.

"O, Father Fisher!" cried Polly, the color flying over her face, "you wouldn't ever do that, I am sure! Why, it would worry Mamsie so, and besides she can't leave King Fisher"—

He interrupted her as she clung to his arm. "I know that, but what can I do? If you'd only promise now, Polly," he added artfully, "that you won't tire yourself all out trying to suit Mrs. Cabot's whims—why, I'd think about taking back what I said about sending your mother down."

"Oh! I won't—I won't," promised Polly gladly. "And now, dear Papa Fisher, you'll take it all back, won't you?" she begged.

"Yes," said Dr. Fisher, glad to see Polly's color back again, and to have her beg him for some favor. So the next half-hour or so they were very cheery—just like old times; just as if there had been no sickness and the shadow of a loss upon them in the past days.

"Though why we should be always acting as if we were in the midst of it now, I don't see," said the little doctor at last. "We're all straightened out, thank God, and Pickering mending so fast that he's a perfect marvel. It would be a sin and a shame for us to be in the dumps forever. Well, now, Polly, remember. Whew! hear that youngster!" This last being brought out by Johnny's lusty shouts in the next room. "I don't envy Mrs. Fargo her bargain, and I do pity myself having to see him safely there."

"Oh! Charlotte will take all the care of him," said Polly quickly. "She's just beautiful with him; you don't know how beautiful, Papa Fisher, because you've been so busy, since you've been here, and Charlotte has kept him away from everybody so he needn't worry any one. And isn't it lovely that he is to have such a beautiful home?" added Polly with shining eyes.

"Um—yes, for Johnny," said Dr. Fisher. "Well, good-by, Polly." He gathered her up in his arms for a final kiss. "Oh! here's Charlotte come to bid you good-by, too."

"Polly," said Charlotte, drawing her off to a quiet corner, as the little doctor went away, leaving the two girls together, "I must say something, and I don't know how to say it."

Polly looked at her with wide eyes.

"It's just this," said Charlotte, plunging on desperately; "Polly, don't let Mrs. Cabot pick at you and talk about duty. Oh! I hate to hear her speak the word," exploded Charlotte, with a volume of wrath in her tone.

"What do you mean, Charlotte?" cried Polly in a puzzled way.

"Oh! she may—never mind how—she's quite peculiar, you know," said Charlotte, finding her way less clear with each word. "Never mind,

Polly; only just fight her if she begins on what is your duty; if she does, then fight her tooth and nail."

"But it may be something that I really ought to do," said Polly.

Charlotte turned on her in horror. "O, never!" she cried. "Don't you do it, Polly Pepper. Just as sure as she says you ought to do it, you may know it would be the worst thing in all the world. Promise me, Polly, that you won't do it."

"But, Charlotte, I ought not to promise until I am quite sure that it wouldn't be my duty to do what Mrs. Cabot advises. Don't you see, Charlotte, that I ought not to promise?"

But Charlotte was too far gone in anxiety to see anything, and she could only reiterate, "Do promise, Polly, do; there's Mr. Higby calling us; the carriage is at the door. Do, Polly! I never will ask you anything else if you'll only promise me this."

But Polly could only shake her head, and say, "I ought not," and then Johnny had to be kissed and wrenched from Phronsie, who insisted on carrying him downstairs to set him in the carriage, and Mrs. Cabot came in, and old Mr. King wanted a last word with Charlotte, so that at last she was in Mr. Higby's carryall, shut in on the back seat looking out over Johnny's head, with a pair of very hopeless eyes. But her lips said, "Do, Polly!"

And still Polly, on the flat door-stone, had to shake her head.

"I shall tell Mrs. Fisher, and beg her to come right down here," determined Charlotte Chatterton to herself, "just as soon as I get in the house. That is exactly what I shall do," she declared savagely, as Mr. Higby whipped up the mare for the quarter-mile drive to the little station.

# CHAPTER XVII

# JASPER

"Halloo, King, Mr. Marlowe wants you." Jasper, his hands full of papers, hurried down the long warehouse, through the piles of books, fresh from the bindery, stacked closely to the ceiling. The busy packers who were filling the boxes, looked up as he threaded his way between them. "Mr. Marlowe is down there," indicating the direction with a nod, while the hands kept mechanically at their task.

"I want to see you about that last lot of paper," Mr. Marlowe began, before Jasper had reached him; "it is thin and of poorer quality than I ordered. The loss must be charged back to Withers & Co."

"Is that so?" exclaimed Jasper. "They assured me that everything should be right, and like the sample that we ordered it from."

"And Jacob Bendel writes that the edition we gave him of *History of Great Cities* to print will be shipped to us within a fortnight, when his contract was to be filled on Thursday. Of course we lose all the Chicago orders by this delay."

"What's the reason?" asked Jasper, feeling all the thrill of the disappointment as keenly as if he were the head of the house.

"Oh! a strike among the printers; his best men have gone out, and he's at the mercy of a lot of inferior workmen who are being intimidated by the strikers; but he thinks he can get the edition to us in ten days or so."

Mr. Marlowe leaned against an empty packing case and viewed the assistant foreman of the manufacturing department calmly, with the air of a man to whom disappointments were in the usual order of things.

"Can't we give it to another printer?" asked Jasper.

"Who?"

"Morse Brothers?"

"They are full and running over with work. I inquired there yesterday; we may want a little extra done as the rush over those Primary Readers is coming on. No, I can't think of a place where we could crowd it in, if we took it away from Bendel."

Jasper's gaze thoughtfully followed the drift of a shaving blown by the draft along the warehouse floor.

"I think I'll send you down to New York to see Bendel, and find out how things are. I don't get any satisfaction from letters," said Mr. Marlowe in a minute. "Beside you can attend to some other matters; and then there is that Troy job; you can do that."

"Very well, sir."

"Can you take the night express?" Mr. Marlowe pulled out his watch. It was ten minutes of three.

"Can I leave the Ransom bills I was checking off? Mr. Parker said they were the most important of the lot."

"Parker must give them to Richard; he knows pretty well how to do them, unless he can find time for them himself."

"I was to be at the Green printing-office at nine to-morrow morning," said Jasper.

"What for?"

"They sent down to Mr. Parker yesterday that we had made a mistake about price for doing those five hundred *Past and Present*; and wanted him to go to their office, and see Mr. Green himself."

"If Mr. Green thinks any mistake has been made, let him come to us," said Mr. Marlowe coolly. "You tell Parker to send a note to that effect; courteously written, of course, but to the point. We don't go running around after people who think mistakes are made. Let them bring their grievances here, if they have any. Is that all that detains you?"

Jasper held out his hand full of papers. "These were to come in between when they could, sir."

"Hem—hem"—Mr. Marlowe read them over with a practiced eye; rolled them up, and handed the roll to Jasper. "Tell Parker to set Danforth on those. Anything more?"

"I was to go to-morrow if there was time to get prices for best calendered paper of Patterson & Co. and Withers; but the next day will do."

"Parker must attend to all that," said Mr. Marlowe decidedly.

"Very well, sir. I believe that is all that hurries particularly."

"Come this way; I'll give you instructions what to say to Bendel," and Mr. Marlowe led the way out to a quiet corner of the warehouse, where he sat down by a desk, and rapidly laid the points of the business before his assistant.

The next morning in New York, Jasper ran across Mr. Whitney on Broadway.

"Well said; that you, Jasper? Why aren't you up at the house?"

"I came on the night express," said Jasper, finding it hard to wait a minute, "on a matter of importance for Mr. Marlowe. Sorry, Brother Mason, but I can't stop now."

"You'll be up to-night, of course," said Mason Whitney.

"I can't; I'm off for Troy," said Jasper concisely, "and I don't come back this way."

"Goodness! what a man your Marlowe is. And your sister Marian wants to hear about Polly and all the others; you've seen them so lately."

"It's impossible," began Jasper; "you see I can't help it, Brother Mason; Mr. Marlowe's orders must be carried out."

"He's a beast, your Marlowe is," declared Mr. Whitney hotly. "I don't know what Marian will say when I tell her you are here in New York and won't stop for even a word with her."

"Sister Marian will say it's all right," said Jasper, a trifle impatiently, and feeling the loss of every moment a thing to be atoned for. "Mr. Marlowe is loaded up with trouble of all kinds. Now I must go."

"Hold on a minute," cried Mason Whitney. "Well, how are you getting on? Seems to me the publishing business doesn't agree with you. You look peaked enough," scanning Jasper's face closely.

"I'm well enough," said Jasper abruptly. "Tell sister Marian I will write her very soon," pulling out his watch; "good-by," and he was lost in the crowd surging down Broadway. Mr. Whitney standing still a moment to look after him, turned, and went directly to his office.

"That call on Hendryx & Co. can wait," he muttered to himself on the way, "but Jasper can't. The boy looks badly, and his father ought to know it; although it seems funny enough for me to be meddling with Jasper's affairs. But I won't leave anything to worry about afterward; they can't say I ought to have told them."

So a letter went out by next mail from Mr. Whitney's office, saying that Jasper looked poorly enough when he was met in New York; that he seemed incapable of breathing any other air than that saturated with business; that he had evidently mistaken his vocation when he chose to be a publisher. "Beside, there isn't any money now in the publishing business," added Mr. Whitney as a clincher; "there are too many of the fellows cutting each other's throats to make it pay; and books are slaughtered right and left, and Jasper much better get into some other business, in my opinion."

Meanwhile Jasper finished, to the letter, the instructions for Jacob Bendel, did up the other matters entrusted to him, and set out on his Troy expedition. Here he was detained a day or two, Mr. Marlowe's instructions being to wait over and telegraph if the business could not be adjusted satisfactorily. But the fourth day after leaving home, Jasper, just from the night express, mounted the stairs to his hotel in the early morning, his bag in his hand, and the expression on his face of a man who has accomplished what he set out to do.

"There's an old gent up in your room," announced Buttons, tumbling off, a sleepy heap, from one of the office chairs, to look at him.

"An old gentleman in my room," repeated Jasper, turning on the stairs. "Why was any person put in my room?"

"We didn't put the person there," said the boy, yawning fearfully, "he put himself there. He's a tiger, he is, and he blows me up reg'lar 'cause you ain't home," he added.

Jasper scaled the rest of the stairs, and tried the knob of his door with no gentle hand. Then he rapped loudly. "Open the door—this is my room."

"Oh! I'm coming," said a voice he knew quite well, and presently old Mr. King stood before him, his velvet cap and morning jacket both awry from impatient fingers.

*"An Old Gentleman In My Room," Repeated Jasper, Turning On The Stairs.*

"Father!" ejaculated Jasper. And "Goodness me, Jasper!" from the old gentleman, "what an unearthly hour to come home in."

Jasper hurried in, set his bag in the corner, then turned and looked at his father anxiously. Meanwhile old Mr. King was studying his son's countenance with no small degree of alarm.

"What is it," cried Jasper at last, coming close to him, "that has brought you?"

"What?—why, you."

"Me?" cried Jasper, in amazement.

"Yes; dear me, Jasper, with all the worries I have had lately, it does seem a pity that you couldn't take care of yourself. It really does," repeated Mr. King, his feelings nowise soothed by picking up his watch and finding it half-past six o'clock. When he made sure of the time, he set down the watch quickly, and stared at Jasper worse than ever.

"Now, father," said Jasper, "there's a mistake somewhere, but never mind now; you must get back to bed again. I don't know when you've been up at this hour." He tried to laugh, while he laid his hand on the old gentleman's arm. "Do get back to bed, father."

"It certainly is a most outrageous hour in which to arise," remarked his father, not able to suppress a yawn, "and I don't mind if I do turn in—but where will you sleep, Jasper?" whirling around on his son. "I've come to look after you, and I shouldn't begin very well to monopolize your bed," with a short laugh.

"Oh, I'll camp out on the lounge," said Jasper carelessly; "in two minutes I could be asleep there or anywhere else. Don't mind me, father."

"If you say so, then I will," said the old gentleman, "and you are too tired to talk before you've had a nap." So he lay down on the bed, Jasper dutifully tucking him up, and presently his regular breathing told that he had picked up the threads of his broken slumber.

Jasper threw himself on the lounge, but unable to close his eyes, his gaze fell on a sheet of paper, lying on the floor just within reach. It was impossible to avoid reading the words: "And Jasper better get into some other business, in my opinion," and signed "Mason Whitney."

Jasper jumped to his feet and strode up and down the room in growing indignation; then seized his hat and darted out to cool himself off before his father should awake. When he returned, old Mr. King was half-dressed, and berating Buttons for his failure to have the morning paper at the door.

"Now for breakfast," cried Jasper, his own toilet quickly made, "then I presume you want to see me in my business surroundings, father?" as they went down the stairs together.

"I most certainly do," said the old gentleman decidedly; and they turned into the breakfast room.

So after a meal in which Jasper, by skillful management of all conversational topics, allowed no chance word of business to intrude, old Mr. King and he started for the publishing house of D. Marlowe & Co., Jasper filling up all gaps that might suggest time for certain questions that seemed to be trembling on the tip of Mr. King's tongue, while that gentleman was making a running commentary to himself something in this wise: "Just like Mason; send me off here when there is not the slightest need of it. The boy is well enough; quite well enough," he added, in his energy speaking the last words aloud.

"What is it, father?" Jasper paused in the midst of a descriptive fire concerning the new buildings going up on either hand, with many side stories of the men who were erecting them; and he paused for an answer.

"Nothing—nothing of importance," said his father hastily. "I only observed that you appeared to be doing quite well; and as if the business agreed with you," he added involuntarily.

"I should think it did, father," cried Jasper enthusiastically, while his cheek glowed; "it's the grandest work a man can do, in my opinion."

"Hem, hem! well, we shall see," observed Mr. King drily, determined not to yield too easily. "You've been at it only six months. You know the old adage, Jasper: 'You must summer and winter' a thing before you decide."

Jasper drew a long breath. "I shall never be anything but a publisher, father," he said quietly.

"Hoity, toity! well, that is for me to decide, I take it," responded his father. "You've never disobeyed me yet, Jasper, and I don't believe you ever will. And if I think it's best for you to change your business, of course you'll do it."

Jasper's brow darkened, and he closed his lips tightly for a moment. Then something Polly said once when his father was in a particularly determined mood, came to his mind: "You better make him happy, Jasper, any way." That "any way" carried the day now.

"It shall be as you wish, father," he said, the frown disappearing; "I want you to be pleased, any way," unconsciously using Polly's word.

"I don't know as I should be at all pleased to have you leave the publishing business, Jasper," said old Mr. King, veering around quickly. "I can't tell till I've seen just how it suits you. But I am going to the root of the matter, now that I am here. Oh! is this the place?" as they came up against a large window, behind whose plate glass, rows and rows of books in all styles of bindings, met the view of the passer-by.

"This is it," said Jasper, with a thrill that he was part of the "it," and the satisfaction in his completed commission, that had been lost by his father's words, now bounded high again. "Now then, father, you must meet Mr. Marlowe," turning up the steps.

Old Mr. King walked down the store-length as if he owned the whole with several others of its kind thrown in, and on Jasper's pausing before a small office-door, marked "private," heard him say through its open window, "Good-morning, Mr. Marlowe."

"Ah, good-morning," came back quickly, and Mr. King saw a pleasant-faced gentleman of middle age, whose keen gray eyes seemed to note everything with lightning-like rapidity—"business all right?"

"Yes, sir," said Jasper.

"Very well; you may come to me in a quarter of an hour and report. I shall be through with these gentlemen," indicating one sitting by his side at the desk, and another awaiting his turn.

"Tell him that I am here, Jasper," said Mr. King pompously, with an admonitory touch upon Jasper's arm.

"It's impossible, father; he can't see you now," said Jasper hurriedly, trying to draw his father off to a quieter corner.

"Impossible? Can't see me? What is there to prevent, pray tell?" cried the old gentleman irately.

*"Good Morning," Said Mr. Marlowe Quickly. "Business All Right?"*

He has business men with him; they'll be through in a quarter of an hour," Jasper brought out in distress that was by no means lightened by the knowledge that half of the clerks through the long salesroom were becoming acquainted with the conversation.

"It's atrocious. I never was kept waiting in my life," fumed Mr. King. "He doesn't know I am here—I will announce myself."

He started forward.

"Father," cried Jasper, darting after him, "let me get you a chair over here by the table and some books to look at."

"I want no books," said the old gentleman, now thoroughly determined, by this time looking in the open window of the private office. "Good-morning, sir," stiffly to the middle-aged gentleman sitting before the desk.

This gentleman looked up, nodded carelessly and said, "Excuse me, but I am at present engaged."

"I am Mr. Jasper King's father," announced the old gentleman with extreme dignity; and again the look of being able to buy out this and several other such establishments, spread over his face.

"I shall be very glad to see you, sir," said the middle-aged man imperturbably, "in a quarter of an hour. Excuse me," and he turned back to finish his sentence to the other business man.

"Jasper," cried Mr. King, taking short, quick steps to where Jasper stood, "give me a sheet of paper so that I may write to this fellow, and take you out of his contemptible trade—or stay, I will write from the hotel," and he started for the door.

"Father," exclaimed Jasper in a low tone, but so distinctly that every one standing near might hear, "Mr Marlowe is just right; he always is."

"Eh?" cried his father, turning and grasping the back of a chair to steady himself.

"Mr. Marlowe is just right about these things. He really couldn't see you, father."

"I have never been obliged to wait for any one in all my life, Jasper," declared his father impressively, "and I never will."

"I wonder what Polly would do now," thought Jasper in despair.

"And that you could tolerate such impertinence to me," continued Mr. King with growing anger, "is more than I can understand; but since you've come into trade it's vastly changed you. If you do not choose to come to the hotel with me, I must go alone," which with great dignity he now proceeded to do.

The first business man who had finished his conference with Mr. Marlowe now came down the salesroom. "How d'ye, King," he said cordially to Jasper in passing.

Jasper's face lighted as he gave an equally cordial response.

"Such familiarity, Jasper!" exclaimed his father in a fresh burst of irritation. "Dear me, I only trust you're not completely spoiled before I get you out of this."

The business man turned around and gave a significant look to a knot of the salesmen, but happening to catch Jasper's eye, he said, "It's a fine day, King," carelessly, and passed out, but not before "Stuck-up old money-bag" fell upon the old gentleman's ear.

"We would better go to the hotel now, I think, father," said Jasper quietly. "Frank," to the nearest salesman, "will you tell Mr. Marlowe when it is ten minutes past," glancing at the clock, "that I was obliged to go with my father, but I will be back at ten o'clock?"

"You need give yourself no such trouble, Jasper, as all this," said his father decidedly; "I will wait if it is absolutely necessary that you see him," with a patronizing wave of his gloved hand toward the private office.

"It is absolutely necessary," said Jasper.

"Very well; I wait, then," said his father, accepting with the air of a martyr, the chair by the table of books.

And just then the private office-door opened and out came the other business man, followed by Mr. Marlowe.

"Frank," he called briskly, "ask Jasper's father to step here."

## CHAPTER XVIII

# MR. KING ATTENDS TO MATTERS

Old Mr. King kept on turning the books with a careless hand.

"Father," begged Jasper in a low voice, and putting his hand on the old gentleman's arm, such a world of entreaty in his face, that his father turned in spite of himself.

"After all I much better have it over with now, I really think," said Mr. King; "yes, Jasper, we will go back," with a marked emphasis on the word "back."

"I can't thank you enough, father," exclaimed Jasper gratefully.

"Well, well, say no more," said old Mr. King abruptly, as they reached the private office.

Mr. Marlowe's hands were mechanically adjusting the loose papers on his desk, so as not to lose an instant's time as Mr. King and Jasper came up, but he turned a face, over which a bright smile shot suddenly, lighting up the gray eyes, then quickly whirled around in his office chair. "Glad to see you," he said, putting out a cordial right hand.

Mr. King bowed, but evidently did not see the hand; which Mr. Marlowe not appearing to notice, the old gentleman was more furious than ever.

"Set a chair for your father, Jasper," said Mr. Marlowe quietly, "and get one for yourself." Then he leaned back in his office chair and pleasantly surveyed old Mr. King, waiting for him to speak.

"I have come, sir," said Mr. King, as he settled his courtly old figure in the chair Jasper had put for him beside the desk, "to see you about my son; I am not satisfied with his appearance, nor, I am sorry to say, with his surroundings."

"Indeed,?" said the head of the publishing house of D. Marlowe & Co., still with a pleasant smile on his face.

"I am very sorry," repeated Jasper's father, "to have to say it, but my attention has been called to the fact, and I cannot now ignore it."

"Hardly by Jasper," remarked Mr. Marlowe, bringing the revolving chair so that he could see Jasper's face.

"Indeed, no," cried Jasper involuntarily, "it is something father has heard elsewhere, Mr. Marlowe, and I know he will feel quite differently when he comes to see things as they really are."

The grave look on Mr. Marlowe's face disappeared as he turned back to old Mr. King.

"Well," he said at last, as the other showed no sign of continuing the conversation, and still playing with the paper cutter on his desk.

"Permit me to say, sir," Mr. King broke out, finding to his astonishment it was not an easy matter to talk to this imperturbable man entrenched behind his own desk, "that I am disappointed in the atmosphere in which I find my son. It smells of trade, sir, too much to suit my fancy."

"Did you suppose for an instant, Mr. King," asked Mr. Marlowe, dropping the paper-cutter to pick up the pencil, "that our books came out ready for libraries, without any intervening process?"

"I certainly supposed Jasper was to be in charge of a literary department of the house, when I gave my consent to his coming here—" declared Mr. King very decidedly.

"Father!" exclaimed Jasper, unable longer to keep silent, "how could I take charge of any department, until I had learned it all myself?"

"You have been through Harvard," his father turned on him, "and it seems to me are fully competent to do the literary work required here."

"And as for the manufacturing department," continued Jasper, finding it more difficult to keep still, "it was the only place for me; I had to begin at the bottom, if I'm ever to be a publisher—which is what my work is to be—"

"Not so fast—not so fast," cried the old gentleman excitedly. "You are not to be a publisher, I take it, if I do not wish it. You've given your word you will not."

"I have given my word, father," said Jasper with a long breath, "and I'll not go back on it," but his lips whitened.

All this while Mr. Marlowe still played with the little articles on his desk, sitting very quietly and watching the two. He now threw them down with an abrupt movement, whirled the revolving chair around suddenly and sent a lightning-like glance of stern inquiry toward old Mr. King.

"Be so kind, sir, as to define exactly what your intentions are as to your son's future. Time is very valuable here, and every fraction squandered has to be made up in some way."

"My intentions are," said the old gentleman, in a lofty way, "to take my son out of the business—entirely out, sir," he waved his hand in a stately and comprehensive manner; then glanced to see the effect on the head of the house.

But there was no effect whatever, except a quick business-like acceptance of the situation on Mr. Marlowe's implacable face. "Father!" began Jasper. But old Mr. King was beyond hearing a word.

"I had intended," he went on condescendingly, "to have my son put in a large interest in the business, supposing it turned out to be the proper one for him. In fact, his and my financial support would have made it one of the finest publishing houses in the world."

Mr. Marlowe bowed. "Thank you," he said politely. "James," turning to the window opening into the book-keeping department, "make out Jasper King's account and settle at once. I believe you wish to go as soon as you can, do you not," to Jasper, "that is, after you have given me the report of the business you did on the trip?"

Jasper could not speak for a moment. Then he said: "But I can't leave my work in this way—it's," and he sprang to his feet.

"Jasper," Mr. Marlowe stopped a moment and seemed to swallow something in his throat, then went on, "your father wishes it, and you will make him happy"—Jasper started at Polly's own words—"that's enough for one life time. I'm sorry to lose you, my boy," he suddenly grasped Jasper's hand, "but allow me to say, sir," turning to old Mr. King, "that for you and your money I have very little consideration. You don't own enough to make it worth while for the house of David Marlowe & Co. to extend an invitation to you to enter it. And now, if you will excuse me, I will hear Jasper's account of the business he was sent on."

With that, seeing it was expected of him, old Mr. King got out of his chair, by the side of the desk, and passed into the long salesroom.

"I hope you'll believe," began Jasper brokenly, feeling as if the whole world were going awry, "that this strange idea was never gained from me. Why, I *love* the business." His gray eyes glowed as he spoke the word.

"My boy," Mr. Marlowe's face was alight with feeling, "don't explain, I understand it all; you've the misfortune to be born into a rich family, and your father probably never had to raise his hand to earn a penny. He isn't to be blamed, only I did hope"—

"That I was different," finished Jasper, his head drooping a bit with the shame of it. "Oh, Mr. Marlowe, father is so splendid—he's just a magnificent man," he added, the head coming up, with Jasper's old habit of throwing it back, "if you only knew him and he could have shown you his old self."

"Don't I know it," responded Mr. Marlowe heartily, "and I also know that you must stick by him. Only I did hope—and now I will finish what I was going to say—that you could stay and help me, for you are after my own heart, Jasper," he added abruptly, a rare tremble in his voice.

Jasper put out his hand instinctively. "Thank you, Mr. Marlowe," he said as the head of the house grasped it warmly, "I shall never forget this."

And then, as if nothing but the ordinary business had occurred, Jasper sat down and went carefully over every detail of the commission he had been sent on, heard Mr. Marlowe's terse, "That's good, Jasper; you've done it all well," and passed out for the last time, from the private office, and joined his father in silence, for the walk to the hotel.

That night Jasper's father wanted to go to a concert, so Jasper got a box, and sat through it all, not seeing anything but Polly's face, and hearing, "I'd make him happy, any way."

Down in the audience sprinkled here and there, or in the galleries, were some of the D. Marlowe & Co. salesmen and workers staring often up at him, and the handsome white-haired old gentleman by his side.

"There's that old snob," they would exclaim at first recognition, to their companions, "look at him," and under pretense of gazing at the stage, the opera glasses would be turned on the box. "Looks as if he owned the whole town, eh?"

"He is awfully handsome, isn't he?" every salesman's companion would exclaim, looking at Jasper pale and quiet, in the most secluded part of the box.

"Yes," said every one of the men, only seeing the old gentleman, "but he's too toploftical to live"—or something to that effect—and then they would forget all about it till the companion's opera glasses leveled in the same direction, brought the conversation around to the old topic.

"They had a flare-up with Mr. Marlowe this morning," confided one salesman to his friend in the *entr'acte*, "and he's off," with a nod over to Jasper's private box.

"Oh dear me!" exclaimed the young girl, with a pang at her heart, "has he left your business?"

"Yes," said the salesman, and a real regret passed over his careless face, "and it's a shame, for no one would have thought he owned a penny; he was just digging at the business all the time, like the rest of us."

"Is he very rich?" asked the young girl.

"Well, I should say," began the salesman, unable to find words to express Jasper's financial condition. Then the curtain rang up.

The next morning, old Mr. King broke the egg into his cup thoughtfully.

"I suppose I might as well look about a bit, now that I'm here, Jasper. I haven't been in this town for twenty years or so."

"Very well, father," said Jasper, trying not to be listless. "Where shall we go to-day?"

"Oh, I'll look around by myself," said his father quickly. "You go to bed—you look all done up," scanning his son's face anxiously.

"Indeed, you will not go alone," said Jasper, rousing himself with shame. "We'll have a good day together."

"Indeed we will not," retorted the old gentleman.

"I shall have a cab and go by myself. You'll go to bed, or I'll call in the doctor. Goodness me, Jasper, you don't look like the same boy that started out in business six months ago; you're all worn out."

Jasper said nothing, only redoubled his efforts on the breakfast before him that now assumed colossal proportions, and as if it could never be eaten in the world, hoping to persuade his father into allowing him to go on the tour of inspection. But it was no use. Mr. King on finishing his morning repast, stalked out to the office, and ordered a carriage, and presently departed, with last injunctions to Jasper, "to lie down and take things easy."

As his father closed the door, Jasper sank into a chair by the table and allowed his head to drop into his hands; but only for a minute, then he sprang to his feet, and paced the floor rapidly.

"If Polly is only happy," he said to himself over and over. How long he walked thus he never knew—it was only by hearing a vigorous knock on the door that he stopped, and called, "Come in."

"They told me," said Jack Loughead, answering the knock, "at the Marlowes,' that I should find you here, unless you had left the town. Are you sick?" he asked with concern.

"No; sit down, do, Loughead," said Jasper, dragging forward a chair, and falling into one himself, just beginning to be conscious of a stiff pair of legs.

Jack Loughead set his hat on the table, and himself in the chair that Jasper proffered. Then he fell to tapping the tip of his shining boot with his walking stick.

"King, I came here to ask you something, that if I didn't trust you so well I could never ask in all the world. But I feel I can trust you."

"Oh, don't—don't," begged Jasper, putting up an unsteady hand to ward off the dreaded subject. "Don't tell me anything, Loughead."

"Well, I will ask you something, then," said Jack Loughead coolly. "I'm a business man, King, and I must come to the point in a business way. First, let me tell you that Uncle and I start for Australia in a fortnight;" Jasper drew a long breath of relief. "Yes, I must get back; and you will see that I cannot go without," Jack Loughead paused—then went on abruptly. "Does Miss Pepper care for Pickering Dodge?"

"How do I know—how can I tell?" cried Jasper desperately, and springing from his chair, he began to pace the floor again. "Excuse me, Loughead, I'm not myself to-day. I've left D. Marlowe & Co. and"—

"Yes, I know," interrupted Jack, and drawing a long breath of relief on his part at being able to speak on this subject now that the ice was broken; "well, I'm glad, of course, King, if you didn't care to stay," he said.

"But I did," cried Jasper, stopping short, to emphasize this. "Mr. Marlowe is a royal man, through and through, and I'd work for him all my life. But my father thought best not; that's enough," he added in the abruptest fashion, beginning to walk again.

"Yes; well, I see," said Jack. "I know a little what well-meaning relatives can do to make a young man's life miserable. I'm sorry, King," and he looked truly wretched over it.

"And you must forgive anything strange about me to-day," said Jasper, walking on hurriedly, "for I am all upset."

"Yes, I know," repeated Jack Loughead, "nothing breaks a man up like wrenching him from his work. King," he sprang to his feet and joined Jasper walking on by his side down the room, "you are Miss Pepper's brother, or as good as one. Can you tell me if I shall wrong Pickering Dodge if I speak to her?"

Jasper was saved from answering by old Mr. King coming in with a "Oh, how d'ye, Loughead? Well, well, Jasper, you've had a good nap, I take it." And then all three went down to luncheon, and Jasper managed not to be left alone with Jack Loughead until at the last when he said, "I shall go and tell the whole story to Mrs. Fisher; of course I must speak to her first."

"Halloo, Dave!" It was such a remarkable cry that David turned at once, although he was almost on a dead run across the campus.

"Hey, there!" shouted Percy Whitney as David turned. "Whew! How you do go, Dave."

"What's the matter?" cried David, running lightly back to stand in front of Percy. "Dear me, Percy, you have lost your eyeglasses!" with a glance at the other's flushed face; "wait, I'll find the things."

"I yelled my lungs sore," said Percy in irritation, dropping down on his knees to pass his hands carefully over the campus grass, "and now I've lost these. Bad luck to you, Dave, for it!"

"Oh! go without 'em," said David, getting gingerly down on all-fours to prowl around on the greensward.

"Go without 'em?" repeated Percy, sitting straight in indignation. "How could I see, pray tell? Don't be a donkey, Dave."

David said nothing, but fell to a more diligent search, while Percy bewailed his loss, watching eagerly David's nimble fingers moving in and out of the little tufts of grass.

"Shades of the departed specs," cried David, also sitting straight and peering with his keen blue eyes in a birdlike way along the sward. "It's a mysteri—oh, Great Caesar!" then he fell on his back on the campus, and rolled and laughed, to bring up red and shining, only to tumble over and roll again.

"Of all the idiots in the universe, Dave Pepper," fumed Percy. "What's the matter?"

"Your trouble has gone to your head," said David faintly. "Feel and see; oh dear!"

***"How You Can Sit There And Laugh When Joe Is In Danger, I Don't See," Exclaimed Percy Irritably.***

Percy's hand flew up to his thick mane of brown hair, that not all his disgust and tireless training could persuade to lie smoothly, when he picked off his beloved glasses, after an angry twitch or two.

"How you can sit there and laugh when Joe is in danger, I don't see," he exclaimed irritably, adjusting them to his nose. "I've nearly killed myself to catch you, and"—

"Joe in danger!" cried David, on his feet in an instant. "Oh, Percy, what do you mean?" his cheeks whitening, and his blue eyes agleam.

"Joel's brought it on himself," said Percy, his irritation not going down. "I must say, Dave, if he'd behave more like the rest of us, he'd be"—

Then Polly's words, "Oh, dear, beautiful Joel!" came to mind, and he coughed violently, holding fast the eyeglasses in their place.

"What danger?" demanded David, in his impatience shaking Percy's arm.

"Well, you must know, after last night's performance over Joe, that they wouldn't let him alone."

"Last night's performance over Joel?" repeated David in astonishment. "What yarn are you spinning now, Percy?"

"Goodness sake, you are yarning yourself," retorted Percy indignantly, "to pretend that you don't know that last night a dozen or more fellows called on Joe, and he handled 'em without gloves, so that Bingley and Dobbs can't hardly step to-day."

"It's the first word I've heard of it," said David slowly, but emphatically, and staggering back a step or two to look at Percy. "I was out all the evening. Oh, magnificent old Joe!"

"Magnificent old Joe!" repeated Percy, "you better say 'poor Joe,' when you know what they are intending to give him."

# CHAPTER XIX

# MOTHER FISHER AND CHARLOTTE

David's blue eyes flashed dangerously. "Tell all you know, Percy," he said briefly.

"Dobbs heads it, as he did the first one," said Percy; "they've changed their tactics, and will get at Joe on their way home from that confounded meeting. Dave, can't you keep him from that?" and Percy, forgetting himself, peered anxiously over his glasses.

"No," said David shortly, "and I sha'n't try."

"You're an idiot," cried Percy, in a passion, "a stupid, blind old donkey! Joe will be mauled dreadfully," he howled, beating his hands together in distress; "no help for it but to keep him away from that old association meeting."

"Anything more to tell?" asked David.

"No," Percy shot out. "Bingley told me all he knew; but they wouldn't let him catch much of it, because he's left the gang"—

David's feet by this time were flying over the Campus, so that Percy was obliged to shout the remainder of the sentence after him. The consequence was that several heads were popped out of as many windows in the long gray dormitory fronting the Campus, their owners all engaged in the pleasing duty of staring at Percy and the flying figure across the grass.

"Now I'm in for it, for there's Dobbs, I vow," exclaimed Percy to himself, in dismay; "he'll guess I've given Dave warning," and he tried to strike a careless attitude, picking off his glasses to hold them up and gaze long and earnestly through them into the nearest tree.

"You can't come it," jeered Dobbs, from his window. "No birdsnesting, I promise you, Whitney; ha, ha!" And the other heads popped farther out than ever, to add a few hisses.

Percy, maddened by the failure of his plan to divert suspicion, now lost his head entirely, and sticking his eyeglasses on again, ran off like lightning to his room, followed by "Little coward, we'll treat you too—Look out!"

"Well, Jasper; now I'm bound for the next thing—Percy and Joel and David," declared old Mr. King as Jack Loughead was cleverly off; "we are so near, it's a pity not to drop down on them."

"Don't you think you ought to hurry back to Brierly?" asked Jasper, having hard work not to show that he cared anything about it one way or the other.

"No, I don't," answered his father, in his crispest fashion. "No one needs me there; Mrs. Cabot is a host in herself, and those boys may—who knows? At any rate, I must see how they are getting on, so we will go as soon as you can get your things packed and sent home," and the old gentleman glanced around the room at the various keepsakes and family adornings that Jasper had brought with him to make life less lonely while he made a business man of himself.

"Very well, father," said Jasper, he could not trust himself to say more; and for the first time had to hurry away that his father might not see his face. But old Mr. King was the farthest removed from carrying the look of a person holding any interest whatever in Jasper's trouble, for he went on to say, "And I do hope you will get it over with as quickly as possible, Jasper, so that we may be off," then he fell to reading the evening paper with great gusto.

Jasper seized his hat, rushed down stairs two steps at a time, nearly overturning Buttons leaning on the post at the foot.

"Oh! beg pardon," said Jasper, quite as if it had been a gentleman he had run against.

"You hain't hurt me none," said Buttons, staggering back to his support, where he craned his neck in curiosity to watch young Mr. King's impatience.

Once out in the park, a half-mile away, his hands thrust in their pockets, Jasper slackened his pace, and breathed freer. Before him seemed to be the little brown house; it was the first time he had seen Mrs. Pepper—and they had just finished their long talk, when the mother had thanked him for rescuing Phronsie from the organ-grinder. The five little Peppers were begging him to come over again to see them, but Mrs. Pepper laid her hand on his arm. "Be sure, Jasper," she warned, "that your father is willing." He could see her black eyes looking down into his face. What would she say now?

Jasper threw himself down on one of the seats under a friendly tree. "At least, Polly, you sha'n't be ashamed of me," he said in a moment or two, "and dear Mrs. Fisher," then he walked quietly off to make the last preparations that his father had ordered.

"Well, now, Charlotte," said Mrs. Fisher, "you needn't worry, not a single bit," and she went on calmly sorting out the small flannel petticoats in her lap. "That is rather thin," she said, holding up one between her eyes and the light; "King Fisher, how you do kick things out!"

"Mrs. Fisher!" exclaimed Charlotte Chatterton in amazement, "how can you sit picking over flannel petticoats, when perhaps Polly will—oh, do excuse me," she broke off hastily, "for speaking so."

"Polly? I'd trust my girl to know what was sense, and what was nonsense," declared Mother Fisher crisply, and not taking off her attention in the slightest from Baby's petticoats.

"Ar-goo—ar-goo!" screamed little King.

"So we would—wouldn't we, Birdie?" she said, nodding at him.

"But people do such very strange things in—in—love," said Charlotte, her face full of distress, "I mean when love is in the question, Mrs. Fisher."

"Polly doesn't," said Mrs. Fisher scornfully. "Polly has never been in love; why, she is only twenty."

Charlotte gave an uneasy whirl and rushed off to the window.

"And there's that dreadful, hateful Mrs. Cabot," she cried, plunging back, her pale eyes afire. "Oh! I feel so wicked, Mrs. Fisher, whenever I think of her, I'd like to tear her, I would, for picking at Polly," she declared with venom.

"You needn't be afraid," repeated Mrs. Fisher calmly, "Polly knows Mrs. Cabot through and through, and will never be influenced by anything she says."

"Oh, dear, dear, dear!" cried Charlotte, wringing her long hands, "and there's that Mr. Loughead, and everything is mixed up, and I can't frighten you."

"Now, just see here, Charlotte," cried Mother Fisher, casting aside the flannel petticoats to look up, "you must just put your mind off from all this; I should never know you, my girl, you are always so sensible and quiet. Why, Charlotte, what has gotten into you?"

"That's just it," cried Charlotte, a pink passion in her sallow cheeks, "everybody thinks because I don't rant every day, that I haven't any more feeling than a stick or a stone. Oh! do excuse me, Mrs. Fisher, but I love Polly so!" And she flung herself down on her knees, burying her face among the little flannel petticoats in Mother Fisher's lap.

"There—there, my dear," said Mrs. Fisher, smoothing Charlotte's pale straight hair, "of course you love Polly; everybody does."

"And I don't—don't want her to marry that Pickering Dodge," mumbled Charlotte.

"Certainly not; and she's no more likely to marry him than you are," said Mrs. Fisher coolly, giving gentle pats to Charlotte's head, while King Fisher screamed and twitched his mother's gown in anger to see the petting going on.

"Well, now I have two babies," said Mother Fisher, with a smile, lifting him up to her lap, where he amused himself by beating on Charlotte's head with both fat fists, till his mother seized them with one hand, while she gently smoothed the girl's hair with the other. "Polly can be trusted anywhere; and when she is in too much of a dilemma, then she brings everything to mother."

Charlotte sat up straight and wiped her eyes.

"And we've got somebody else to worry about much more, and all our sympathies ought to go out to him," said Mrs. Fisher gravely.

"Charlotte, I don't mind telling you that I am dreadfully sorry that Grandpapa has taken Jasper away from his business." She sat King Fisher abruptly on the floor, all the little petticoats tumbling after him, and walked away so that Charlotte could not see her face. "Poor Jasper, he loved his work so."

*"Well, Now I Have Two Babies," Said Mother Fisher*

"And that's just it," gasped Charlotte, somehow finding her feet to hurry over to Mrs. Fisher, "Jasper has lost his work, and now oh dear!—oh! can't you see, Mrs. Fisher"—and then frightened at her boldness, she ran back to Baby.

"Charlotte Chatterton!" exclaimed Mrs. Fisher. There was something so dreadful in her tone, that Charlotte, without a word, ran out of the room—to meet little Dr. Fisher hurrying upstairs with his hands full of letters. "A whole budget from Brierly," he announced joyfully; "two for you, my girl," casting them into her hands. "And the folks are coming home next week; that is, our folks—good news—eh, Charlotte?" then he sped on to find his wife.

And at dinner Charlotte, sitting pale and immovable amidst all the chat, let the news of Mr. and Mrs. Mason Whitney's and Dick's determination to come on to greet the arrivals from the Brierly farmhouse, fall on apparently unheeding ears.

"Charlotte!" cried Dr. Fisher at last, looking at her through his big spectacles, "why, I thought you would rejoice with us," he added reproachfully.

"Adoniram," exclaimed Mrs. Fisher across the table, for the first time in her life looking as if she would like to step on his toes. The little doctor stared at her a moment—"Oh—er—never mind, my dear," he cried abruptly, turning to Charlotte. "I suppose you do not feel well."

"Yes, I do feel well," said Charlotte truthfully, not daring to look at Mrs. Fisher, but keeping her eyes on the tablecloth.

"I have a letter from Mr. King—a very long one; he is going to see Joel and David," Mother Fisher made haste to say; "I hope he hasn't heard anything wrong about them," and a little anxious pucker came on her forehead.

Charlotte Chatterton glanced up quickly, and seeing it, "Oh, I do believe everything is all right, Mrs. Fisher," she exclaimed involuntarily.

Mother Fisher looked straight at her with one of her brightest smiles. "I guess so," she said, her brow clearing.

And after they had pulled back their chairs from the table, and the little doctor had gone into his office for a minute, Mrs. Fisher followed Charlotte out into the hall.

"Charlotte," and she put both hands on the girl's shoulders, "you and I won't meddle with the Lord's will for Polly. Promise me that you'll not say one word of what we were talking, to any one."

"I won't!" said Charlotte Chatterton.

"And now," said Mother Fisher, dropping her arms and resuming her usual cheery manner, "you and I, Charlotte, have got to put our minds on getting ready for the Whitneys and the home-coming, and we must make it just the brightest time that ever was. I'm no good at thinking up ways to celebrate," added Mrs. Fisher, with a little laugh, "Polly always did that; so you must do it for me, you and the doctor, Charlotte. And you better run in to his office now and make a beginning, for next week will come before we know it," and with a motherly pat, and a "run along, child," Mrs. Fisher waited to see Charlotte well on the way before she turned to her own duties.

"Come in!" cried little Dr. Fisher, as she rapped at the office door. "Oh, it's you, Charlotte," with a sigh of relief; "I'm sure I don't feel much like dragging on my boots and going off to the Land's End to-night, on a call."

"Mrs. Fisher thought I ought to come and see you, sir, about getting up a plan to celebrate the home-coming next week," said Charlotte, feeling her heart bounding already with delight. Would they really all be together in a week?

"Now that's something like," exclaimed Dr. Fisher joyfully, and pushing aside with a reckless hand his books and vials on the table; "sit down, do, Charlotte; there," as Charlotte settled her long figure in the opposite chair. "Now then!"

"I never got up a plan to celebrate anything in my life," said Charlotte, folding her hands in dismay.

"Nor I either," confessed the little doctor in an equal tremor, "Polly was always great at those things. But I suppose that's the reason my wife set us two together, Charlotte, for she's the wisest of women, and perhaps we ought to learn how to get up celebrations."

"If only Phronsie were home," breathed Charlotte wistfully. "I'm so afraid our affair will be worse than nothing."

"I dare say," replied the little doctor cheerily, "but we can try, and that goes a great way, Charlotte—trying does."

***"I've Always Found," Said Dr. Fisher, "That All You Had To Do To Start A Thing, Was To Begin."***

Charlotte drew a long breath and moved uneasily in her chair. "If we only knew how to begin," she said at last doubtfully.

"I've always found," said Dr. Fisher, springing from his chair, "that all you had to do to start a thing was to—begin."

"Yes, that's just it," ruminated Charlotte, bringing up her hands to hold her head with, "I think we are in a tight place, Dr. Fisher."

"Hum, that may be," assented the little man, "I like tight places. Now, then, Charlotte, how do you say begin?"

Charlotte sat lost in thought for a minute, then she said, "Any way, I think it would be best for us to get up something very simple, so long as we are beginners."

"I think so too," agreed Dr. Fisher, "so that's settled. Now for the first thing; what do you say we should do, Charlotte?"

"How would it do," asked Charlotte suddenly, "to invite everybody after they have gotten over the first of the home-coming—after dinner, I mean—into the drawing-room, and then tell them that we are not smart enough to think up things, and ask them to give a recitation apiece, or something of that sort?"

"Charlotte Chatterton!" exclaimed the little doctor, cramming his hands into the side pockets of his office coat and staring at her.

"I am ashamed of you! that would be shabby enough—not so bad either," he added quickly, a sudden thought striking him, "as you'll do your part in singing."

"Oh! I couldn't sing," cried Charlotte, drawing back into her shell of coldness again, "they don't any of them care for it; they've heard me so much," she finished, trying to smooth her refusal over.

"You'll sing," declared the little doctor decidedly, "we could never be tired of hearing you; and for the rest, I have a notion that this might suit. See here," and he threw himself into his office chair, and looked Charlotte squarely in the face, "why not ask Alexia and Cathie and the others, to take hold and get up some fandango—eh?"

Charlotte caught herself on the edge of saying "No," then drew a long breath and said, "Well," trying not to seem indifferent over the plan.

"Don't like it—eh?" asked Dr. Fisher, regarding her keenly.

"It might be the best thing in the world," said Charlotte slowly. "Those girls act splendidly; they've had little plays so often, and Polly has drilled them, that they'll know just how to go to work, and it will please Polly. Oh, yes, do let us have that," she cried, beginning to wax quite enthusiastic.

"It will please them too," said the little man, not withdrawing his gaze.

"Yes, it will please them," said Charlotte, after a minute, "and I will run over in the morning and ask them."

"That's good!" cried Dr. Fisher, bringing his hands together with a joyful clap; and getting out of his chair he began to skip up and down like a boy. "And let Amy Loughead do the piano music, do; that will please Polly to see how the child has gone ahead. I can't hardly believe Miss Salisbury; she tells me the chit practices every minute she can save from other things. Be sure to have her asked, Charlotte, child."

"I will ask Amy," promised Charlotte, with a pang at the thought of the delight over Jack Loughead's handsome face at her invitation.

"And you are to sing," cried the little doctor jubilantly. "Now we are all capitally fixed. It takes you and me to get up celebrations, doesn't it?" and he stood as tall as he could and beamed at her. "I'd go over as early as I could, Charlotte," he advised, "and tell those girls, because you know a week isn't much to get ready in."

"I will," said Charlotte, "go the very first thing after breakfast."

And after breakfast, the next morning, she tied her hat on, and not trusting herself to think of her expedition, actually ran down the long carriage drive to the avenue—then walking at her best pace, she stood before Alexia Rhys' door and rang the bell.

"There, now, I can't go back," she said to herself, and in a minute or two she was in the reception room, and Alexia Rhys was running over the stairs and standing with a puzzled expression on her face, before her.

"Oh, my goodness me—oh, oh!" exclaimed Alexia, with a little laugh. "Is this you, Miss Chatterton?"

"Yes," said Charlotte Chatterton, "I came to ask if you would get up something nice to celebrate the home-coming of all the family from Brierly; and Mr. Whitney's family are to come too, next week. Will you, Miss Rhys?"

"Well, I never!" cried Alexia Rhys, sinking into the first chair she could find. "You want me—I shouldn't think you would," she added truthfully.

"I didn't at first," said Charlotte Chatterton, "but I do now, Miss Rhys—oh! very much, you and Miss Harrison, and all those girls—you can get up something beautiful; and Dr. Fisher and I don't in the least know how, and we want you to do it." Then she sat quite still.

"Well, I declare!" cried Alexia Rhys, unable to find another word. Then she looked out of the window. "Oh, here's Clem," and, rushing out, Charlotte could hear a whispered consultation with, "Did you ever?" and "I'm awfully ashamed," while Clem's voice said, "So am I."

"Well, come in," said Alexia audibly at last, dragging Clem after her into the reception room, "we've got to do what's right now, any way."

"I'm awfully ashamed, Miss Chatterton," said Clem Forsythe, going straight to Charlotte's chair and putting out her hand; "we girls haven't been right to you since you came, and I, for one, want to ask your pardon."

"Dear me, so do I," cried Alexia, crowding in between with an eager hand stretched out, "but what good will that do—we said things, at least I did the most. Oh, my hateful tongue!"

"If you'll only take hold and make a nice celebration for Polly and all the others, that will be all I'd want," said Charlotte. "Thank you, you are so good," she brought up happily.

"And then we'll do something for you some time," declared Alexia, "all for yourself, won't we, Clem—something perfectly elegantly splendid?"

# CHAPTER XX

# STRAIGHTENING OUT AFFAIRS

Two days after, old Mr. King was walking over the college campus, bound for Joel's and David's room in the "Old Brick Dormitory."

"I am glad I sent Jasper ahead to the hotel; I much rather pop in on the boys by myself," soliloquized the old gentleman in great satisfaction. "Ah, here it is," beginning to mount the stairs.

"Come in," yelled a voice, as he rapped with his walking-stick on the door of No. 19, "and don't make such a piece of work breaking the door down—oh, beg pardon!" as Mr. King obeyed the order.

A tall figure sprawled in the biggest chair, his long legs carried up to the mantel, where his boots neatly reposed; while a cloud of smoke filling the room, made Mr. King cough violently in spite of himself.

"'Tis a nasty air," said the tall young man, getting his legs down in haste from the mantel, and himself out of the chair, though with much difficulty; "take a glass of water, sir," hobbling over to a side table, and pouring one out, to work his way with it to old Mr. King.

"Thank you," said the old gentleman, when he could speak, and accepting it quickly, "you say truly, the air is beastly," glancing around the room in displeasure at the plentiful signs of its inmates' idea of having a good time at college. "Are Joel and David Pepper soon to be in?" As he spoke, he lifted up the cover of a French novel thrown on the lounge near him, and dropped it quickly as he read the title.

"Hey? oh! I see—a little mistake," exclaimed the tall youth, going unsteadily back to his chair. "Their room is 19, in the extension. I am Robert Bingley, sir."

"I'm very glad," cried old Mr. King heartily, "for I don't mind telling you, my young friend, that I shouldn't want Joel's and David's room to look like this."

"I don't blame you in the least, sir," said Bingley, nowise abashed, "but you needn't worry, for the Peppers aren't my kind. You must be Grandfather King?" he added.

"Yes, I am," said old Mr. King, straightening up, and throwing back his white hair with a proud gesture. "So you've heard about me?" he asked, in a gratified way.

"I should rather think we had," said Bingley, "why, all of us know about you, sir." Here he got out of his chair again. "You won't care to, after you know all, but I should like to shake hands with you, sir."

"Most certainly," responded the old gentleman heartily, "although your room isn't to your credit." Thereupon he bestowed a courtly hand-shake upon the young man, with the utmost cordiality, making Bingley, who seemed to have a good deal of trouble with his legs, to retreat to his chair in a high state of satisfaction.

"It was mean of me to ask you such a favor, sir," said Bingley, gazing up at the ceiling, "before I had told you all, but I couldn't help it, some way, and I knew you wouldn't touch my hand after you'd heard. Well, I was one of a gang who went to Joe Pepper's room last week for the purpose of l amming him."

"You went to Joe Pepper's room for the purpose of lamming him?" repeated old Mr. King, darting out of his chair.

"Yes, sir"—Bingley still kept his gaze glued to the ceiling—"but we didn't do it, though; Joe lammed us."

"Oh!"

"So the rest of the gang are going for him to-night; I'm not able to," said Bingley, trying to appear careless.

"Joel to be in such business—how could he!" fumed old Mr. King. "A gentleman—and I thought so much of his turning out well. It will kill his mother—oh, how could he?" turning fiercely on Bingley.

"See here, now," cried that individual, tearing his gaze from the ceiling, to send a sharp glance at the white-haired old gentleman, "Joe is all right; straight as a brick. You can bet your money on that, sir."

"Oh—oh!" cried Mr. King, more and more horrified, "is this what you all come to college for? I should consider, sir," very sternly, "it a place to keep up the dignity of one's family in, and that of such a venerable institution," waving both shapely hands to include the entire pile of buildings by which they were surrounded.

Bingley gave vent to an uncontrollable laugh. "Beg pardon, sir, but the dignity isn't worth a rush. We are in the old hole, and all we look out for is to have a good time, and scrape through."

"Old hole—and scrape through! Oh, dear—oh, dear!" groaned old Mr. King.

"That's what our set do," said Bingley, to give him time to recover, "Joe and Davina—ah, I mean David—don't train in our crowd; the other one, Whitney"—

"Don't tell me that he does," interrupted Percy's grandfather sharply. "It wouldn't be possible."

"No, he doesn't affect us," said Bingley coolly, "it's all he can do to take care of those eyeglasses of his; and he'd muss his clothes. Whitney is something of a softy, sir."

Old Mr. King drew a long breath of relief. But he looked so troubled, that Bingley for the life of him couldn't keep up his assumed carelessness.

"Sit down again, do, sir," he begged involuntarily, "and I will tell you all about it," and Mr. King, resuming his chair, presently had a graphic account of Joel's course in college, with a description of the trouble in his room, till the whole thing was laid bare.

"How I wish I had been here to see my boy," exclaimed the old gentleman, with sparkling eyes; "I might have helped him a bit." He stretched out a handsome fist and looked at it as admiringly as any college athlete could view his own. "Well," dropping his arm, "I am interrupting you, Mr."—groping for the name.

"Bingley, sir."

"Ah, yes; Bingley. Well, Mr. Bingley, pray go on. Did you not say that another attempt was to be made on my grandson?"

Bingley nodded. "To-night after he comes from the Association rooms," he added.

"We shall see—we shall see," exclaimed the old gentleman drily, in a manner that delighted Bingley and made him tingle all over to "be in at the death" himself.

"Dobbs has planned it to"—

"Dobbs?" interrupted the old gentleman sharply, "what family? Not the Ingoldsby Dobbs, I trust"—

"This chap's name is Ingoldsby Dobbs," said Bingley; "he's a high-flyer, I tell you! Lives up to his name, I suppose he thinks."

"Oh, I'm so sorry," mourned Mr. King; "I have known his father ever since we were boys; he's capital stock. Well, go on, Mr. Bingley, and let me know what this young rascal is up to," he added, with extreme irritation.

"He is going to have his men close in on Joe in the middle of the park.

Pepper often comes that way to 'Old Brick'—short, you know, for 'Old Brick Dormitory'—with a poor miserable cuss—excuse me, sir—he's trying to get up on to sober legs. There are twenty fellows pledged to do the job, I've found out."

Bingley didn't think it worth while to mention how the plan was discovered, nor that heavy vengeance was vowed upon his head if he divulged it.

"I gave it away to Whitney. I couldn't get at Davi—er, Dave, to see if it wasn't possible to keep Joe away from that meeting."

"It would come some time—it better be to-night," said the old gentleman briefly. "Well, is that all?"

"Yes, sir; only that they are to toss a cloak over Joe's head, and carry him off for a little initiation fun."

"Ah!" Old Mr. King sat quite straight. "Thank you, Mr. Bingley," he said, getting out of his chair. He didn't offer to shake hands, and Bingley, though pretending not to notice any omission of that sort, felt considerably crest-fallen about it.

The moment the door was shut and he heard Mr. King go down the stairs, Robert Bingley ran his fingers through his hair, giving a savage pull at the innocent locks.

"Curse my luck!" he growled, taking out the angry fingers to shake them at his legs, "tied here by these two beggars, and he thinks that I'm sneaking out of standing up for Joe!"

Old Mr. King fumed to himself all the way down the stairs, becoming more angry with each step. When he reached the lower hall he turned and passed through the building instead of going out, and meeting a young collegian on a run, asked, "Have the goodness to tell me, sir, does Mr. Ingoldsby Dobbs room in this building?"

"No. 23-4-5 in the extension," said the undergraduate, not slackening speed, and pointing the direction. So the old gentleman climbed the staircase to the wing, and presently rapped on the door marked 23.

Uproarious shouts of laughter greeted him as he opened the door in response to a loud "Come in!" The noise stopped as suddenly as it was possible for the inmates of the room to check it when they saw the visitor, but not before "We'll season Pepper well and make the deacon howl!" came distinctly to his ears.

"Good afternoon, young gentlemen," said old Mr. King, bowing his white head; and holding his hat in his hand, he advanced to the table, around which sat six or eight of them. "I beg of you not to go," as some of them made a sudden movement to leave; "I should like to see you all, though I called especially upon Mr. Ingoldsby Dobbs."

A tall, wiry youth with sallow face and high-bred nose, disentangled himself from the group and came forward. "I don't remember where I have met you, sir," he said, yet extending his hand, with his best manner on.

"Aristocratic old party," whispered one man to his neighbor, "Dobbsey needn't be afraid to claim him."

"I am very thankful to say I never have met you before, young man," observed Mr. King coolly, not seeing the slender hand waiting for his, "your father honors me with his friendship. This may tell you who I am," and he threw a card upon the table.

Young Dobbs' sallow face turned a shade paler as he picked up the card and read it.

"Glad to see you—sit down, won't you?" he mumbled, dragging up a comfortable chair. "Any friend of father's is welcome here," he went on awkwardly, while the rest of the men stared at him, one of them exclaiming under his breath, "First time Dobbs' cheek deserted him, I'll wager."

The old gentleman looked first into Ingoldsby Dobbs' thin face, then surveyed them all quite leisurely. "I understand you paid my grandson, Joel Pepper, a call a short time since, when instead of abusing him, some of you got your deserts."

The men started, and angry exclamations went around the room: "He's turned coward, the mean sneak! We'll pay him up!" and remarks of a like nature being quite audible.

Old Mr. King turned on them. "Silence!" he commanded. "My grandson Joel doesn't know I am here. I heard the story since my arrival. If any one says one word against him, I'll cane him from the top of the stairs to the bottom," and he looked as if he could do it.

"'Twas Bingley, then," said Dobbs sullenly.

The old gentleman completely ignored him, addressing his words to the crowd. "There are four men in this class who are going to be protected from your insults. Those are my three grandsons and Mr. Robert Bingley; and this is to be done without appealing to the college authorities either. That puts a stop to your fine plan, Mr. Dobbs," at last looking at him, "and any other idea of the same sort your fertile brain may chance to think up. The first intimation of any hostility, and your father and the fathers of these men here with you," waving his hand at them all, "and of the others in this interesting plan, will be informed, and you will be dealt with exactly like any other disturber of the peace—villains in college or out of it ought to be served to the same punishment, in my opinion. Now have any of you remarks to make?"

It was so like Joel's invitation to "Come on and have it out now," that not a single man of them stirred.

"Then I will have the pleasure of bidding you good-by," said Mr. King, and the next moment he was outside of No. 23, while perfect silence reigned within.

Polly came slowly down Mrs. Higby's front stairs and looked at Phronsie standing at the further end of the entry.

"What's the matter, Phronsie?" at last she asked.

For the first time in her life Phronsie seemed unable to answer Polly, and she stood quite still, her gaze fastened on the big-flowered muslin curtain that swung back and forth in the breeze that came through the open window.

"Now, Phronsie," said Polly very decidedly, and going up to her, "you must tell me what the matter is."

"I can't," said Phronsie, in a low tone, "don't ask me, Polly."

"Can't tell me everything?" cried Polly. "Dear me, what nonsense, Phronsie. Come now, begin, there's a dear."

"But I am not to tell," persisted Phronsie, shaking her head. Then she drew a long breath, and looked as if she were going to cry.

"Who has been telling you things?" cried Polly, her brown eyes flashing, "that you are not to tell? It is Mrs. Cabot. I know it is, for there is no one else here who would do it."

"Don't ask me," pleaded Phronsie in great distress, and clutching Polly's gown. "Oh, don't say anything more about it, Polly."

"Indeed I shall," declared Polly. "No one has a right to command you in this way, and I shall just speak to Mrs. Cabot about it."

"Oh, no, no," protested Phronsie, huddling up closer to Polly in dismay; "please, Polly, don't say anything to her about it, please."

"Mamsie wouldn't ever allow you to be annoyed about anything," said Polly, with increasing irritation, "and if Mrs. Cabot has said anything to you, Phronsie, to make you feel badly, why, I must know it. Don't you see, child, that I really ought to be told?"

Phronsie folded her hands tightly together, trying to keep them quiet, and her cheeks turned so very white that Polly hastened to put her well arm around her, saying quickly, "There, there, child, you needn't tell me now if you don't want to. Wait a bit."

"I had rather tell it now," said Phronsie, "but oh, I do wish that Grandpapa was here," she added sadly.

"Whatever can have been said to you, Phronsie?" exclaimed Polly in dismay. "You frighten me, child. Do tell me at once what it was."

"Jasper isn't going to be at Mr. Marlowe's any more," said Phronsie, with distinctness.

"Jasper isn't going to be at Mr. Marlowe's any more." repeated Polly wildly, and holding Phronsie so closely that she winced. "Oh, what do you mean! who has told you such nonsense?"

"Mrs. Cabot," said Phronsie; "she told me this morning—and I was not to tell you, Polly. But I did not promise not to. Indeed I didn't."

"What perfect nonsense!" exclaimed Polly, recovering herself, and trying to laugh, "well, Phronsie, child, didn't you know better than to believe any story that Mrs. Cabot might tell? How in the world could she know of Jasper's affairs, pray tell?" and she laughed again, this time quite gaily.

"Ah, but," said Phronsie, shaking her head, "she had a letter from Mr. Cabot; it came in this morning's mail; she opened it and said out loud this dreadful thing about Jasper, and then she saw me, and she said I was not to tell you."

Polly dropped Phronsie's arm and rushed down the hall.

"Where are you going?" cried Phronsie, hurrying after—"Oh, Polly!"

"I am going to make Mrs. Cabot tell me everything she knows," said Polly hoarsely, and not looking back; "she shall let me have every syllable. It can't be true!" She threw wide the door of Mrs. Higby's "keeping-room" where that lady was engaged in putting a patch on the chintz-covered sofa, and talking gossip with a neighbor at the same time.

"I thought as this was a-going so fast, Mr. Higby sets it out so, and we were all so comfortable to-day, I'd get at it kinder early," said Mrs. Higby apologetically; "anything I can do, Miss Polly?" she asked, flying away from her patch, and dropping her scissors on the floor.

"No," said Polly, turning back hastily. "Never mind, Mrs. Higby."

"Now 'twas something you wanted me for," cried Mrs. Higby, ambling toward the door, "I ain't a mite busy, Miss Polly; that old patch can wait. La! I can tell Mr. Higby to set on the other end till I get time to attend to it. What was it, Miss Polly?"

Polly turned back, Mrs. Higby's tone was so full of entreaty. "Oh, nothing, only if it isn't too much trouble, would you ask Mrs. Cabot to come down stairs a moment, I want to see her."

"Oh, cert'in," cried Mrs. Higby, ambling off toward the stairs. And presently Mrs. Cabot in a pink morning gown came down the hall toward Polly, and put both arms around her.

***"Phronsie, get a glass of water; be quick, child!"***

"What is it, dear?" she asked caressingly.

"Come out of doors," begged Polly, "I can't breathe here. Come, Mrs. Cabot."

And Mrs. Cabot, her arms still around Polly, was drawn out to the old porch, Phronsie following. Then Polly shook herself free.

"Is it true?" she began—"I made Phronsie tell me—that Jasper," she caught her breath, but went on again hurriedly, "has left Mr. Marlowe?"

"Oh, dear me!" exclaimed Mrs. Cabot in consternation, "what shall I do? Yes; but I wasn't to tell you; Mr. King is coming back. Do wait, Polly, and ask him about it."

"I shall not wait," declared Polly passionately, facing her. "Tell me all you know, Mrs. Cabot; every single word."

"I don't know a thing about it," cried Mrs. Cabot in a frightened way, "only Mr. Cabot writes that Mr. King has made Jasper leave Mr. Marlowe. That's all I know about it, Polly," she added desperately, "and I wish Mr. Cabot had been asleep before he wrote it. Phronsie, oh! get a glass of water; be quick, child!" as Polly sank down on the old stone floor of the porch.

# CHAPTER XXI

# POLLY TRIES TO HELP JASPER

"I think it was a mean shame," began Dick wrathfully.

"Dick—Dick!" exclaimed his mother gently.

Mr. Whitney tapped his knee with a letter he had just placed within its envelope, then threw it on the table. "It's the best job I ever did," he cried jubilantly, "to get Jasper out of that business."

Dick sent his two hands deep within their pockets. "Oh! how can you say so?" he cried.

"And how can you question what your father does?" exclaimed Mrs. Whitney. "Why, that isn't like you, Dick!" with a face full of reproach.

"Oh! let the boy say what he wants to, Marian," broke in her husband easily. "So, Dicky, my lad, you don't think I did just the right thing for Jasper—eh?"

He leaned back in his chair, and surveyed his young son with a twinkle in his eye.

"No, I don't," declared Dick, beginning to rage up and down the room on young indignant feet. "I say it's mean to meddle with a fellow's business. I wouldn't stand it!" he added stoutly.

Mr. Whitney laughed long and loud, despite his wife's shocked, "Dicky, don't, dear!"

"Well, if I didn't know that in a year's time Jasper will come to me and say, 'I thank you!' I should never have gone through with the job in the world," said his father, when he came out of his amusement. "It isn't the pleasantest piece of work a man could select, 'to meddle,' as you call it, with another's affairs."

"Jasper never will thank you in the world—never!" exclaimed Dick, cramming his irritated hands deeper in their pockets, and turning on his father.

"You see," said his father, nodding easily.

"And you see, papa," cried Dick, turning hastily in front of him, looking so exactly like his father that Mrs. Whitney forgot to chide, in admiring them both.

"And I think it's too bad," went on Dick. "Everybody pitches into Jasper, and wants him to do things; and Grandpapa is always picking at him. I'd—I'd fight—sometimes," he added.

"Softly—softly there, my boy," said Mr. Whitney; "you'll have plenty of practice for all your fighting powers by and by; a fourteen-year-old chap doesn't know everything."

"Well, I know one thing," declared Dick, more positively, "Grandpapa has always been meddling with Jasper, and you know it, papa."

"That's because he expects great things from Jasper, and that he will hold up the King name; we all do," replied his father.

Dick turned on an impatient heel. "And so he would have done, if you'd let him be a publisher," he declared.

His father laughed again, and leaned out of his chair to pinch his son's ear, but Dick, resenting this indignity, retreated to a safe position, declaring, "And I'm going to be one when I'm through college—so!"

"Mr. King's a-coming down the road, and Mr. Jasper!" screamed Mrs. Higby, coming out suddenly to the porch. "I see 'em from the keepin'-room window. My! what's the matter with Miss Polly?"

***"I Think It Was A Mean Shame' Began Dick Wrathfully.***

"Nothing," said Polly, opening her eyes; "that is, not much," and sitting up straight. "Are Grandpapa and Jasper really coming?" she asked.

"Dear me, Polly," exclaimed Mrs. Cabot, before Mrs. Higby could answer, and putting shaking hands on Polly's shoulders, "I never was so frightened in my life! I thought your arm was worse—and you so near well! O, dear! are you sure you are right?" peering around into her face. "Here comes Phronsie with the water—that's good!"

Polly took the glass and smiled up reassuringly into Phronsie's troubled face. "Oh! how good that is, Phronsie," she cried. "There now, I'm all right. Don't let Grandpapa or Jasper know," and she sprang to her feet, while Mrs. Higby hurried off to see if her preparations for dinner were all right, now that Mr. King had come back a day sooner than he wrote he intended.

"Phronsie, you go and meet them; do, dear," begged Polly; and as Phronsie ran off obediently, Polly walked up and down the porch with hasty steps, holding her hands as tightly locked together as the injured arm would allow. "Oh! if I only had time to think—but I ought to try, even if I don't say just exactly the right words, for Mr. Marlowe may not be able to take him back if I wait," and then Grandpapa came hurrying out with, "Where's Polly?" and she was kissed and her cheeks patted—he not seeming to notice anything amiss in her—he was so glad to get back; and through it all, Polly saw only Jasper's face, and, although everything seemed to turn around before her, she made up her mind that she would tell Grandpapa just what she thought, and beg him to change his mind, the very first instant she could.

And so, before the first greetings of the homecoming were fairly over, Polly, afraid her courage would give out if she waited a moment longer, put her hand on Mr. King's arm. "What is it, dear?" asked the old gentleman, busy with Phronsie, who hung around his neck, while she tried to tell him everything that had happened during his absence; and he peered over her shoulder into Polly's face.

"Grandpapa," cried Polly in a tremor, "could you let me talk to you a little just now? Please, Grandpapa."

"Well, yes, dear, after Phronsie has"—

"Oh! Phronsie will wait," cried Polly, guilty of interrupting; "I know she will."

For the first time in her life, Phronsie said rebelliously, "Oh! I don't want to wait, Polly. Dear Grandpapa has just got home, and I must tell him things."

"So you shall, Phronsie," declared old Mr. King, drawing her off beyond Polly's reach. "There, now you and I will get into this quiet corner," and he sat down and drew Phronsie to his knee. "Now, Pet, so you are glad to get your old Grandpapa home, eh?"

Polly, in an agony at being misunderstood, followed, and without stopping to think, she threw her arms around Phronsie and cried, "O, Phronsie! do trust me, dear, and let Grandpapa go. I must see him now!"

Mr. King gave Polly's burning cheeks a keen glance, then he set Phronsie on the floor abruptly. "Phronsie, see, dear, Polly really needs me. Come, child," and he gathered up Polly's hand into his own, and marched out of the room with her.

"Suppose we go in here," said the old gentleman, "and have our talk," unceremoniously opening the door of Mrs. Higby's best room as he spoke; "nobody is likely to disturb us here."

Polly, not caring where she went, but with the words she must speak weighing heavily on her mind, followed him unsteadily into the parlor, and while he threw open a blind or two to light up the gloom that usually hung over Mrs. Higby's best room, she busied herself trying to think how she should begin.

"There, now, my dear," said Mr. King, coming up to her, and drawing her off to a big haircloth sofa, standing stiffly against the wall, "we will sit down here, and then we can go over it comfortably together and settle what is on your mind," he added, feeling immensely gratified at the impending confidence.

"Grandpapa," cried Polly in desperation, and springing from the sofa, where he had placed her by his side, to stand in front of him, "I don't know where to begin. Oh! do help me." She clasped her hands, and stood the picture of distress, unable to say another word.

"Why, how can I help you to tell me, child," cried old Mr. King in astonishment, "when I don't know in the least what it is you want to say?"

"Oh! I know it," cried Polly, twisting her hands, unable to hold them quite still. "O, dear! what shall I do? Grandpapa, it's just"—

"Well, what, my dear?" asked the old gentleman, and taking one of her hands encouragingly. "Are you afraid of me? Why, Polly!"

Polly started at his tone of reproach, and threw her well arm around his neck, exactly as Phronsie would have done, which so pleased the old gentleman that it was easier for her to begin again to tell him what was on her mind. But when she had gotten as far as "It's just this"—she stopped again.

"Well, now, Polly," said Mr. King, sitting straight on the sofa, with displeasure, "I must say, I am surprised at you. I should never think this was you, Polly, never in all the world," which so unnerved her, that she plunged at once into what she had set herself to do, saying the most dreadful thing that was possible.

"O, Grandpapa!" she cried, "do you think it can be right to take Jasper away from his work?"

"Hoity-toity! Well, I must say, Polly," exclaimed the old gentleman in the greatest displeasure, and rising abruptly from the sofa, brushing her aside as he did so, "that I never have been so surprised in my life, as to have you come to teach me my duty. Right? Of course it is—it must be, if I wish it. I have always looked out for Jasper's good," with that he walked up and down the parlor, fuming at every step, and looking so very dreadful, that Polly, rooted to the spot, had only to stand still, and watch him in despair.

"If you could have seen Jasper, the way he was when I found him," said Mr. King, tired at last of vituperating, and coming up to Polly sternly, "you would be glad to have me get him out of the wretched business. It smelt so of trade, and everybody was grossly familiar; while that Mr. Marlowe—I have no words for him, Polly. He insulted me."

"Oh!—oh!" cried Polly, with clasped hands and flaming cheeks. "How could he, Grandpapa? Jasper has always said he was such a gentleman."

"Jasper's ideas of what a gentleman should be, and mine, are very different," exploded the old gentleman, beginning to walk up and down the parlor again. "I tell you, Polly, that my boy is sadly changed since he went into that contemptible trade."

"But Jasper loves his work," mourned Polly, her color dying down.

"Loves his work? Well, he shouldn't," cried Mr. King in extreme irritation. "It's no sort of a work for him to love, brought up as he has been. A profession is the only thing for him. Now he studies law"—

"O, Grandpapa!" cried Polly, quite white now, and she precipitated herself in front of the old gentleman's angry feet, "Jasper just hates the law. I know, for he has often said so; and if you do fasten him down all his life to what he don't like, and make him be a lawyer, it will kill him. He'll do it, Grandpapa"—Polly rushed on, regardless of the lightning gleam of anger in the sharp eyes above her; and, although she knew that after this she should never be the same Polly to him as of old, she kept on steadily—"because you want him to; he'll do anything to please you, and make you happy, Grandpapa, and he won't say anything, but it will kill him; it surely will, for he loves his work with Mr. Marlowe so." Then Polly stopped, aghast at the effect of her words.

"And what am I to do now, pray, to please you?" asked old Mr. King, and drawing off to look at her quite coldly.

"Oh! nothing to please me," cried poor Polly; "only for Jasper. Do let him go back to Mr. Marlowe, Grandpapa."

"He shall never go back to Mr. Marlowe with my consent," declared the old gentleman stiffly, his anger rising again, "and you have displeased me very much, Polly Pepper, by all this. Now you may go; and remember, not another word about Jasper and his work. I will arrange everything concerning him without interference." And Polly, not knowing how crept out of Mrs. Higby's parlor, and shut the door.

*"Oh, Why Did I Speak?" Cried Polly Over And Over.*

"Polly!" somebody called, as she hurried on unsteady feet over the stairs to her own little room that she had begged under the farmhouse eaves. But she didn't even answer, only rushed on, and locked the door behind her. Then she threw herself on her knees by the bed, and buried her face in her hands. This was worse than the day so long ago when she sat in the old rocking-chair in the little brown house, with eyes bound closely to shut out all outside things; and all of them had been afraid she was going to be blind. For now she felt sure that she had spoiled whatever chance there might have been for Jasper. "Oh! why did I speak—why did I?" she cried, over and over in her distress, as she buried her face deeper yet in Mrs. Higby's gay patch bedquilt.

After a while—Polly never could tell how long she had staid there—somebody rapped at the door. It was Phronsie; and she cried in a grieved little voice, "Polly, are you here? I've been under the apple-trees—and just everywhere for you. Do let me in."

"I can't now, Pet," cried Polly, trying not to let her voice sound choked with tears; "you run away, dear; Polly will let you in by and by."

"Are you sick, Polly?" cried Phronsie anxiously, and kneeling down to put her mouth to the keyhole.

"No, not a bit," said Polly hastily, and trying to speak cheerfully.

"Really, Polly?"

"Really and truly, Phronsie; there, run away, dear, if you love me."

Phronsie, at this, unwillingly crept off, and still Polly knelt on, with the wild remorse tugging at her heart that she had been the one to injure Jasper's prospects for life.

And then the dinner-bell rang, and Polly, who was never known to be late at a meal, heard Mrs. Higby come out into the hall again, and shake the big bell till it seemed to fill the whole farmhouse with its noise.

"Oh! I can't go down—I can't!" moaned poor Polly to herself, quite lost to everything but the dreadful distress at the mischief she had wrought. And then Phronsie came again, this time imploring, with tears—for Polly felt quite sure that she could hear her crying—that Polly would only open the door, "and let me see you just once, Polly!"

And even Mrs. Cabot came, and Polly thought she should go wild to have her stand outside there and beg and insist that Polly should come down to them all.

***"Are You Sick, Polly?" Cried Phronsie A[Illustration: "Are You Sick, Polly?" Cried Phronsie Anxiously.]Nxiously.***

"I don't want any dinner," said Polly over and over. "I just must be alone a little while," and at last she spoke quickly to Mrs. Cabot's persistent pleadings, "Have the goodness, Mrs. Cabot, not to call me again." And then she was sorry the minute she had spoken the words, and she opened her door a little crack to call after Mrs. Cabot, as she sailed downstairs in great displeasure, "Oh! do forgive me, dear Mrs. Cabot, for speaking so. I am very sorry, but I cannot come down just yet."

"I shall send you up your dinner, then," said Mrs. Cabot, only half appeased, and pausing on the stairs.

"No, no!" begged Polly, and she seemed so distressed at the mere thought, that Mrs. Cabot unwillingly let her have her way about it.

It was in the middle of the afternoon, and Polly, exhausted by weeping, had fallen asleep just where she was, on her knees by the bed, her head on the gay bedquilt, when a low knock on the door startled her and made her rub her eyes and listen.

"Polly," said a voice—it was Jasper's—"won't you undo the door? I want to speak to you."

"O, Jasper!" cried Polly, springing to her feet, and running over to the door, "I can't; don't ask me—not just yet."

"I won't ask you again," said Jasper, "if you don't wish it, Polly."

His voice showed his disappointment, and Polly, full of dismay at the trouble she had made for him, couldn't find it in her heart to cause him this new worry.

"You won't want to speak to me, Jasper," she cried, unlocking the door with trembling fingers, "when you know what I have done."

"What, Polly?" he cried, trying not to show how he felt at sight of the swollen eyelids and downcast face. Meanwhile he drew her out gently into the hall. "There, let us sit down here," pausing before the wide window-seat; "it's quiet here, and nobody will be likely to come here." He waited till Polly sat down, then made a place for himself beside her.

"Jasper," cried Polly, lifting her brown eyes, now filling with tears again, "you can't think what I've done. I've ruined your whole life for you!"

"How, Polly?" Jasper's face grew pale to his lips. "Oh! do tell me at once," yet he seemed to be afraid of what she was about to say.

"O, Jasper! I thought perhaps I could help you. I never knew till this morning, just before you came, that you had lost your place. Mrs. Cabot had a letter from her husband, and she told me. And I spoke to Grandpapa and begged him to let you go back, and, O, Jasper!" here Polly's tears, despite all her efforts to keep them back, fell in a shower, "you can't guess how dreadfully

Grandpapa feels, and he says—oh! he says that you are to study law, and never, never go back to Mr. Marlowe."

"Is that all?" exclaimed Jasper in such a tone of relief that Polly sprang to her feet and stared at him through dry eyes.

"All?" she gasped. "O, Jasper! I thought you loved your work."

# CHAPTER XXII

# MR KING AND POLLY

"So I do love my work," cried Jasper in a glow, "but, Polly," and he sprang to his feet and walked away so that she couldn't see his face, "I thought that you were going to say something about yourself."

Then he turned around and faced her again.

"O, Jasper!" exclaimed Polly reproachfully, "what could I possibly have to say about myself! How can I think of anything when you are in trouble?"

"Forgive me, Polly," broke in Jasper eagerly, and he took her hand, "and don't worry about me; I mean, don't think that what you said to Grandpapa made any difference."

"But indeed it did, Jasper," declared Polly truthfully; "oh! I know it did, and I have done it all."

"Polly—Polly!" begged Jasper in great distress, "don't, dear!"

"And now you must give it all up and go into the law—oh! the horrid, hateful law; oh! what will you do, Jasper?" And she gazed up into his face pityingly.

"I shall have to go," said Jasper, drawing his breath hard, and looking at her steadily. "You know you yourself told me long ago to make my father happy any way, Polly." He smiled as he emphasized the last word.

"Oh! I know," cried Polly in despair, "but I didn't think it could ever be anything as bad as this, Jasper."

"'Any way' means pretty hard lines sometimes, Polly," said Jasper. "Well, there's no help for it now, so you must help me to go through with it."

"And just think," mourned Polly, looking as if the shower were about to fall again, "how I've made it worse for you with Grandpapa. O, Jasper! I shall never be any help to you."

"Polly!" exclaimed Jasper, in such a tone that she stopped to look at him in astonishment. "There, now, I'll tell you all about it," he added with his usual manner, and sitting down beside her again, "and then you'll see that nothing on earth made any difference to father. This was the way of it," and Jasper proceeded to lay before her every detail of Mr. King's visit to him, and all the circumstances at the store, not omitting Mr. Whitney's part in the affair, as shown by the letter that Jasper had seen.

"Oh, oh! how mean," interrupted Polly at this point, with flashing brown eyes; "how could he?" and her lips curled disdainfully.

"Oh! Mason thought he was doing me the greatest favor in the world, I don't doubt," answered Jasper. "You know, Polly, he never could bear to hear of the publishing business, and he was so disappointed when I wouldn't go into the law."

"I know," said Polly, "but this was dreadful, to meddle—after you had once decided; very, very dreadful!"

"I think so," said Jasper, with a laugh; feeling surprisingly light-hearted, it was so beautiful to be talking it all over with Polly, "but the trouble is, Mason don't. Well, and then came that dreadful misunderstanding about Mr. Marlowe; that hurt me worse than all. O, Polly! if you only knew the man," and Jasper relapsed into gloom once more.

"O, dear, dear!" cried Polly sympathetically, and clasping her hands. "What can we do; isn't there anything to do?"

"No," said Jasper, "absolutely nothing. When father once makes up his mind about anything, it's made up for all time. I must just lose the friendship of that man, as well as my place." With that his gloom deepened, and Polly, feeling powerless to utter a word, slipped her hand within his as it lay on his knee.

He looked up and smiled gratefully. "You see, Polly, we can't say anything to him."

"Oh! no, no," cried Polly in horror at the mere thought; "I've only made it a great deal worse."

"No, you haven't made it worse, dear; but we shouldn't do any good to talk to him about it."

"I don't believe I could live," cried Polly, off her guard, "to have him look at me, and to hear him speak so again, Jasper."

Jasper started, while a frown spread over his face. "I can bear anything but that you should be hurt, Polly," he exclaimed, his fingers tightening over hers.

"Oh! I don't mind it so much," cried Polly, recovering herself hastily, "if I hadn't made mischief for you."

"And that you never must think of again. Promise me, Polly."

"I'll try not to," said Polly.

"You must just put the notion out of your mind whenever it comes in," said Jasper decidedly; "you'll promise that, Polly, I know you will."

"Well," said Polly reluctantly, "I will, Jasper."

"All right," exclaimed Jasper, in great satisfaction.

"Polly—Polly." Phronsie's yellow head came up above the stairs, and presently Phronsie came running up to them in great haste.

"O, Polly!" and she threw her arms hungrily around Polly and hugged her closely. "O, dear!" letting her arms fall, "I wasn't to stop a minute. Grandpapa wants you to drive with him, Polly, and you are to go right down as soon as you get your hat on."

"Grandpapa!" screamed Polly, jumping off from the window-seat so hastily that Phronsie nearly fell over, while Jasper was hardly less excited. "Why, Phronsie, you can't mean it. He"—

"Father really wants you, Polly, I know," broke in Jasper, with a look into the brown eyes. But his voice shook, and if Phronsie hadn't been so worried over Polly, she would certainly have noticed it.

"Polly hasn't had any dinner," she said in a troubled way.

"Oh! I don't care for dinner," cried Polly, with another look at Jasper, and beginning to dance off to her room for her hat.

"But you must have some," declared Phronsie in gentle authority, going toward the stairs, "and I shall just ask Grandpapa to wait for you to get it. Mrs. Higby saved your dinner for you, Polly"—

"Oh! I couldn't eat a morsel," protested Polly from her little room, "and don't ask Grandpapa to wait an instant, whatever you do, Phronsie. See, I'm ready," and she ran out into the hall, putting on her hat as she spoke.

"Get her a glass of milk, Phronsie," called Jasper, standing by the stair-railing; "that's a good child."

Polly flashed him a grateful look as she dashed down the stairs, drawing on her gloves, and not daring to look forward to meeting Grandpapa.

But when she came out to the back piazza, Phronsie following her with the glass, and begging her to drink up the rest left in it, old Mr. King, standing by the little old-fashioned chaise, received her exactly as if nothing had happened.

"Well, I declare, Polly," he said, turning to her with a smile, "I never saw anybody get ready so quickly as you can. There, hop in, child," and he put aside her dress from the wheel in his most courtly manner possible.

"Polly hasn't had all the milk," said Phronsie, by the chaise-step, holding up the glass anxiously.

"Well, I don't believe she wants it," said old Mr. King.

***"Polly Hasn't Had All The Milk," Said Phronsie***

"No, I don't," said Polly, from the depths of the old chaise. "I couldn't drink it, dear."

Mr. King bent his white head to kiss Phronsie, and then they drove away, and left her standing in the lilac-shaded path, her glass in her hand, and looking after them.

All sorts of things Mr. King talked of in the cheeriest manner possible, just as if Polly and he were in the habit of taking a drive like this every morning; and he never seemed to notice her swollen eyelids, or whether she answered, but kept on bravely with the conversation. At last Polly, at something he said, laughed in her old merry fashion; then Mr. King drew a long breath, and relaxed his efforts.

"I declare, Polly," he said, leaning back in a comfortable way against the old cushion, and allowing the neighbor's horse, hired for the occasion, to amble along in its own fashion, "now we are so cosy, I believe I'll tell you a secret."

Polly stopped laughing and gazed at him.

"How would you like to take a little journey, just you and I, to-morrow?" he asked, looking down into her face.

"A journey, Grandpapa?" asked Polly wonderingly.

"Yes; about as far as—-say, well, to the place where Jasper has been all winter. The fact is, Polly," went on Mr. King very rapidly, as if with the fear that if he stopped he would not be able to finish at all, "I want you to look over the ground—Jasper's work, I mean. It seems an abominable place to me—a perfectly abominable one," confided the old gentleman in a burst of feeling, "but there," pulling himself up, "maybe I'm not the one to say it. You see, Polly, I never did a stroke of work in my life, and I really can't tell how working-places ought to look. And I suppose a working man like Mr. Marlowe might be different from me, and yet be a decent sort of a person, after all. Well, will you go?" he asked abruptly.

"O, Grandpapa!" cried Polly, aghast, and turning in the chaise to look at him with wide eyes.

"Yes, I really mean it," nodded old Mr. King, in his most decided fashion, "although I don't blame you for thinking me funny, child."

"I was only thinking how good you are Grandpapa!" exclaimed Polly fervently, and creeping up close to his side.

"There—there, Polly, child," said the old gentleman, "no more of that, else we shall have a scene, and that's what I never did like, dear, you know. Well, will you go with me—you haven't said yes yet."

"Oh! yes, yes, yes," cried Polly, in a rapturous shout, not taking her glowing eyes off from his face.

"Take care, you'll scare the natives," warned old Mr. King, beaming at her. "Brierly folks couldn't have any such transports, Polly," as they turned down a shady lane and ambled by a quiet farmhouse.

"Well, they ought to," replied Polly merrily, peering out at the still, big house. "O, Grandpapa! I just want to get out and jump and scream. I don't feel any bigger than Phronsie."

"Well, I much rather have you here in this carriage with me," said the old gentleman composedly. "Now that's settled that we are going, Polly. Of course I asked the doctor; I sent down a letter to him after dinner, to ask if your arm would let you take a little journey with me, and of course he said 'yes,' like a sensible man. Why shouldn't he, pray tell—when we were all going home in a day or two? Now, of course, that must be postponed a bit."

"Never mind," Polly hastened to say, "if Jasper is only fixed up."

"Now, Polly," Mr. King shifted his position a bit, so that he might see her the better, "perhaps Mr. Marlowe won't take Jasper back. Judging from what I know of the man, I don't think he will," and the old gentleman's face, despite his extreme care, began to look troubled at once.

"Oh! maybe he will," cried Polly warmly. "Grandpapa, I shouldn't wonder at all—he must!" she added positively.

"I don't know, Polly," he said, in a worried way. "I think it's very doubtful; indeed, from what I know of business now, I don't believe at all that he will. But then, we can try."

"Oh! we can try," echoed Polly hopefully, and feeling as if, since God was good, he would let Jasper back into his chosen life-work.

"Well, we'll start early to-morrow morning on our little trip, Polly," said the old gentleman, catching her infectious spirit, and giving the old horse a fillip with the whip. "Meantime, not a word, my dear, of our little plan!"

So Polly promised the deepest secrecy, and that no one should even have a hint from her looks, of what Grandpapa and she were to do.

And the next morning, although everybody was nearly devoured by curiosity, no one dared to ask questions; so old Mr. King and Polly, with two well-filled portmanteaus, departed for a journey of apparently a few days; and Polly didn't dare to trust herself alone with Jasper, but ran a race with him around all the angles of the old farmhouse, always cleverly disappearing with a merry laugh when there was the least chance of his overtaking her and cornering her for an explanation.

And Pickering Dodge, in his invalid chair drawn close to the window, heard the merry preparations for the journey, and fretfully declared "that people seem to be happy, with never a thought for a poor dog like me," while old Mr. Loughead, who, despite Doctor Bryce's verdict, had never seemed quite well enough in his own estimation for his departure from the "Higby hospital," on the contrary brightened up, exclaiming, "Now, that is something like—to hear Miss Polly laugh like that—bless her!"

"Good-by, Pickering," said Polly, coming into his room, old Mr. King close behind; "I am going away with Grandpapa for a day or two," and she came up in her traveling hat and gown close to his chair.

"So I heard," said Pickering, lifting his pale face, and trying to seem glad, for Polly's joy was bubbling over. But he made rather a poor show of it.

"Good-by to you, my boy," said Mr. King, laying a soft palm over the thin fingers on Pickering's knee. "Now see that you get up a little more vigor by the time we are back. Goodness! all you want is a trifle more backbone. Why, an old fellow like me would beat you there, I do believe. I am surprised at you," cried the old gentleman, shaking his fingers at Mr. Loughead, with whom he was on the best of terms, but never feeling the necessity to weigh his words, "that you, being chief nurse, don't set up with that boy and make him get on his feet quicker."

"So I could do," cried old Mr. Loughead, whose chief object in life since Pickering had been pronounced out of danger, had been to browbeat the trained nurse, and usurp the authority in Pickering's sick-room, "if Mrs. Cabot would keep out, or take it into her head to return home. To state it mildly," continued the old gentleman, not lowering his tone in the least, "that lady doesn't seem to be gifted with the qualities of a nurse. Providence never intended that she should be one, in my opinion."

"Don't tell him to bully me worse than he does," cried Pickering. "He shows a frightful hand when he wants his own way."

"That's it," cried old Mr. King delightedly; "only just keep it up. You'll get well fast, as long as you can fight. Come on, Polly, my girl, or we shall be late for the train."

The evening before, Jack Loughead ran up the steps to Miss Salisbury's "Select School for Young Ladies," and pulled the bell hastily.

Amy ran down as quickly to the little room where she was always allowed to see her brother.

"Well, Amy, child," cried Jack, when they had gone through with the preliminaries always religiously observed on his visits: how she had progressed in her music under the new teacher Miss Pepper had recommended during her enforced absence, and how far she had pleased Miss Salisbury, and all the other things an elder brother who had come to his conscience rather late, would be apt to look into. "And so you really think you are getting on in your practice?"

"O, yes, Jack!" cried Amy confidently. "Come and see; I've a new Beethoven for you," and she laid hold of his arm with eager fingers. "Now, you'll be immensely surprised, Jack—immensely."

"No doubt, no doubt," answered Jack hastily, and not offering to get up from the sofa, "but you needn't play it now."

"Why, Jack," cried Amy, no little offended, "what's the matter? You've asked me regularly to play you my pieces, and now to-night when I offer to, you won't have any of it," and she began to pout.

"That's shabby in me," declared Jack, with remorse; and getting off the sofa, to his feet, he dutifully spread the music on the rack, and paid his little sister such attention, that she was soon smilingly launched into the new piece, and lost to everything else but her own melody.

"That's fine!" pronounced Jack, as Amy declared herself through, and whirled around on the music-stool for his applause. But his heart wasn't in it, and Amy's blue eyes soon found it out.

"You're not a bit like yourself to-night, Brother Jack," she cried, with another pout and staring at him.

"You're right; I'm not, Amy," declared Jack. "Come over to the sofa, and I'll tell you about it."

So the two turned their backs on the piano; and pretty soon, Amy, her hand in her brother's big brown palm, was nestled up against him, and hearing a confidence that made her small soul swell with delight.

"Amy," said Jack, putting his arm closer around her, "when Miss Pepper had the courage to tell me of my duty to you, I made up my mind that you should never want for anything that my hand could supply."

"And I never have," cried little Amy, poking her head up from its nest to look at him. "All the girls say you are just splendid to me; that they never saw such a brother; and I don't believe they ever did, Jack," she added proudly.

"So now, what I am about to do," said Jack, speaking with great effort, "isn't to bring anything but the greatest happiness to you, Amy, as well as to me. If only I can secure it!" he added under his breath.

"What are you going to do, Jack?" demanded Amy, springing away from him to stare into his bronzed face. "Oh! I know; you are going to Europe again, and will take me this time—oh! goody, goody!" She screamed like a child, clapping her hands gaily.

"Hush, Amy," cried Jack, trying to speak lightly, "or Miss Salisbury will come in, and send me off, saying I spoil your manners. There, come back here to me; I can talk better then," and he drew her to his side again. "No, it is something much more beautiful than any trip to Europe would be."

"It can't be. Jack," cried Amy positively, and burrowing her sunny head into his waistcoat.

"Listen—and don't interrupt again," said her big brother. "Amy—how can I tell it? Amy, if Miss Pepper will—will marry me, I will bless God all my life!"

This time Amy sprang to the middle of the floor of Miss Salisbury's small reception-room. "Marry you, Brother Jack!" she screamed. "Oh! how perfectly elegant! It's too lovely for anything—oh! my darling Miss Pepper," and so on, till Jack couldn't make her hear a word.

"Amy—Amy," at last he said, getting up to her, to lay an imperative hand on her arm, "what would Miss Pepper say—don't get so excitable, child—to see you now? Do hush!"

"I know it," said Amy, stopping instantly, and creeping humbly back to the sofa; "Miss Pepper was always telling me how to stop screaming at everything I liked; and not to cry at things I didn't like," she confessed frankly.

"Well, then, if you love her," said Jack, going back to sit down by her again, "you will try to do what she says. And you do love her, I am quite sure, Amy."

***Amy.***

"I love her so," declared Amy, "that I would do any and everything she ever asked me to, Brother Jack."

"I thought so," said Jack. "Well, now, Amy, I must tell you that I went to see Mrs. Fisher to-day, to ask her if I may speak to Miss Pepper. And she gives me full permission; and so I shall go to Brierly to-morrow, and try my fate."

"It won't be any trying at all," cried Amy superbly, and stretching her neck to look up with immense pride at her tall brother. "She can't help loving you, Jack! Oh! I am so happy."

Jack Loughead's dark face had a grave look on it as he glanced down at her. "I hope so," he said simply.

## CHAPTER XXIII

# THAT SETTLES MANY THINGS

"It's perfectly dreadful," cried Alexia Rhys, wrinkling her brows, "to try to get up anything with Polly away. If we only had Joel to help us, that would be something"—

"Well, it's got to be done," said Clem Forsythe, in a matter-of-fact way.

"Of course it has," cried Alexia gustily. "Dear me," in a tone of horror, "did you suppose that we'd let Polly Pepper go on year after year getting up perfectly elegant things for us, and then we not celebrate for her, when she comes home, and with a broken arm, too? The idea, Clem!"

"Well, then I think we much better set to work to think up something," observed Clem wisely, "if we are going to do anything."

"We can't think of a single thing—not one," bemoaned Alexia; "it will be a perfectly horrid fright, whatever we get up. Oh, dear! what shall we do, girls?"

"Alexia, you are enough to drive anybody wild," cried Sally Moore; "it's bad enough to know there isn't an idea in all our heads put together, without having you tell us of it every minute. Cathie Harrison, why don't you say something, instead of staring that wall out of countenance?"

"Because I haven't anything to say," replied Cathie, laughing grimly and leaning back in her chair resignedly. "Oh, dear! I think just as Alexia does, it will be utterly horrid whatever we do."

"Don't you be a wet blanket," cried two or three of the girls, "if Alexia is. Oh, dear! Miss Chatterton, you are the only one of sense in this company. Now do give us an idea," added one.

"I don't know in the least how to help," said Charlotte Chatterton slowly, and leaning her elbows on her knees she rested her head in her hands. "I never got up a play or tableau, nor anything of the kind in my life; and we never celebrated anything either; there was never anything to celebrate—but I should think perhaps it would be better not to try to do great things."

"Why, Miss Chatterton," exclaimed Alexia Rhys, in great disapproval, and starting forward in the pretty pink-trimmed basket chair. "I'm perfectly surprised at you—nothing can be too good for Polly Pepper. We must get up something perfectly magnificent, or else I shall die!" she cried tragically.

"Nothing can be too good for Polly," repeated Charlotte, taking her head out of her hands and looking at Alexia, "but isn't it better not to try to be too grand, and have something simple, because, whatever we do, Polly must always have had things so much nicer."

"In other words, it's better to hit what you aim at, than to shoot at the clouds and bring down nothing," said Clem sententiously.

"Yes—yes, I think so," cried Cathie, clapping her hands; "it's awfully vulgar to try to cut a dash—that is, if you can't do it," she added quickly.

***"Nothing Can Be Too Good For Polly Pepper!" Cried Alexia, Starting Forward.***

"Don't say 'awfully,'" corrected Alexia, readjusting herself in her pink-and-white chair. "Well, I suppose you are right, Miss Chatterton; you're always right; being, as I said, a person of sense."

Charlotte gave a short laugh, but with a little bitter edge to it. Why would the girls who now seemed to be so glad to have her in the center of all their plans, persist in calling her Miss Chatterton? It gave her a chill every time, and she fairly hated the name.

"And now since we are going to follow your advice," went on Alexia, "be so good as to tell us a little bit more. Now what shall we do in the way of a simple, appropriate fandango—a perfect idyl of a thing, you know?"

"Well," said Charlotte quietly, "you know in the olden time at Christmas"—

"But this isn't Christmas," cried Alexia, interrupting with an uneasy gesture.

"Do be still," cried the other girls, pulling at her, "and let Miss Chatterton finish"—

"At Christmas ages ago, when special honor was done to entertain the King wherever he was lodged," went on Charlotte, "there was a Lord of Misrule, who gathered together a company of ladies and gentlemen, who rummaged the old castles for grotesque costumes and furbelows. And then masked, they all came in and marched before the King, and danced, oh—everything—we might have Minuets and Highland Flings, and all the rest. And they did everything the Lord of Misrule directed, and"—

"Charlotte Chatterton, you are a jewel!" cried Alexia, tumbling out of her chair, and flying at her, which example was followed by all the other girls.

"Thank you," cried Charlotte, with glistening eyes.

"Thank you? I guess we do thank you," cried Sally Moore heartily, "for getting us out of this scrape."

"Oh! I don't mean that," said Charlotte indifferently, "I mean because you called me by my first name, the same as you girls always talk to each other."

There was a little pause. "Oh! we didn't know as you'd like it," broke in Alexia hastily, "you are so tall, and you never seem in a hurry, nor as if you cared a straw about being like a girl, and we didn't dare. But now, oh, Charlotte—Charlotte!" And she gave her a hug that well repaid Charlotte for all the past.

"That's a regular bear-hug," she cried at last, releasing her and taking a long breath, "and equal to a few dozen common every-day ones."

"If Charlotte can breathe after that," said Clem, turning on Charlotte a pair of glowing eyes, "she'll do well. We are just as glad to call you Charlotte, aren't we, girls," whirling around on the group, "as Alexia, for all her bear-hug."

"Yes—yes," cried the whole bevy.

"Well, now, girls," said Alexia, running over to give Clem a small shake, "let's to business. There isn't any time to waste. Charlotte Chatterton, will you tell us the rest of it, and who will be the Lord of Misrule?—dear me, if we only had Joel here!"

"I think Doctor Fisher would be the Lord of Misrule," said Charlotte; "he said he'd do anything we wanted of him, to help out."

The girls one and all gave a small howl, and clapped their hands, crying, "Capital—capital!"

"Let's go and ask him now!" cried Alexia, who wasn't anything if not energetic; and running to her closet, she picked off her hat from the shelf and tossed it on her head. "Oh, how slow you are, girls—do hurry!" as the others flew to the bed where their different head-gear had been thrown.

"But it's his office hours," said Charlotte, hating in her new-found happiness at being one with the girls, to put a damper on their plan.

"Bother! supposing it is," exclaimed Alexia, in front of her pink-and-white draped mirror, while she ran the long hat pins through her fluffy hair, "it's as important to take care of us girls, as if we were a lot of patients. We shall be, if we don't get this fixed. Come on, girls!" she seized a lace scarf from some mysterious corner, and pranced to the door, shaking her gloves at the group.

"I don't think we ought to go, now," said Charlotte distinctly, not offering to join the merry scramble for the wearing apparel on the bed.

"Charlotte Chatterton!" cried Alexia, thoroughly annoyed, "aren't you ashamed of yourself? Don't listen to her, girls, but come on," and she ran out to the head of the stairs.

The other girls all stopped short.

"I don't think Polly would like it, and it isn't right," said Charlotte, hating to preach, but standing her ground. At this Alexia, out in the hall, came running back.

"Oh! dear—dear, it's perfectly dreadful to be with such good people! There, now, Charlotte, don't look like that," rushing up to the tall girl and standing on tiptoe to drop a kiss on the sallow cheek—"we won't go; we'll stay at home and be martyrs," and she began to tear off her hat with a tragic air.

"Why not go to Madam Dyce's and ask her to loan us some of her old brocades and bonnets?" proposed Cathie Harrison suddenly. "She's got a perfect lot of horrible antiques."

"The very thing!" cried Alexia, the others coming in as chorus.

Charlotte Chatterton rushed as happily as any of them for her walking things. "And then Doctor Fisher's office hours may be over, and we may stop there on our way home," she cried.

Doctor Fisher's office hours were not only over, but the little doctor assured one and all of the eager group that precipitated themselves upon him, that nothing would give him greater delight than to be a Lord of Misrule at the celebration to be gotten up for the home-coming.

"And it's a very appropriate way to celebrate, my dears," he said, beaming at them over his large spectacles; "for it will be for the coming of the King; King by name as well as nature," and he laughed enjoyably at his own pun. "And I'm sure nobody ever did rule his kingdom so well as our Grandpapa. So let's have a splendid mummery, or masquing, or whatever you call it; and in my opinion, you were very smart to think it up."

Thereupon Alexia pulled Charlotte Chatterton unwillingly into the center of the group that surrounded the little doctor. "We didn't; it was all Charlotte," she said.

Doctor Fisher took a long look at the pink spot on Charlotte's sallow cheek, and into her happy eyes, then he turned and surveyed the bevy.

"We'll have a good time, my dears," he said.

"Now, Polly," exclaimed old Mr. King, drawing her back an instant before stepping into Farmer Higby's big carryall, waiting at the station as the train came in, "you mustn't even look as if you had any secret on your mind—oh, come now, that won't do, my dear," turning her around to study the dancing eyes and rosy cheeks. "I can't take you home looking like that, I really can't, my dear."

Polly tried to pull down her face, but with such poor success that the old gentleman sighed in dismay.

"Well, you must be careful to keep away from everybody as much as you can," he whispered, as he helped her into the ancient vehicle, "and whatever you do, don't say much to Jasper, or you'll surely let the whole thing out," and he got in beside her. "There, drive on, do, Mr. Higby."

"You'll tell Jasper that he is to go back to Mr. Marlowe?" Polly leaned over and was guilty of whispering behind Farmer Higby's broad back. "Oh, Grandpapa! you won't keep him waiting to know that, will you?" she begged anxiously.

"No; that shall be at once, as soon as I see my boy," replied the old gentleman; "but, the rest, Polly; how Mr. Marlowe is coming to look in upon us at our own home, and to meet us the very evening we arrive—that's to be kept as dark as possible."

"Yes, indeed," cried Polly, getting back into her own corner with a happy little wriggle, all unconscious of Grandpapa's conspiracy with Mother Fisher in regard to the home-coming.

"For if I can't have the surprise party I started for," declared the old gentleman to himself, "I'll have a jollification at the other end." So he had telegraphed to Mrs. Fisher an additional message to his many letters, all on the same subject—"Have what celebration you like, and invite whom you like. And let it be gay, for the College boys have got leave, and they bring a friend."

And at such intervals when he could take his mind from Jasper and his affairs, it afforded Mr. King infinite delight to tap a certain letter in his breast pocket, that opened, might have revealed in bold characters, a great deal of gratitude for his kindness in inviting the writer on with Joel, which was gladly accepted and signed Robert Bingley.

"Where's Jasper?" said Mr. King, as he and Polly got out of the carryall into the bustle of the farmhouse delight over their return.

"He's gone fishing with Phronsie," said Mrs. Cabot; "we didn't any of us expect you till this afternoon."

"Goodness me! couldn't they go fishing any other day?" cried the old gentleman irascibly. "Well, I suppose there's no help for it. Ah! Loughead, that you?" extending a cordial hand to the tall figure waiting at the end of the porch till the family greetings were over; "glad to see you."

But Jack Loughead had no eyes for anybody but Polly's happy face; and he barely touched the extended palm, while he mumbled something about being glad to be there; then awkwardly stood still.

Mrs. Cabot, who evidently did not regard him in the friendliest of lights, turned her back upon him, keeping her arm around Polly. "Pickering is waiting to see you," she said, and trying to draw her off.

"I'll come in a minute," said Polly, breaking away from her, and taking a step toward Jack Loughead.

"How do you do?" she said, putting out her hand.

Jack Loughead seized it eagerly. "May I see you—just now?" he asked in a quick, low voice. "I have your mother's permission to tell you something"—

"From Mamsie," cried Polly, her beaming face breaking into fresh smiles; "yes, indeed, Mr. Loughead."

"About—myself," stumbled Jack truthfully, "but your mother gave me permission to speak to you. Will you go down the lane, Miss Pepper, while I can tell you?"

So Polly, despite Mrs. Cabot's calls "Come, Polly," nodded to Grandpapa, who said, "All right, child, don't be gone long," and moved off with Jack Loughead "down the lane," fresh with spring blossoms and gay with bird songs.

"I don't know how," said Jack Loughead, after a moment's pause, during which Polly had lifted her face to look at him wonderingly, "to tell you. I have never been among ladies, and my mother died when I was fifteen; since that I

***He Walked Off, Leaving Polly Alone In The Lane***

have been working hard, and known no other life. You have been so kind to Amy," he said suddenly, as if there were a refuge in the words.

"Oh, don't put it that way," cried Polly, full of sympathy, "Amy is a dear little thing; I am very fond of her."

He turned glad eyes on her. "Yes, I know. And when you spoke to me and showed me my duty, I"—

"Oh!" cried Polly, with cheeks aflame, "don't make me think of that time. How could I speak so, and to you, who know so much more of duty than I ever could imagine? Pray forget it, Mr. Loughead," she begged.

"I can't," said Jack Loughead gravely, "for it was the kindest thing I ever supposed one could say to another—and then—I from that time—loved you, Miss Pepper!"

Polly Pepper stopped short in the lane. "Oh, don't—don't!" she begged, and covered her face with her hands.

"I must tell you," said Jack Loughead, still gravely, and standing quietly to look at her; "and I have come to ask you to marry me."

"Oh!" cried Polly again, and not daring to look at him, "I am so sorry," she cried, "I wouldn't hurt you for all the world, Mr. Loughead."

"I know it," he said, waiting for her to finish.

"For—for, I do like you so much—so very much," cried poor Polly, wishing the birds wouldn't sing so loud. "You have taught me so much, oh, so much, I can't tell you, Mr. Loughead, about being true and noble, and"—

He waited patiently till she began again.

"But I couldn't marry you; oh, I couldn't," here Polly forced herself to look at him, but her head went down again at sight of his face.

***"My! What A Sight Of Fish! Exclaimed Mrs. Higby, Dropping To Her Knees Beside The Basket.***

"You sha'n't be troubled," said Jack Loughead gently, "I'll take myself out of the way, and make all excuses at the house."

"Oh! do forgive me," Polly sprang after him, to call.

He turned and tried to smile, then walked off, leaving Polly standing in the lane.

"Jasper," said Mrs. Cabot in great irritation, when Jasper and Phronsie wandered into Mrs. Farmer Higby's neat kitchen a half-hour later, with torn garments and muddy shoes, "they got home while you were away, and that tiresome Mr. Loughead came a little before them; and he made Polly go to walk with him; actually made her!" Mrs. Cabot leaned her jeweled hands on

Mrs. Higby's spotless pine table, and regarded him in great distress.

Jasper bent his broad straw hat over the basket of fish a minute.

"Oh!" screamed Phronsie, clapping grimy little hands and darting off, "have they come?"

"My! what a sight of fish," exclaimed Mrs. Higby, getting down on her knees before the basket. "Now I s'pose you want some fried for dinner, don't you, Mr. Jasper?"

"Yes," said Jasper, bringing his gaze off from the fish, "I think they better be, Mrs. Higby," and he went out of the kitchen without looking at Mrs. Cabot.

Up at the head of the stairs he ran against Jack Loughead.

"It's all against me, King," said Jack unsteadily.

Jasper lifted heavy eyes, that, all at once, held a lightning gleam. Then he put his good right hand on Jack's shoulder.

"I'm sorry for you," he said.

"One thing, King," said Jack gratefully, "will you have an eye to my uncle? He won't come with me now, but insists on going with your father who kindly invited us both to go home with you all. And when he is ready, just telegraph me and I will meet him at New York."

"I'll do it gladly," said Jasper, quite shocked at Jack's appearance; "anything more, Loughead? Do let me help you."

"Nothing," said Jack, without looking back.

# CHAPTER XXIV

# HOME

"I don't want to leave you, Mrs. Higby," said Phronsie slowly.

Mrs. Higby looked as if she were about to throw her apron over her head again. "You blessed child!" she exclaimed, half-crying and allowing her hands to rest on the rim of the dish-pan.

"You have been so very good to us," continued Phronsie, shaking her yellow head decidedly. "I love you, Mrs. Higby, very much indeed." With that she clasped the farmer's wife around her stout waist and held her closely.

"Dear—dear!" cried Mrs. Higby, violently caressing Phronsie; "you precious lamb, you, to think I sha'n't hear you pattering around any more, nor asking questions."

"I've made you ever so much trouble, Mrs. Higby," said Phronsie, in a penitent little voice, and enjoying to the fullest extent the petting she was receiving. "And I'm so sorry."

"Trouble!" exploded the farmer's wife, smoothing Phronsie's yellow hair with her large red hands, "the land! it's only a sight of comfort you've been. Why, I've just set by you!"

"I've come in here," said Phronsie, reflectively peering around at the spotless kitchen floor, "with muddy boots on and spoiled it; and I've talked when you wanted to weigh out things, and make cake, and once, don't you remember, Mrs. Higby, I left the pantry door open and the cat got in and ate up part of the custard pudding."

"Bless your heart!" exclaimed Mrs. Higby, with another squeeze, "I've forgot all about it."

"But I haven't," said Phronsie, with a sigh, "and I'm sorry."

"Well, now," said the farmer's wife, "I'll tell you how we will settle that; if you'll come again to the farm, and give my old eyes a sight of you, that'll make it all right."

"You're not old," cried Phronsie, wriggling enough out of Mrs. Higby's arms to look at the round red cheeks and bright eyes. "Oh, Mrs. Higby! and you're just as nice!" With that she clasped her impulsively around the neck. "And Pickering likes you too, Mrs. Higby," continued Phronsie, "he says you're as good as gold."

"You don't say so!" cried Mrs. Farmer Higby, intensely gratified; "well, he's as nice a boy as ever lived, I'm sure, and I'm just as tickled as I can be that that fever was broke up so sudden, for you see, Phronsie, he's got the making of being a right smart man yet."

"Grandpapa is going to have Pickering go home with us," said Phronsie, confidentially, and edging away from the farmer's wife to facilitate conversation. "And he's going to stay at our house with us till he gets nice and strong."

"Well, I'm dreadful glad of that," declared Mrs. Higby heartily, "for that a'nt of his—well, there, Phronsie, she ain't to my taste; she is such a making sort of woman—she comes in here and she wants to make me do this, and do that, till I'm most out of my wits, and I'd like to take my broom and say 'scat' as I do to the cat," and a black frown settled on Mrs. Higby's pleasant face.

Phronsie began to look quite grave. "She loves Pickering," she said thoughtfully, "and when he was so bad she cried almost all the time, Mrs. Higby."

"Oh! she loves him well enough," answered Mrs. Higby, "but she fusses over him so, and wants her way all the same. It would be good if she thought somebody else knew something once in a while," and she began to splash in the dish-pan vigorously to make up for lost time, quickly heaping up a pile of dishes to drain on the little old tray.

"Let me wipe them, do, Mrs. Higby," begged Phronsie eagerly, and without waiting for the permission she felt quite sure of, Phronsie picked up the long brown towel and set to work.

Upstairs Jasper and his father were going over again all the incidents of Mr. King's and Polly's trip, that the old gentleman was willing to communicate, and Jasper, despite his eagerness to know all the whys and wherefores, held himself in check as well as he could, scarcely realizing that he was really to go back to Mr. Marlowe's.

And Polly and Mrs. Cabot were busily packing, with the aid of a farmer's daughter who lived near, while Polly, who dearly loved to do it all herself, was forced to stand by and direct matters; and old Mr. Loughead divided his time between stalking out to the piazza where Pickering was slowly pacing back and forth in his "constitutional," to insist that he shouldn't "walks his legs off," and calling Polly from her work, "just to help me a bit, my dear"—when he got into a tight place over the packing that he insisted should be done by none but his own two hands.

And the whole farmhouse was soon thrown into such a bustle and ferment, that any one looking in would have known without the telling, that "Mr. King's family are going home." And after a day or so of all this, Farmer Higby carried a wagon-load of trunks down to the little station, and his wife drove the carryall, in the back of which Pickering was carefully tucked with Mrs. Cabot, who insisted on being beside him, and old Mr. Loughead in front—the others of the party merrily following in a large old vehicle of no particular pattern whatever—and before anybody could hardly realize it, the train came rushing in, and there were hurried good-bys, and hand-shakes, and they were off—Phronsie crying as she held to her, "I wish you were going too, I do, dear Mrs. Higby." And the farmer and his wife were left on the platform, staring after them with sorry eyes.

"Well, now, Phronsie," said Mr. King, as they quieted down, and Phronsie turned back after the last look at the little station, "I think it is time to answer your question, so as to let you go home without anything on your mind."

"About Charlotte, you mean, Grandpapa?" whispered Phronsie softly, with wide eyes, and glancing back to see that no one else heard.

"To be sure—about Charlotte," said the old gentleman. "Well, I've concluded you ought to have your way, and make Charlotte a gift of some money, if you want to."

"Oh, Grandpapa!" cried Phronsie, in a suppressed scream, and having great difficulty not to clap her hands; "oh, how good!" then she sat quite still, and folded them in silent rapture.

"And I'll see that it is fixed as soon as may be after we get home," said the old gentleman, "and I'm sure I'm glad you've done it, Phronsie, for I think Charlotte is a very good sort of a girl."

"Charlotte is just lovely," cried Phronsie, with warmth, "and I think, Grandpapa, that dear Mrs. Chatterton up in heaven, is glad too, that I've done it."

Old Mr. King turned away with a mild snort, and then not finding any words to say, picked up the newspaper, and Phronsie, full of her new happiness, looked out the window as the cars sped along.

"There's Thomas!" cried Jasper, at sight of that functionary waiting on his carriage-box as he had waited so many other times for them; now for the jolliest of all home-comings.

"And the girls," finished Polly, craning her neck to look out the car window at a knot of them restlessly curbing their impatience on the platform as the train moved into the station and—"why, Mamsie. Oh, Jasper! how slow we are!"

Pickering Dodge shook his long legs impatiently as he got out of his seat. "Don't try to help me, Mr. Loughead," he said testily, as the old gentleman offered his arm; "I'm not sick now. No, thanks, I'll go out alone."

Jasper now ran up, but he didn't offer to help, but waited patiently for Pickering's slow movements as he worked his way unsteadily down the aisle.

"Don't stop by me," said Pickering, rather crossly, "go ahead, Jasper, and get the fun."

"Nonsense!" exclaimed Jasper, yet feeling his heart bound at the merry din as Polly was surrounded, and the babel of voices waxed louder; for everybody was now out of the car but Pickering and himself—"here we are now," as they neared the car step.

Alexia Rhys, back on the platform hanging to Polly who had one hand in Mother Fisher's at the expense of all the other girls who couldn't get the chance, looked up and saw Pickering Dodge, and dropping Polly's arm she ran lightly across the stream of passengers and put out her hand.

"How do you do, Pickering? it's so good to see you back."

Pickering shot her an astonished glance, then he said gratefully, "Thank you, Alexia," and he actually let her help him down the steps, which so astonished her that it took away her breath and left her without a word to say.

And the rest was all bustle and confusion—Mr. King declaring it was worse than a boarding-school—everybody talking together—and Jasper ran off to see to the luggage for the whole party, followed by Ben trying to help. And old Mr. Loughead had to be introduced all around, and little Doctor Fisher tried to get them all settled in the carriages, but at last gave it up in despair.

"Charlotte, my girl, go and tell Polly to get in, will you?" he said, turning to Charlotte Chatterton. "Phronsie won't stir till Polly is settled."

"Oh, Polly! let me drive you home; I've got my dog-cart here," cried Clem Forsythe alluringly, and trying to pull her off as Charlotte ran up with her message.

"No, no," cried Sally Moore, "I brought my phaeton on purpose; you know I did, Clem—come with me, Polly, do."

"You'll have to get in here," called Doctor Fisher, waiting at the carriage, "to end it."

"Yes, I think I shall," said Polly merrily, and running to him followed by Phronsie. "Girls, come over this evening, won't you?" she looked back to call after them.

"Yes, we'll be over this evening," cried the girls back again, and Phronsie hopping in after her, the carriage-door was shut, and off they rolled.

And old Turner was waiting at the steps as the carriage rolled up the winding drive, with a monstrous bouquet of his choicest blossoms for Polly, and one exactly like it only a little smaller, for Phronsie; and Prince came rushing out getting in every one's way and nearly devouring Phronsie; and there was King Fisher running away on toddling feet from his nurse to meet them, screaming with all his might; and Mrs. Fargo with Johnny in her arms crowing with delight—all stood on the broad stone porch.

"Oh—oh!" cried Polly, jumping out, her cheeks aflame; "are we really at home!"

"Oh—oh!" echoed Phronsie, flying at them all, and trying to keep hold of Prince at the same time.

And there in the wide hall drawn back within the shadow of the oaken door, were Mr. and Mrs. Whitney and Dick ready to pounce upon them in a moment.

And no one ever hinted a suspicion that the college boys were steaming along as fast as they could, for the evening's festivities; and old Mr. King appeared superbly indifferent to the fact that Mr. Marlowe was waiting at a hotel for that hour to arrive; and everybody rushed off to get ready for dinner, with the exception of Polly and Jasper and Phronsie.

"Oh! we must go in the conservatory just for a minute," begged Phronsie, flying off on eager feet.

"We'll only take one peep," said Polly, just as eagerly, "come on, Jasper."

And then Polly had to run into the long drawing-room, and just look at her piano, and lay her fingers lovingly on the keys.

"Don't try it with your lame hand, Polly," begged Jasper, close beside.

"No, I won't," promised Polly, running light scales with the fingers of the other hand. "But oh! Jasper, I do verily believe I could. My arm feels so well."

"Well, don't, Polly," begged Jasper again.

"No, of course I won't," said Polly, with a little laugh, "but it won't be many weeks, you dear"—this to the piano, as she unwillingly got up from the music-stool, and let Jasper lead her off—"before you and I have all our good times together!"

Polly, in a soft white gown, sat on a low seat by Mother Fisher's side, her head in Mamsie's lap. It was after dinner, and the gas was turned low.

"Mamsie," said Polly, and she threw one hand over her head to clasp Mother Fisher's strong fingers closer, "it's so good to be home—oh! you can't think how I wanted you."

Just then somebody looked into Mother Fisher's bedroom.

"Oh! beg pardon," said Jasper, as he saw them. But there was so much longing in the voice that Polly called out, "Oh! come, Jasper. May he, Mamsie?"

"Yes," said Mrs. Fisher; "come in, Jasper."

Jasper came in quickly and stood a moment looking down at them. "It's so lovely to be home, Jasper," said Polly, looking up at him and playing with her mother's fingers.

"Isn't it?" cried Jasper, with feeling, "there never was anything so nice! Mrs. Fisher, may I sit down by you here?" and he went over to her where she sat on the sofa—it was the same big comfortable affair where Joel had flung himself, when he declared he could not keep on at school; and where Mamsie had often sat when the children brought her their troubles, declaring it was easier to tell her everything on the roomy, old-fashioned sofa, than anywhere else.

"Yes, indeed!" cried Mrs. Fisher cordially, and making way for him to sit down by her side.

"Now isn't this nice!" breathed Polly, lifting her head out of her mother's lap to look at him on Mamsie's other side. "Now, Jasper, you begin, and we'll tell her all about it, as we always do, you know, when we get home from places."

"I want to tell her something—and to you too, Polly," began Jasper quietly. "Mrs. Fisher—may I speak?" He leaned over and looked into the black eyes above Polly's shining brown hair.

"Yes," said Mother Fisher as quietly.

"How funny you are, Jasper," cried Polly with a laugh, "asking Mamsie in such a solemn way. There now, begin, do."

"Polly," said Jasper, "look at me, do, dear!"

Polly lifted her brown eyes quietly. "Why, Jasper?"

"I waited because I thought I ought," said Jasper, trying not to speak too quickly. "It seemed at one time as if you were going to be happy, and I should spoil it, Polly, if I spoke; but now—oh, Polly!" He put out his hand, and Polly instinctively laid her own warm palm within it. "Do you think you could love me—I've loved you ever since the Little Brown House days, dear!"

"Oh, Jasper!" Polly cried, with a glad ring in her voice, "how good you are," and she clung to his hand across Mamsie's lap.

"Will you, Polly?" cried Jasper, holding her hand so tightly that she winced a bit, "tell me quickly, dear."

"Will I what?" asked Polly wonderingly.

"Love me, Polly."

***"Now, Jasper, You Begin," Cried Polly, "And We'll Tell Mamsie All About It, As We Always Do When We Get Home!"***

"Oh! I do—I do," she cried; "you know it, Jasper. I love you with all my heart."

"Polly, will you marry me? Tell her, Mrs. Fisher, do, and make her understand," begged Jasper, turning to Mother Fisher imploringly.

"Polly, child," said Mamsie, putting both arms around her, careful not to disturb Jasper's hand over Polly's, "Jasper wants you to be his wife—do you love him enough for that?"

Polly, not taking her brown eyes from Jasper's face, laid her other hand upon his, "I love him enough," she said, "for that; oh, Jasper!"

Old Mr. King walked proudly down the long drawing-room with Polly on his arm. Everybody was in the highest possible spirits. The Lord of Misrule had made a triumphant entree, covering himself with glory and winning great applause for his long train of masquers; whose costumes if not gotten up on strict historical lines, made up any lack by the variety of other contrivances, each one following his own sweet will in dressing. They had gone through with the minuet and the pantomimes; and Charlotte, in a peaked hat and a big flowered brocade gown rich with tambour lace, had sung "like a nightingale," as more than one declared, and now the room was in a buzz of applause.

Old Mr. King took this time to walk up and down the long room with Polly several times quite pompously; and once in a while the little Lord of Misrule would rush up to them, say something very earnest, seize Polly's hand

and give it a shake and then dart away; which proceeding Joel would imitate, at such times leaving Robert Bingley to his own devices—until Joel, evidently struck by remorse, would as suddenly fly back and introduce his college friend violently to right and left, to make up for lost time.

"That's three times you've introduced me to that girl in blue," said Bingley, on one of these occasions, when he could get Joel aside for a minute. "Do let me alone—I was having a good enough time where I was."

"Did I?" cried Joel, opening his black eyes at him, "oh! beg pardon," and off he rushed at Polly again.

"How queerly they do act!" cried Alexia, to a knot of the girls. "And just look at Mr. King, he holds on to Polly every minute—I'm going to see what it's all about."

So she hurried across the room as fast as her high-heeled slippers would let her. "Polly—Polly, did you really like it all?" she asked breathlessly. "Oh! dear me, this ruff will be the death of me," picking at it with impatient fingers.

"Don't, Alexia," cried Polly, "it's so pretty—it was all just as fine as could be, and splendidly gotten up!"

"Well, it nearly killed us," declared Alexia, fanning herself violently, "and this old ruff will end me. There!" and she made a little break in the starched affair under her chin, "that's one degree less of misery."

"What would Queen Bess do to you?" cried Polly, saying the first thing that came in her head, to keep off questions she saw trembling on Alexia's tongue.

"Queen Bess was an old goose to wear such a thing," retorted Alexia. "Oh, Polly! do come with us. Let her, do, Mr. King," to the old gentleman who made all sorts of signs that served to show he meant to keep Polly to himself. "We girls want her now," she added saucily.

"You keep away," said old Mr. King, with an emphatic nod and a twinkle in his eye, "and the other girls; I'm going to have Polly tonight; you can come over in the morning and see her." And he moved off coolly, carrying Polly with him.

Alexia stood a moment transfixed with astonishment. "Joel—Joel, what is it?" she cried in a stage whisper, as that individual pranced by in one of his fits of remorse looking up Bingley. "Do tell me what's come over Polly, and why does Mr. King act so queerly?"

Joel flashed her a smile, but wouldn't say anything, and his eyes twinkled so exactly like Mr. King's, that Alexia lost all patience.

"Oh! you horrid boy," she cried, and ran back dismally to the girls, with nothing to tell.

***"Polly, Do Come With Us!"***

And Charlotte Chatterton walked as if she disdained the ground, her peaked hat towering threateningly, while her sallow face was wreathed with smiles; and it seemed as if she couldn't sing enough, throwing in encores in a perfectly reckless fashion.

"What is it? oh! I shall die if I don't know," exclaimed Alexia, over and over. "Girls, if some of you don't find out what's going on, I shall fly crazy!"

And the room buzzed and buzzed with delight, the growing mystery not lessening the hilarity.

"That's an uncommonly fine fellow I've just been talking with," said Mason Whitney, coming up to old Mr. King still keeping Polly by his side; "I haven't met such a man in one spell; he's a thorough-going intellectual chap, and he's been around the world a good deal, it's easy to see by his fine manner. Where did you pick him up?"

"Whom are you talking of, Mason?" asked Mr. King, in his crispest fashion.

"Why, that new man—Mr.—Mr.—I didn't catch the name when I was introduced, that you invited here to-night," said Mr. Whitney, with a little touch of the asperity yet remaining over the failure of his plan for Jasper, and he jerked his head in the direction of Mr. Marlowe.

"He?—oh! that's Jasper's publisher, Mr. Marlowe," said the old gentleman, trying to speak carelessly; then he burst into a laugh at Mr. Whitney's face.

"Whew!" exclaimed that gentleman, as soon as he could speak, "I've got to eat humble pie before my fourteen-year-old son Dick, and you've taken my breath away, Polly," looking at her blooming cheeks and happy eyes, "with that piece of news, and"—

"What news—oh, what news?" cried Alexia, coming up, too frantic to remember her manners. "Please tell us girls, for we are dying to know."

"You come away!" retorted Mr. Whitney unceremoniously, and Mr. King laughed, and Polly shook her white fan at them as the two moved off, and it was just as bad as ever!

"Pickering, do you know?" at last demanded Alexia, as he leaned against the doorway surveying the bright crowd.

"Yes, I know enough—that is, I can guess—don't ask me."

"Oh, what!" breathlessly cried Alexia, seizing his arm; "do tell me, Pickering, that is a dear—oh, I thought I was talking to the girls—I don't know what I'm doing anyway, Polly has so upset me."

"Well, she has upset me, too, Alexia," said Pickering gloomily, "but it isn't her fault; she couldn't help it."

Alexia, feeling that here was coming something quite worth her while to hear, waited patiently.

"You all know I've loved Polly for years," said Pickering steadily; "I made no secret of it."

"I know it," said Alexia, full of sympathy, and not daring to breathe, lest she should spoil it all. "Well, go on."

"And when I was sick, I hoped that things might be different—for Polly was sorry for me. But one day Aunt was talking about it to me, in a way that made me mad, and I knew that Polly would be bothered awfully if she ever got at her, so I told Polly the first chance I got, that she was never to be sorry for me any more, for I'd made up my mind not to think of her in that way again; which was an awful lie," declared Pickering suddenly, standing quite erect, "for I can't help it."

"Oh, dear—dear!" exclaimed Alexia, quite gone in sympathy, "aren't things just shameful in the world! Of course you oughtn't to be allowed to marry Polly, for you are not half good enough for her, Pickering," she added frankly, "but I'm so sorry for you!" and she put out her hand instinctively.

Pickering took it, and held it a minute in a calm grasp, with the air of a man considering it better to take the little, since he couldn't get all he wanted.

"But now tell why Polly and Mr. King and all the family act so funnily?" cried Alexia, pulling away her hand and suddenly awaking to the fact that this important piece of news had not been made known to her.

***"And You Will Be My Own Brother, Jasper," Said Phronsie.***

"Can't you see for yourself?" cried Pickering, with an impatient stare. "Why, Alexia, where are your eyes?" which was all she could get him to say, as Pickering walked off immediately.

Jasper all this while seemed to find it impossible to be separated from Mother Fisher; and together they wandered up and down the drawing-room, Phronsie clinging to his hand. "I always longed since the Little Brown House days, to call you Mamsie," he said affectionately, looking down into Mrs. Fisher's face, "and now I can!"

"And you will really and truly be my very own brother, Jasper," said Phronsie, as they walked on.